A Kingdom of the Mind

Scotland is a place in the sun and the rain,
but it is more than that; it is a kingdom
of the mind ... The old love for it endures,
whatever [a Scot's] reason or necessity for
living elsewhere.

Frederick Niven

McGILL-QUEEN'S STUDIES IN ETHNIC HISTORY

SERIES ONE
Donald Harman Akenson, Editor

1 *Irish Migrants in the Canadas*
A New Approach
Bruce S. Elliott
(Second edition, 2004)

2 *Critical Years in Immigration*
Canada and Australia Compared
Freda Hawkins
(Second edition, 1991)

3 *Italians in Toronto*
Development of a National
Identity, 1875–1935
John E. Zucchi

4 *Linguistics and Poetics of Latvian Folk Songs*
Essays in Honour of the
Sesquicentennial of the Birth
of Kr. Barons
Vaira Vikis-Freibergs

5 *Johan Schroder's Travels in Canada, 1863*
Orm Øverland

6 *Class, Ethnicity, and Social Inequality*
Christopher McAll

7 *The Victorian Interpretation of Racial Conflict*
The Maori, the British, and the
New Zealand Wars
James Belich

8 *White Canada Forever*
Popular Attitudes and Public
Policy toward Orientals in
British Columbia
W. Peter Ward
(Third edition, 2002)

9 *The People of Glengarry*
Highlanders in Transition,
1745–1820
Marianne McLean

10 *Vancouver's Chinatown*
Racial Discourse in Canada,
1875–1980
Kay J. Anderson

11 *Best Left as Indians*
Native-White Relations in the
Yukon Territory, 1840–1973
Ken Coates

12 *Such Hardworking People*
Italian Immigrants in Postwar
Toronto
Franca Iacovetta

13 *The Little Slaves of the Harp*
Italian Child Street Musicians in
Nineteenth-Century Paris, London,
and New York
John E. Zucchi

14 *The Light of Nature and the Law of God*
Antislavery in Ontario, 1833–1877
Allen P. Stouffer

15 *Drum Songs*
Glimpses of Dene History
Kerry Abel

16 *Louis Rosenberg*
Canada's Jews
(Reprint of 1939 original)
Edited by Morton Weinfeld

17 *A New Lease on Life*
Landlords, Tenants, and
Immigrants in Ireland and Canada
Catharine Anne Wilson

18 *In Search of Paradise*
The Odyssey of an Italian Family
Susan Gabori

19 *Ethnicity in the Mainstream*
Three Studies of English Canadian
Culture in Ontario
Pauline Greenhill

20 *Patriots and Proletarians*
The Politicization of Hungarian
Immigrants in Canada,
1923–1939
Carmela Patrias

21 *The Four Quarters of the Night*
The Life-Journey of an
Emigrant Sikh
Tara Singh Bains
and Hugh Johnston

22 *Cultural Power, Resistance,
and Pluralism*
Colonial Guyana, 1838–1900
Brian L. Moore

23 *Search Out the Land*
The Jews and the Growth of
Equality in British Colonial
America, 1740-1867
Sheldon J. Godfrey
and Judith C. Godfrey

24 *The Development of Elites
in Acadian New Brunswick,
1861–1881*
Sheila M. Andrew

25 *Journey to Vaja*
Reconstructing the World of
a Hungarian-Jewish Family
Elaine Kalman Naves

MCGILL-QUEEN'S STUDIES IN ETHNIC HISTORY

SERIES TWO
John Zucchi, Editor

1 *Inside Ethnic Families*
Three Generations of
Portuguese-Canadians
Edite Noivo

2 *A House of Words*
Jewish Writing, Identity,
and Memory
Norman Ravvin

3 *Oatmeal and the Catechism*
Scottish Gaelic Settlers in Quebec
Margaret Bennett

4 *With Scarcely a Ripple*
Anglo-Canadian Migration into
the United States and Western
Canada, 1880–1920
Randy William Widdis

5 *Creating Societies*
Immigrant Lives in Canada
Dirk Hoerder

6 *Social Discredit*
Anti-Semitism, Social Credit,
and the Jewish Response
Janine Stingel

7 *Coalescence of Styles*
The Ethnic Heritage of St John
River Valley Regional Furniture,
1763–1851
Jane L. Cook

8 *Brigh an Orain / A Story
in Every Song*
The Songs and Tales of
Lauchie MacLellan
Translated and edited by John Shaw

9 *Demography, State and Society*
   Irish Migration to Britain,
   1921–1971
   Enda Delaney

10 *The West Indians of Costa Rica*
   Race, Class, and the Integration
   of an Ethnic Minority
   Ronald N. Harpelle

11 *Canada and the Ukrainian
   Question, 1939–1945*
   Bohdan S. Kordan

12 *Tortillas and Tomatoes*
   Transmigrant Mexican Harvesters
   in Canada
   Tanya Basok

13 *Old and New World Highland
   Bagpiping*
   John G. Gibson

14 *Nationalism from the Margins*
   The Negotiation of Nationalism
   and Ethnic Identities among
   Italian Immigrants in Alberta and
   British Columbia
   Patricia Wood

15 *Colonization and Community*
   The Vancouver Island Coalfield
   and the Making of the British
   Columbia Working Class
   John Douglas Belshaw

16 *Enemy Aliens, Prisoners of War*
   Internment in Canada during the
   Great War
   Bohdan S. Kordan

17 *Like Our Mountains*
   A History of Armenians in
   Canada
   Isabel Kaprielian-Churchill

18 *Exiles and Islanders*
   The Irish Settlers of Prince
   Edward Island
   Brendan O'Grady

19 *Ethnic Relations in Canada*
   Institutional Dynamics
   Raymond Breton
   Edited by Jeffrey G. Reitz

19 *Ethnic Relations in Canada*
   Institutional Dynamics
   Raymond Bréton

20 *A Kingdom of the Mind*
   How the Scots Helped
   Make Canada
   Edited by Peter E. Rider
   and Heather McNabb

A Kingdom of the Mind

of the Mind

How the Scots Helped Make Canada

Edited by Peter E. Rider and Heather McNabb

McGILL-QUEEN'S
UNIVERSITY PRESS
Montreal & Kingston · London · Ithaca

© McGill-Queen's University Press 2006

ISBN-13: 978-0-7735-2989-2 ISBN-10: 0-7735-2989-6 (cloth)
ISBN-13: 978-0-7735-2990-8 ISBN-10: 0-7735-2990-X (paper)

Legal deposit first quarter 2006
Bibliothèque nationale du Québec

Printed in Canada on acid-free paper that is 100% ancient forest
free (100% post-consumer recycled), processed chlorine free.

This book has been published with the help of a grant from the
McCord Museum

McGill-Queen's University Press acknowledges the support of the
Canada Council for the Arts for our publishing program. We also
acknowledge the financial support of the Government of Canada
through the Book Publishing Industry Development Program (BPIDP)
for our publishing activities.

Library and Archives Canada Cataloguing in Publication

A kingdom of the mind : how the Scots helped make Canada /
Edited by Peter E. Rider and Heather McNabb.

(McGill-Queen's studies in ethnic history)
Includes bibliographical references and index.
ISBN-13: 978-0-7735-2989-2 ISBN-10: 0-7735-2989-6 (bnd)
ISBN-13: 978-0-7735-2990-8 ISBN-10: 0-7735-2990-X (pbk)

1. Scots–Canada–History. 2. Scottish Canadians–History. I. Rider,
Peter E., 1944– II. McNabb, Heather, 1963– III. Series.

FC106.S3K56 2005   971'.00491'63   2005-905328-3

This book was designed and typeset by studio oneonone
in Sabon 10.5/14

Contents

Illustrations | xi

Tables | xiii

Introduction: PETER E. RIDER AND HEATHER MCNABB | XV

PART ONE: SHAPING

1 *The Scots' Imaging of Canada* | 3
EDWARD J. (TED) COWAN

2 *Exiles or Entrepreneurs? Snapshots of the Scots in Canada* | 22
MARJORY HARPER

3 *A Man's a Man because of That: The Scots in the Canadian
Military Experience* | 40
H.P. KLEPAK

4 *The Curious Tale of the Scots and the Fur Trade:
An Historiographical Account* | 60
J.M. BUMSTED

5 *Sojourners in the Snow? The Scots in Business
in Nineteenth-Century Canada* | 76
DOUGLAS McCALLA

PART TWO: CREATING

6 *Thistles in the North: The Direct and Indirect Scottish Influence
on James Bay Cree Material Culture* | 99
CATH OBERHOLTZER

CONTENTS

7 *Aspects of Scottish-Canadian Material Culture: Heart Brooches and Scottish Pottery* | 122
GEORGE R. DALGLEISH

8 *A Scottish-born Silversmith in Montreal: Robert Cruikshank* | 137
RENÉ VILLENEUVE

9 *"Bonnie Lassies" and a "Coat of Many Colours": Highland-Inspired Clothing at the McCord Museum* | 149
EILEEN STACK

PART THREE: BUILDING
10 *Sir William Logan and Sir J.W. Dawson: Victorian Geology as Scottish Science in a New World Environment* | 167
SUZANNE ZELLER

11 *The Seed, the Soil, and the Climate: The Scottish Influence on Canadian Medical Education and Practice, 1775–1875* | 183
JOCK MURRAY AND JANET MURRAY

12 *A Scout of the Past: Ramsay Traquair and the Legacy of the National Art Survey of Scotland in Quebec* | 201
IRENA MURRAY

13 *Scottish Identity and British Loyalty in Early-Nineteenth-Century Montreal* | 211
GILLIAN I. LEITCH

14 *"In the Hallowed Name of Religion": Scots and Public Education in Nineteenth-Century Montreal* | 227
RODERICK MACLEOD

15 *Butcher, Baker, Cabinetmaker? A View of Montreal's Scottish Immigrant Community from 1835 to 1865* | 242
HEATHER MCNABB

Acknowledgments | 261
Contributors | 263
Index | 265

Illustrations

James McGill memorial plaque at the University of Glasgow | 9

Memorial to Lord Selkirk's settlement at Belfast, Prince Edward
Island | 25

Canadian government press advertisement for farmers | 28

D Company, Royal Scots | 42–3

Captain Bovey and Officers of the 5th Royal Highlanders | 51

Beaver Club medal belonging to James McGill | 71

Donald Smith Driving the Last Spike | 79

Silk-embroidered caribou hide octopus bag | 101

Beaded panel bag | 103

Moccasins collected by Lord Strathcona | 104

Model cradleboard collected by Dr John Rae | 106

Model cradleboard made for Alice Malloch | 106

Infant in a cradleboard | 107

Short Neck's Wife and Daughter | 108

Beaded hood | 113

Alice Malloch wearing a Cree-made outfit | 115

Model cradleboard | 116

Double-heart brooch | 126

Group of Scottish heart brooches | 127

Pocahontas and Her Son Thomas Rolfe | 128

Earthenware bowl with Portneuf spongeware decoration | 131

Earthenware jug decorated with *Canadian Sports* pattern | 131

Tissue transfer print, *Wolfe's Monument* | 133
Robert Cruickshank, *Pair of Salt Spoons* | 139
Robert Cruickshank, *Pair of Salt Cellars* | 140
Robert Cruickshank, *Tea Service* | 141
Robert Cruickshank, *Sweetmeat Basket* | 143
Robert Cruickshank, *Monstrance* | 144
Robert Cruickshank, *Circular Brooch* | 145
Sergeants of the 78th Fraser Highlanders | 151
Duncan McIntyre, 1892 | 153
Evening dress in silk tartan | 154
Joseph Family Members | 155
Young Boys in Highland Costume | 156
Master Hugh Allan, Montreal | 158
Waistcoat, about 1840 | 159
Sir William Edmond Logan, 1865 | 169
Sir William Dawson, 1895 | 170
Anatomy Study, McGill Medical Students | 194–5
Argyll Lodging, Stirling | 204
Argyll Lodging, Stirling | 205
The High Altar of the Chapel, Hôpital général, Québec | 206
Hôpital général, Québec | 207
Hôpital général, Québec | 208
Photographs of the old silver of Quebec | 208
Saint Andrew, patron saint of Scotland | 219
Saint Andrew's Society Ball, Montreal, 1878 | 221
Alex McGibbon, 1866 | 245
John Ritchie, 1886 | 246

Tables

5.1 Scots in Canadian Business Circles, Selected Evidence | 81
15.1 Origins of the Scottish Immigrant Population in Montreal | 247
15.2 Occupations of Scottish-Born Montrealers, by Ward | 249
15.3 Occupations of Males in the Saint Gabriel Street Church Records,
     1835 | 252
15.4 Occupations at Montreal's Secession Church, 1835–65 | 254
15.5 Occupational Profiles of Montreal's Presbyterian Churches,
     1835 | 254

Introduction

Branding is serious business. A corporation's economic future rides on the creation of a proper image. Similarly, an ethnic group or a whole nation may invest a tremendous amount of emotion in the establishment of an identity or tradition that sustains its collective existence. Canadians have to go no further than the supposedly distinctive use of "eh" or the myth of our Northern hardiness to discover how flimsy these assertions of cultural markers may actually be. The accuracy of the image, though, is often beside the point. What counts is the belief that certain traditions or traits are representative. Canadians continue to pride themselves on being, and having been, a compassionate, egalitarian, peace-loving nation. Yet some critics of government would argue that certain current domestic and foreign policies fail to meet those standards. Many Canadians would also now admit that our past treatment of ethnic minorities in wartime belies our comfortable self-image. What we are and what we imagine ourselves to be are often two quite different things. So what do we make of the tartan ribbon, that band of Scottishness that wraps itself around so much of our civic life and intellectual discourse? Is it reality, a romantic fantasy, or a little of both?

An awareness of being Scottish is bred-in-the-bone for many Canadians – Easterner or Westerner, anglophone or francophone, urban or rural, a broad spectrum of us. More than the 10 percent of Canadians who actually consider their origins to be Scottish can trace one or more of their ancestors to the Scottish part of Great Britain. Further, there is something about being Canadian that seems to exude a sense of Scotland. Perhaps it is the long association with a part of the world that helped to mould our economy, society, and culture, or perhaps it is a shared *volksgeist* of being an ambitious but marginal people living beside a larger, dominant people, but Scotland, and things Scottish, resonate with who we are and what we think and do to a remarkable degree.

Part of Scottish identity is its tenacity and assertiveness in the face of English domination. Whether conquered, quelled, co-opted, convinced, or opportunistic (a word that breaks the alliterative chain but still has an authentic ring), the Scots, once linked to the English, took up the cause of imperialism. As colonizers who often used English power for their own advantage, the Scots helped set Canada on its own fervent imperialist path in the late nineteenth and early twentieth centuries. In describing Canada in Scottish terms, early Scots inhabitants inadvertently gave it a non-English tone and ensured that it was British rather than English. Many Canadians, too, shared a sense of empire. Citizens of the "Great Dominion" used the imperial connection for their own ends, either to gain admission to the seat of world power, like financier Max Aitken, who became Lord Beaverbrook, and Sir Edward Peacock, Glengarry County–born director of the Bank of England, or to shore up the bulwark of a separate identity as a defence against the republic to the south. The British connection was useful to Canadians, and Canada's Scottishness was an important manifestation of that link.

Scots settled in various parts of Canada, and their influence was pervasive. Those who first came to Montreal were attracted by the administrative and commercial possibilities of the place in the days immediately following its capture from France. They soon assumed leadership roles in the fur trade, an activity in which Scots had long been engaged through the Hudson's Bay Company. They subsequently turned their attentions to the timber trade, banking, commerce, and industry. Advancement was facilitated by their intellectual formation, a Calvinistic acquisitiveness and work ethic, and clannishness in business and politics. Of course, not all Scots succeeded spectacularly; most led unremarkable lives, and some failed utterly. As new arrivals joined their compatriots, they similarly experienced a wide range of fates.

From their vantage point in Montreal, Scottish migrants grasped one of the great realities of North America: the huge hinterland of the St Lawrence River, stretching deep into the continent's interior and accessed via the Upper St Lawrence and Ottawa Rivers and the Great Lakes. Montreal was the portal to this vast, resource-rich geographical area. With vigour and enterprise, Montreal business interests could dominate half of North America. They moved quickly to respond, soon eclipsing the older city of Quebec. Following the American Revolution, a political boundary split this territory, but Montreal was still left with apparently limitless economic advantages and a role as the social and cultural focus of an emerging Canadian state. In the view of Donald Creighton, who so ably propounded this Laurentian interpretation of Canadian history, Scottish success in the city and beyond would have been rooted in the interplay of character and circumstance.

The Scots formed a vibrant community within Montreal that sought to perpetuate Scottish traditions in education and moral probity. Schools and institutions of higher learning were created in which science and moral philosophy, a subject that stressed the moral purpose of life, were emphasized. These shared predispositions, however, did not exclude disputes among Scots in many facets of life. Commercial rivalries, religious splits, and political differences were common. In politics Scots provided leaders for both reform and conservative sides.

By the 1880s Montreal was the business and intellectual centre of Canada. Half of Canada's industrial leaders were either native to Scotland or had Scottish-born fathers, and many lived in Montreal. Migrants of Scottish origin born in the rest of Canada, such as Sir William Dawson and Sir William Macdonald, were attracted to and nurtured by, and in turn strengthened, Montreal's Scottish community. This pattern tended further to enhance the city's primacy within Canada. The presence of the Scots in Montreal helped make it Canada's central place and gave it a spirit and institutions marked by traits that have their origins in the hills and glens, the myths and realities, and the struggles and triumphs of Scotland.

The question remains, however, as to the extent to which Canada's Scottish qualities are real or imagined. This volume seeks to examine some of the dimensions of that question. Some impacts are relatively amenable to documentation and are even measurable. Others are intangible and lie within the complex workings of our national consciousness. These are, at best, open to subjective assessment. At times our collective identity seems as variable as the dapples of light on a wind-swept lake, shaped by the breezes of contemporary popular culture, society, and politics. On other occasions it appears more like a snowball rolling down a hill, growing as it moves. Accretive layers are covered in succession, but the early ones give shape and substance to the mass as a whole. History is constructed from events we choose to remember; identity arises from traits we wish to honour. Both are a kind of kingdom of the mind.

It is this concept of the kingdom of the mind to which Ted Cowan turns in the opening chapter of the book. Cowan examines the Scottish influence on how Canada was perceived in the late eighteenth and early nineteenth century. This critical phase in the formation of the image of English Canada, at least, took place when the Scots were both influential and relatively numerous. Imbued with concepts of the cultural awakening in their homeland, they projected images inspired by them onto their new surroundings and marked the setting as their own. In the second chapter of part I Marjorie Harper explores the ways in which the Scots who came to Canada perpetuated their identity. They relied on ties of religion, education, and charitable organizations and on careful selection of desirable aspects of their homeland to be remembered. Strands of these cultural traditions were ultimately woven into the tartanized identity of twentieth-century Canada.

Traditions have to be useful, however, to thrive, and Hal Klepak demonstrates that in the armed forces, Scottishness proved to be highly so. The Highland ethos came with the British military at the time of the Conquest, and it settled comfortably into colonial militia units and blossomed, in particular, during World War I. In time Canada's military appropriated Scottish, particularly Highland, identity as its own. The process of selecting elements of the past to be commemorated in history intrigues Jack Bumsted in his examination of the literature on the fur trade. While the significance of the Scots as fur traders is not a matter of dispute, their ethnic identity has not been given a great deal of attention until recently, in part, perhaps, because historians have traditionally tended to deny or downplay the importance of ethnicity in Canada. Such reticence can limit historical understanding. Douglas McCalla demonstrates how the Scots, by no means the numerically dominant ethnic group, came in the nineteenth century to play a leading economic role. Ties of kinship and business and personal relationships facilitated the accumulation of wealth among migrant Scots, but an inability to repatriate their wealth to the homeland entrenched their presence here.

The second part of this book looks at some physical evidence of the Scottish influence on Canadian material culture. Although examples of cultural transference may become scarce with time, the artifacts that do survive can offer powerful testimony documenting intellectual trends. Cath Oberholtzer, in her essay on the impact of the Scots on the material expression of the James Bay Cree, demonstrates how these influences were both direct and indirect. Design motifs, such as the thistle and the heart, worked their way into the fabrication of First Nations handiwork. Through the introduction of Scottish tartan cloth and the opening of markets for Native-made souvenirs by Scots traders, the material culture of the Cree was indirectly altered.

George Dalgleish elucidates two specific contributions of Scottish business to our material history. The Scottish-born Montreal silversmith Robert Cruickshank became a major manufacturer of Indian trade silver and incorporated heart, or "luckenbooth," brooches into his production. Back in Scotland, the pottery industry found the expanding Canadian market an attractive outlet for its wares. John Marshall and Company in Bo'ness and Robert Cochran and James Fleming at the Britannia factory in Glasgow employed Canadian scenes to appeal to local consumers in Canada. While their products are found in many private and museum collections in this country, they remain remarkably unknown in their land of origin. René Villeneuve also focuses on Robert Cruickshank but reviews a broader selection of his oeuvre, including his domestic and ecclesiastical pieces. Here we find a Scot who brought designs inspired not only by the traditions of his homeland but also by the latest trends in British neoclassical taste. In addition, he pioneered new forms that reflect considerable artistic originality and technical sophistication.

Eileen Stack completes part 2. She uses the rich and varied collection of the McCord Museum to show the incorporation of Highland costume or Highland-inspired textiles into the wardrobes of Montrealers and Canadians generally. Either through the reaffirmation of Scottish identity or the popularization of Highland fashion by the British royal family, Canadian taste in costume in the Victorian era was tartanized. This influence spread far beyond the segment of the population that traced its roots to Scotland.

Part 3 focuses on the way in which the Scots contributed to the building of society in their newly adopted surroundings. Suzanne Zeller looks in particular at the influence of Sir William Logan and Sir J.W. Dawson on the study of natural history in British North America. Pursuing trends of thought then current in Scotland, they melded their interests with the broader community of scientific enquiry that flourished in Canada in the nineteenth century and reached conclusions that had significant political implications. In medicine, as well, Scots decisively affected their new homeland, and Jock Murray and Janet Murray trace the Scottish impact on the Canadian medical profession in its formative years from 1775 to 1875. Because Scotland was at the time the acknowledged leader in medical practice and training, Scottish-trained physicians frequently assumed leadership roles in the establishment of hospitals and medical schools and even the Canadian Medical Association. In proceeding with these tasks, they used Scottish concepts and traditions as their models.

Irena Murray turns to architecture and the legacy left by one Scot, Ramsay Traquair. In implementing a survey of architecture in Quebec modelled on the National Art Survey of Scotland, he ensured the survival of a tradition that was native to his adopted country. Gillian Leitch explores an aspect of the Scottish presence that, at times, was viewed less positively by the Scots' francophone compatriots. Through Montreal's St Andrew's Society the city's Scots were able to affirm their British identity and attachment to the imperial Crown. The society was founded in response to the political uncertainties of the 1830s but endured to foster fellowship and mutual support among Montreal's Scots. In doing so, it retained its patriotic tone. Roderick MacLeod also deals specifically with Montreal in his study of the influence of Scots on public education. Their influence was felt initially in prying control of non–Roman Catholic education in the city out of the grip of the Anglicans. Primary education was instead vested with a Protestant board of education that the Scots ultimately dominated. They then endowed the board with a philosophy of education that reflected the Scottish tradition of publicly funded, widely accessible schools in which biblical teaching was a cornerstone.

In the closing chapter of part 3 – and of the book – Heather McNabb gives a timely reminder that not all Scots in Montreal or in Canada were rich and powerful. Using censuses, cemetery inscriptions, and Presbyterian church records, she classifies Scottish Montrealers according to the model proposed by Michael Katz in his study of Hamilton, Canada West. She finds that the bulk of Scots were the middling sort with few at the lower end of the occupational scale and few, as well, at the upper end.

The essays that compose this volume are based on papers presented at a colloquium held in Montreal at the McCord Museum of Canadian History on 9–11 May 2002. Entitled Character and Circumstance: The Scots in Montreal and Canada, the colloquium placed a special emphasis on the Scottish community in that city but was not limited to it. Nor was such a restriction possible. As Canada's central place for well over a century, Montreal to a degree both represented the whole country and was shaped by it. The interplay of Scots and Canada, Scots and Montreal, and Montreal and Canada forms part of a single story in which expatriates from the periphery of Great Britain established themselves at the centre of a new land and left an indelible mark on it. Thus the chapters in this book speak of a nation as well as a city. And they speak with a distinct burr.

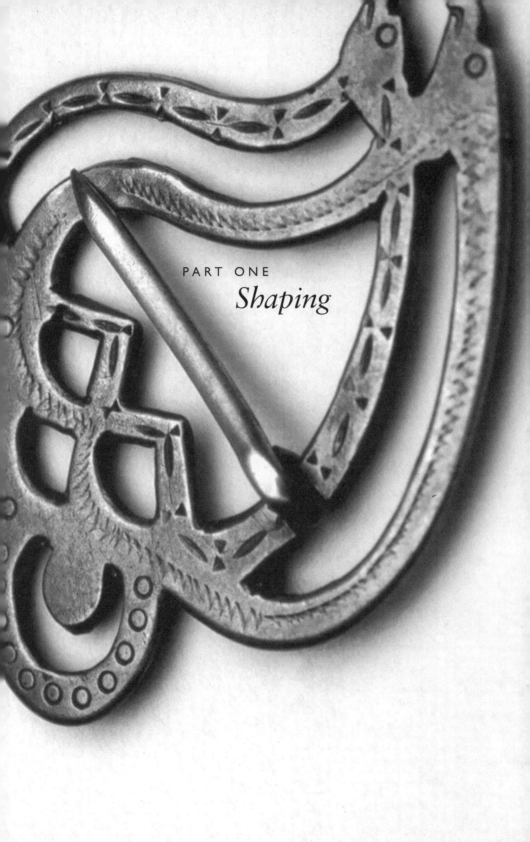

PART ONE
Shaping

ONE

The Scots' Imaging of Canada

Edward J. (Ted) Cowan

From the lone shieling of the misty island
Mountains divide us, and the waste of seas –
Yet still the blood is strong, the heart is Highland.
And we in dreams behold the Hebrides.[1]

When "The Canadian Boat Song," surely the best-known example of the literature of loss in the shared annals of Scotland and Canada, was published in *Blackwood's Edinburgh Magazine* in 1829, it was debated by John Wilson and his co-conspirators of the *Blackwood's* circle.[2] They were indulging once again in one of their fictive *Noctes Ambrosianae*,[3] and the mood was ambivalent. "As for Canada, why it's as Scotch as Lochaber – whatever of it is not French I mean. Even omitting our friend John Galt, have we not [today] our Bishop Macdonell for the papists, our Archdeacon Strachan for the Episcopals and our Tiger Dunlop for the Presbyterians? and tis the same I believe all downwards." Scotland, however, was losing her identity through anglicisation, desertion by the nobility, and the erosion of Scots law. From a kingdom Scotland had sunk to provincial status and would soon be a colony. James Hogg, the Ettrick Shepherd,[4] said in his usual couthy fashion:

Ah wae's me – I hear the Duke of Hamilton's cottars are a gaun away, man and mither's son, frae the Isle o Arran. Pity on us! Was there a bonnier sight in the warld than to sail by yon green shores on a braw summer's evening, and see the smoke risin frae the puir bodies' bit shielings, ilk ane wi its peatstack and its twa three auld donnerd pines or saughs or elms, sugh-sughin owre the thack in the gloamin breese.[5]

Poor James Hogg, ever the butt of the *Blackwood's* group, was sentimentalizing the Auld Country – braw summer's evenings with the smoke rising from the thack in the gloamin breese. While no one would ever take the ramblings of the *Noctes* crowd completely seriously, this particular example does invoke the Scottish emigrant experience that is the central theme of this book. It also strongly hints that Scottish aspirations, then being checked at home, would have greater chance of realization through emigration, and it provides a fine articulation of what I have elsewhere described as the myth of Scotch Canada, which this paper seeks to further develop.[6] That there was a symbiotic relationship between Scotland and Canada can scarcely be doubted. It may be further suggested that this relationship was without parallel – by reason of various historical accidents and coincidences there is perhaps no other example as graphic and striking of one country being described in terms of another. This is not to deny that there was also a French imaging of Canada, just as there was an English one, and undeniably every component of the Canadian multicultural mosaic made its own contribution. But to a remarkable degree it was the Scots, particularly in the earlier period, who were responsible for creating the image of the great new country to which so many of them went. Their efforts were born of extensive travel and yielded an immense literary output encompassing fiction, memoir, science, and the literature of exploration and emigration. And it all started, as it should, almost at the beginning.

When William Alexander, Earl of Stirling, Viscount Canada, and Sir Robert Gordon of Kenmure produced their tracts on the desirability of Canadian colonization in the 1620s, they attempted to render the exotic familiar by applying Scottish names to rivers and waterways. Thus Tweed, Solway, Clyde, and Forth appeared on the map. It has been overlooked in the past that both men were extremely interested in what would be described today as the potential for scientific knowledge arising from Scottish exposure to the New World. Both Alexander and Gordon were interested in, among other things, geography, botany, natural history, and the ethnology and languages of the First Peoples. Some of the material they included in their tracts was almost certainly derived from Jacques Cartier's published accounts, translated into English by Hakluyt in 1600.[7]

Victoria Dickenson has shown the importance of science in early contacts between Britain and Canada,[8] and so far as the Scots were concerned this sort of interaction remained crucial right through to the age of Daniel Wilson and Sanford Fleming.[9] From the Scottish perspective science was just as much a catalyst in the exploration of Canada as was the idea of colonization, and numeracy would prove as important as literacy in abetting the success of Scottish emigrants. There is still much research to be done on the democratization of science in this period – in the seventeenth century, men gathered in Masonic lodges throughout Lowland Scotland to discuss not only literature and potentially applied subjects such as mathematics (including algebra and geometry) but also other subjects that would now be classified as science.[10] Certainly the Scots never lost the scientific interest that fed into the Scottish Enlightenment of the 1680s and 1690s.[11] But because of what might be described as an overprovision of university and college education in Scotland at this time, Scots found themselves at the cutting edge of scientific exploration just as Britain set about to colonize the world.[12]

The extraordinary career of David Douglas, the botanist and naturalist for whom the Douglas fir was named, illustrates not only one man's appetite for scientific knowledge but also the truly remarkable number of Scots who could be encountered in one of the greatest wildernesses on the planet.[13] Douglas arrived at the mouth of the Columbia River on the West Coast accompanied by John Scoular, a Glasgow surgeon, in 1825.[14] At Fort Astoria (later renamed Fort George) Douglas encountered Donald Mackenzie and Dr John MacLoughlin, chief factors of the Hudson's Bay Company. The latter was born in Quebec and always referred to himself as an Irishman, but he was Scots on his mother's side, and his Western experience was marked by its share of Scottish connections. He owned a gun that had belonged to Alexander Mackenzie when the explorer made his great trek to the Pacific in 1793, and when MacLoughlin and Governor George Simpson arrived at Fort George in 1824, they were welcomed by a piper in full Highland regalia.[15] Indeed, MacLoughlin's travels suggest that until George IV's visit to Edinburgh in 1822, when Sir Walter Scott orchestrated a kind of tartan orgy,[16] the most likely place to see kilts was probably the Canadian frontier – most of them having been acquired from, or used for self-decoration by, demobbed soldiers.

In the Northwest, Douglas associated with such luminaries as the McGillivray brothers (Duncan, William, and Simon), with Angus Bethune, Norman Macleod, Simon Fraser,[17] Simon MacTavish, Cuthbert Grant, and John Macleod. He named a set of rapids after David Thompson, an Englishman, but one who was heavily contaminated through his contacts with legions of Scots. The botanist also encountered individuals who symbolized the mix of Native, French, and Scot in the fur trade, like Jacques Rafael Finlay and Jean Baptiste Desportes Mackay, who presented Douglas with his first sugar pinecone. At Fort Walla Walla he met his namesake, James Douglas, whose father was a Glaswegian plantation owner in Demerara and whose mother was a freed slave. Educated in Scotland and England, he eventually became governor of Vancouver Island and British Columbia.[18] Further Scottish associations were with James MacMillan, who established Fort Langley on the Fraser River, and Aemilius Simpson, who developed the America-China trade and who is credited with growing the first apple trees on the Northwest Coast.

At this point Douglas took the so-called Hudson's Bay Express overland from the Columbia River to the Great Bay, accompanied by John Macleod and Mr Archibald Macdonald, who was en route to the Okanagan. At Revelstoke he thought daily of home. On his journey Scots popped up everywhere, including George MacDougall, who had almost starved crossing the mountains from Jasper, and John Stuart, who had accompanied Simon Fraser on his Western expedition. He met with men associated with the polar explorers John Ross and James Clark Ross from Galloway.[19] On his way down the Saskatchewan River he aided the notorious buffalo wrestler Finnan Macdonald, captain of the militia in Glengarry County and a Canadian MP. Douglas is the best source on Macdonald's buffalo encounter: the politician was believed to be dead, but he later explained that although badly injured he had survived by holding onto the animal's "wig." Douglas conveyed the wounded Finnan to Norway House to be treated by Dr John Richardson from Dumfries, who was to write his own sensational account of his Arctic expedition with Franklin.[20]

The search for the Northwest Passage was romantic, mythic, heroic, and tragic. It was also perhaps one of the cruelest hoaxes in Canadian history. At age sixty-one Richardson led an expedition in search of Franklin with John Rae from Orkney. Cannibalism on an earlier expedition had permitted Richardson's survival; Rae's similar revelations about members of Franklin's company led to the Orcadian's lifetime disgrace. One of Richardson's associates was Robert McVicar, chief trader of the HBC at Fort Resolution. Mrs McVicar gave birth to a son in 1827, "the first Scot that was ever born at Slave Lake."[21] Richardson gave instructions on how to preserve bird specimens to William Fraser Tolmie, another physician-naturalist and a recent graduate of Glasgow University, who kept a detailed diary of his voyage from Scotland to the Columbia and of his subsequent adventures in the fur trade. Tolmie later became a member of the Vancouver Island legislature.[22]

Franklin himself turned up and gave Douglas a ride in his canoe across Lake Winnipeg and down the Red River to the Settlement, where he received hospitality from Donald Mackenzie, "Governor of the Colony." This in turn brought him in touch with numerous acquaintances of the recently deceased Lord Selkirk. A further encounter was with Thomas Drummond from Forfar, yet another botanist-explorer who had transported some of Douglas's specimens all the way from the West Coast. It took Douglas a further eighteen days to reach York Factory, where he was greeted by John Mac-Tavish and the ship that would take him home.

So it was that these men who played a crucial role in the history of the Northwest (in both Canada and the United States) kept running up against each other in one of the world's vastest wildernesses. They haunted their own metaphor.

The amount of writing by Scots about pre-Confederation Canada is truly staggering. Travelogues, novels, memoirs, poetry, journals, reports, guides for emigrants, and periodical articles abound. One of the most famous and talented of those who investigated and described the Canadian aspects of the Scottish Empire was John Galt, whose interest was sparked as a small boy when he was transported by a print of Niagara Falls; he described this as "an event which has had a singular influence on my life."[23] Between 1827 and 1829 he founded the towns of Guelph and Goderich on behalf of the Canada Company, and he had earlier produced the "Statistical Account of Canada," drawing upon information provided by William Gilkison, founder of Elora in Canada West. His account was a modest affair inspired by – but which does not merit comparison with – Sir John Sinclair's preeminent series for Scotland in the 1790s. Galt was to write two novels about the emigrant experience: *Lawrie Todd* was set in America and *Bogle Corbet* partly in Canada, as was the lugubrious short story "The Metropolitan Emigrant." Galt the entrepreneur was regarded as a failure in his own day, and indeed he was bankrupt when, on his return to England, he wrote his American stories. Nonetheless, today he is credited with being far-sighted, idealistic, and visionary, a man whose greater schemes were thwarted by lesser minds and professional jealousy.[24]

Galt's friend William "Tiger" Dunlop acquired his soubriquet in India. He was a highly colourful character who wrote fairly extensively. His most notable publication was probably *The Backwoodsman*, an influential guide for emigrants,[25] but he also produced a number of articles for such magazines as *Blackwood's* and *Frasers* while penning an absorbing and informative journal. Dunlop was heavily involved in Canadian politics, but he lived an almost aggressively Scottish existence. When he travelled he made a point of stopping only at inns where "the bagpipes shrilled, the whiskey flowed." At his log mansion of Garbraid he founded the *Noctes Ambrosianae Canadiensis*, on the *Blackwood's* model, for literary and political discussion, as well as for bouts of drinking and eating.[26] An associate, Major Samuel Strickland, was not a Scot but almost an honorary one, since he associated with so many of them in his adopted country, as described in his *Twenty Years in Canada West* (1848). His more famous sisters, Catherine Traill and Susanna Moodie, published widely read accounts of pioneer life and were both married to Scots.[27] Adam Fergusson from Perthshire, founder of Fergus, Ontario, also published on his travels in Upper Canada.[28] Even William Cattermole, an Eng-

THIS MEMORIAL STONE
IS PLACED HERE BY
McGILL UNIVERSITY
IN HONOUR OF
JAMES McGILL
1744–1813
STUDENT IN ARTS OF THE
UNIVERSITY OF GLASGOW
TRADER SOLDIER AND
STATESMAN IN CANADA
AND
FOUNDER OF McGILL UNIVERSITY
MONTREAL

James McGill memorial plaque at the University of
Glasgow. Courtesy of the University of Glasgow

lishman, included significant information about Scots in his book
Emigration (1831).[29] These people were all contemporaries of Galt,
as was William Dickson, who founded Dumfries Township and who
named the town of Galt after the novelist. Dickson's brother Thomas
was an associate of James McGill, who founded Montreal's famous
university.

When the prosperous Lizars family from Edinburgh arrived on the
shores of Lake Huron they assembled a large library (part of which
still survives at the University of Guelph)[30] and sang Scottish ballads
and Jacobite songs in the backwoods. Back home many of these people would have been part of the circle of Sir Walter Scott, who, with

Galt and Hogg, was busily providing Scotland with a literary identity at exactly the same time the poetry of Robert Burns was becoming widely known. It was a period that witnessed one of the greatest re-brandings of the country in Scottish history. Indeed, a descendant described Daniel Lizars as a radical belonging to a party, which made the weeping Scott exclaim, "Little by little, whatever your wishes may be, you will destroy and undermine until nothing of what makes Scotland Scotland, shall remain."[31] The refrain was the same as that rehearsed in *Blackwood's* in 1829, discussed above. Despite his political sympathies Lizars and others obviously agreed in part with Scott, to the extent that they assiduously cultivated their Scottish heritage. Such émigrés looked backwards and forwards at the same time. They were somewhat disingenuous in their nostalgia for the Old Country, since they were desperate to prosper in the New, and they did not greatly care how they came by their fortunes. But they also contributed to the forging of a literary identity for Canada. For them the great new country was to become the Scotland they had lost.

John MacTaggart provided interesting comment on these matters in his *Three Years in Canada: An Account of the Actual State of the Country in 1826-7-8* (1829). A native of Galloway, he is best known for his *Scottish Gallovidian Encyclopedia* (1824), a gloriously idiosyncratic production written in a vigorous and often hilarious style. The book's less decorous passages offended both local and literary sensibilities, resulting in its suppression. The author wished to send a copy to "our friends in the wilds of Canada ... I know they would like to laugh at my folly on the Banks of the Eerie [sic]."[32] Towards the end of his short life (1791–1830) he was appointed clerk of works on the Rideau Canal. He noted, "the majority of the inhabitants of Montreal are French but the Scottish and Irish taken by themselves, outnumber the English." He was surprised that in the city the Scotch brogue was not only considered vulgar but also highly offensive: "How they turn up their noses when they hear me speak." Ever the comedian, he confessed that "to please them I have set to work to study the English lisp and I dare say time will make a beau of my grannie.[33] How polite I find myself getting! Soon I shall not know where to look for Scotland on a map of the world; and as to Sir Walter's writings, his Scotch characters do indeed disgust me."

Behind this banter, of course, lurks the spectre of Scots who were already quite unpopular because of their number and influence.

According to MacTaggart those Scots who unthinkingly aped the manners of the English were termed "Canadianized Scotchmen." He advised emigration agents such as Galt and Dunlop to "keep out Yankee characters who cannot bear to be laughed at." Another visitor, John Howison, noted in 1821 that the ultimate in vanity, impudence, and rascality was thought to be comprised under the epithet "Scotch Yankey."[34] Galt's *Lawrie Todd* further illustrates MacTaggart's observation. In it Zerobabel L. Hoskins is the archetypal "stirring and adventurous old Yankee," always one with "a sharp eye to the main chance," forever planning a "grand spec."[35] He is, in short, exactly the type of character that virtually every Scottish immigrant aspired to be, including Lawrie himself and the legions of Scots who seemed to inhabit the city and state of New York. Furthermore, *Bogle Corbet* has been described as "the first major work to define Canadianism by reference to an American alternative."[36] It is also a towering contribution to the literature of emigration and Scotland's role within the empire. Bogle, a disconnected, self-reflective and somewhat melancholy individual, believes that "the Yankies are a real upsetting folk, and have no a right restraint of moderation anent their own ferlies [marvels]," by which he means they could not tolerate criticism. He admits, however, that artisans would do better to settle in New York, while Canada was more suited to agricultural labourers, since it was much less developed.[37]

A Scots doctor appears in the second paragraph of Susanna Moodie's *Roughing it in the Bush* (1852), and thereafter his countrymen seldom stray far from her pages, although Americans are also in evidence. Chapter 7 introduces Uncle Joe: "No thin, weasel-faced Yankee was he, looking as if he had lived upon cute ideas and speculations all his life." Yet Yankee he was by birth and in mind, "for a more knowing fellow at a bargain never crossed the lakes to abuse British institutions, and locate himself comfortably among the despised Britishers."[38] So far as Mrs Moodie was concerned "Yankee" and "conman" were interchangeable terms. On the other hand Robert MacDougall, like many of his fellow countrymen, confessed to a healthy admiration for American enterprise; men of ambition should "go over to the Yankees."[39] Nonetheless, Scots on the make in Canada had to ensure that they did not come across as being too overtly ambitious, enterprising, or calculating. Those who proved aggressively successful were regarded as no better than Yankees.

John MacTaggart related all that he saw to Scotland, or at least pretended so to do, for he was almost certainly satirizing the parochialism of himself and his fellow Scots. Thus, one place in the Gatineau, which sat on a bed of iron-ore, might one day become the "Muirkirk of Canada."[40] "Go not to Glengarry [Ontario]," he cautioned, "if you be not a Highlandman."[41] He visited Captain Andrew Wilson at his home, Ossian Hall, on the banks of the Rideau. In a superb example of parochial particularism he remarked of a casual acquaintance, "all the humour of Dunscore was depicted in his countenance."[42] His Canadian experience inspired MacTaggart to poesy:

> Sax months here are frost and snaw
> Up to the oxters wading,
> But what o' that! Success to sleighs
> To fun and cavalcading.

More seriously, he noted that while Scots such as Mackenzie and Richardson had seen the "utmost limits of Canada," the interior had been ignored. He wrote of such luminaries as Selkirk of Red River and John Galt. In a letter to Tiger Dunlop he remarked that the Canada Company's advertisements had resulted in an explosion in emigration. Before the company was founded, only poor emigrants had ventured to British North America, most of them, he thought, Scots. Thereafter there were many of the better sort (of Scots) and many more English.[43] Few in the Old Country were in a position to contradict him. He noted that James Scott from Glasgow, publisher of the *Montreal Herald*, had recently produced a report lamenting British ignorance of Canada.[44]

By the mid-nineteenth century the Scottishness of Canada had become a literary assumption – at least so far as Scots were concerned. Robert MacDougall's *Emigrant's Guide*, written in Gaelic, set out to demonstrate that Canada would make a most conducive destination for Gaelic speakers in particular, though he thought that more ambitious types should make for the United States. He deplored the obliteration or displacement of Native place-names by ridiculously inappropriate European ones. "When the British began to shape everything as they saw fit in Canada, they began to give these places the names they saw fit as well." MacDougall's particular spin was to indicate that many of those place-names, like the languages of the Native peoples, derived from Gaelic. For example, Ottawa he derived as *ath-a-tuath*, or "the north ford," Niagara as *Abhainn-na-Gàirich*, "roaring river." Unfortunately for his theory, French names were also given Gaelic roots: Montreal was explained as *Monadh thri allt*, "mount of three streams," while Rideau reminded him of *ruith dubh*, Gaelic for "black river." He considered Montreal a "most handsome town, brimming over with food and drink and with many types of work which are always easy for emigrants to find." He knew of Gaels who had arrived there with only a shilling to their name but who were "wealthy men today, accustomed to the common language of that country, and independent of the world." Even the name of the great Tecumseh was rendered from *deadh chuise*, "straight aim."[45] Obviously Gaels could expect to feel at home in Canada.

The deeply entrenched idea that the North American First Peoples spoke Gaelic can be traced to David Malcolme, minister of Duddingston, Edinburgh, who in the early eighteenth century interviewed the veterans of the Darien expeditions on the matter of language.[46] He subsequently convinced a committee of the Church of Scotland that the Dariens did indeed speak Gaelic, as did the inhabitants of the entire American continent. This utterly deluded notion was thus one of the longest-lasting legacies of the Darien disaster (1698–1700) and is not yet completely discredited in certain quarters.

The underlying theme of MacDougall's short book is that Canada was the place of choice for Scots and especially Gaels, and he did proffer some useful advice. Like many writers he observed the weather: "any man who has never been away from Scotland may talk, read, imagine, and dream of cold until he goes grey, but as long as he lives, he will never comprehend the extent of the cold in Canada." Since Gaelic did not have the words to describe it, he gave up hope "that there is any other language that can." He included several evocative lines on mosquitoes, and he warned that snakes in Upper Canada were even more plentiful than "midges in the Black Forest of Rannoch on a July night." He complained of English writers who went over to America (meaning Canada and the United States), running "through the country like a clucking hen on a hot griddle, and who then come back and shout at the top of their voices" about advice for emigrants. He preferred to give sensible counsel about choosing land and livestock, realistic appraisal of economic conditions, and honest opinions about the nature of Canadian society. In a highly sympathetic chapter on the First Nations, in which he detected many customs in common between them and his own folk, he praised their "commanding valiant men," observing that he never expected to encounter people who were "more respectful towards others."[47]

American "Indians" had often been cited by writers of the Scottish Enlightenment, particularly those in pursuit of "conjectural history," which involved substituting anthropological material when discussing historical periods for which there was little or no evidence. Thus the stage of "civilization" achieved by the Native population of the Americas was deemed to replicate that of Scotland at some time in its past – and one not very far distant when surveying the history of the Gaels. Scottish emigrants who described their experiences of the First Nations of Canada may actually have believed that they witnessed an earlier stage of their own history. Scientific interest was present when Alexander and Gordon, in their Nova Scotia tracts, pointed to the nobility of the Native Peoples, their potential value as allies, and the desirability of learning something of their language. It is striking in subsequent literature that Scots wrote most approvingly of Native culture and customs, suggesting a certain empathy extending to linguistics, ethnography, and anthropology, all of which were reinforced by Enlightenment writers. There is certainly a subject here – the relationship between Scots and North American First Peoples – which merits much closer investigation.

Space does not permit discussion of the practical scientific observations of dozens of Scots who were motivated as much by humanity and sympathy as they were by the fad for classification and categorization. Andrew Graham's scrupulous observations of Hudson Bay in the later eighteenth century, for example, are prime sources for the Native Peoples of the area.[48] Alexander Mackenzie's pessimistic prognosis for the future of the tribes to the west of the Great Lakes is well known.[49] John Richardson[50] and John Rae[51] paid close attention to the customs and practices of the inhabitants during their Arctic expeditions. By midcentury, as in MacDougall's effusion, laudatory passages on the Natives were almost mandatory. Robert Brown, on the Vancouver Island Expedition of 1864 at the tender age of twenty-two, wrote extensively about the Natives he encountered and their culture, sprinkling his text with Scotticisms. He provided an account of a potlatch, as well as a collection of Native legendary and mythical material.[52]

The Reverend George Grant, who famously chronicled Sandford Fleming's expedition of 1872, adhered to the well-worn clichés of high regard for the "noble savages" and of the Scottish predisposition towards recognition of the familiar in the wilderness. So prevalent were Scots and things Scottish that Grant could write, "although in a new land we were still in our own country." Parts of Manitoba reminded him of Moffatdale and many other similar valleys in the south of Scotland, "but here there had never been bold moss troopers and there were no 'Tales of the Borders.' Crees and Sioux and Ojibbeways may have gone on the warpath against each other ... but there has been no Walter Scott ... to gather up and record their legends and hand down the fame of their braves," or so, in his literate-centric fashion, he thought. August 12 found the party up early "as if near a Highland moor," with plentiful supplies of snipe, plover, and duck. Canadian sites frequently reminded Grant of the Pentlands, the Highlands, or the Borders, but even in his sympathetic pages – and he was, after all, a minister – a new tone is to be detected:

When a Scotchman married a squaw, her position was not much higher than a servant's. He was the "superior person" of the house. He continued Christian after his fashion, she continued pagan. The granite of his nature resisted fusion in spite of family and tribal influences, the attrition of all surrounding circumstances and the total absence of civilisation; and the wife was too completely separated from him to be able to raise herself to his level.

Racism had raised its ugly head and white supremacy was emphatically endorsed.[53]

With hindsight it can be said that the heyday of Confederation and the creation of Sir John A. Macdonald's Dominion marked the high point of Scottish influence in Canada.⁵⁴ The year 1867 inspired an outpouring of patriotic poetry on the part of Alexander McLachlan, who emigrated from Renfrewshire in 1840, aged twenty-two. He composed such poems as "The Men of the Dominion," "Hurrah for the New Dominion," and "Young Canada or Jack's as Goods His Master." He never lost the Chartist ideals of his youth or a lifelong Burns-like concern for the plight of humanity. He tried to keep alive in his verse a sense of Scottish identity, but in much of his poetry, notably the complex and ambitious multipart sequence entitled "The Emigrant," he also attempted to create a poetic identity for his adopted country. Although the poem was a failure, Elizabeth Waterston is not entirely correct to suggest that it was such because McLachlan "remained an emigrant, not an immigrant," that "he was too tied to his native range of awareness to be able to move on and adjust as poet to his new homeland," or that "it was a mark of his limitation as well as of his achievement that he was always called 'the Burns of Canada.'"⁵⁵ Frederick Niven, the Scottish novelist who made his home in British Columbia, observed that "Scotland is a place in the sun and the rain, but it is more than that; it is a kingdom of the mind ... The old love for it endures, whatever [a Scot's] reason or necessity for living elsewhere."⁵⁶ By 1867 it could be said that Canada was well and truly "Scotched," but it was the very strength of an awareness of Scottishness, of "the kingdom of the mind," that stimulated McLachlan and others like him, such as Robert Service⁵⁷ or Niven himself, to confer a similar boon on their homeland of choice.

NOTES

1 From "The Canadian Boat Song." The poem's title is still uncritically accepted in Canada, even today, although its referents are almost entirely Scottish. Despite the efforts of several enquirers the author remains unknown. See, among others, George M. Fraser, *The Lone Shieling, or the Authorship of the Canadian Boat Song* (Aberdeen 1908); Thomas Newbigging, *The Canadian Boat Song and Other Papers* (London: Sherrat R. Hughes 1912); Edward MacCurdy, *A Literary Enigma, The Canadian Boat Song: Its Authorship and Associations* (Stirling: Eneas Mackay 1935); and "The 'Canadian Boat-Song': A Mosaic," compiled by D.M.R. Bentley, *Canadian Poetry* 6 (1980): 69–79.
2 *Blackwood's Edinburgh Magazine* was a monthly periodical begun by Scots publisher William Blackwood (1776–1834) as a rival to the *Edinburgh Re-*

view. Also known as "the Maga," it ran in one form or another from 1817 to 1980.

3 The *Noctes Ambrosianae* were a popular series of dialogues presenting a romanticized and whimsical view of Scotland. They were devised by the writer and critic J.G. Lockhart (1794–1854) and published in *Blackwood's* from 1822 to 1835.

4 Hogg was a poet, novelist, essayist and storyteller from the Ettrick Valley in the Scottish Borders (1772–1835).

5 "*Noctes Ambrosianae*," no. 46, *Blackwood's Edinburgh Magazine*, September 1829, 399–400.

6 Edward J. Cowan, "The Myth of Scotch Canada," in *Myth, Migration and the Making of Memory: Scotia and Nova Scotia, c. 1700–1990*, ed. Marjory Harper and Michael Vance (Halifax: Fernwood Publishing/John Donald 1999), 49–72.

7 H.S. Burrage, *Early English and French Voyages: Chiefly from Hakluyt, 1534–1608* (New York: Scribners 1906). The Scots may have been at a disadvantage as far as the Auld Alliance between Scotland and France (1295–1560) was concerned, so often exploited militarily by their ally with little or no benefit to themselves. Nonetheless, Scottish intellectuals continued to be hugely influenced by French ideas long after the Reformation.

8 Victoria Dickenson, *Drawn from Life: Science and Art in the Portrayal of the New World* (Toronto: University of Toronto Press 1998).

9 Both Wilson and Fleming were "time lords" in their own right, the former organizing the epochs of prehistory, the latter standardizing world time. See Marinell Ash, *Thinking with Both Hands: Sir Daniel Wilson in the Old World and the New*, ed. Elizabeth Hulse (Toronto: University of Toronto Press 1999), especially articles by M. Ash (60–80), B. Trigger (81–100), B. McCardle (101–14), and S. Zeller (115–38); and Clark Blaise, *Time Lord: The Remarkable Canadian Who Missed His Train and Changed the World* (Toronto: Alfred A. Knopf Canada 2000).

10 The Masonic order originated in Scotland in 1598 as a craft guild to which those who were not members of the craft soon sought admission. When the Royal Society was established in 1660, its first president was a Scot, Sir Robert Moray; the latter was also a Mason. See David Stevenson, *The Origins of Freemasonry: Scotland's Century* (Cambridge: Cambridge University Press 1988) and *The First Freemasons Scotland's Early Lodges and Their Members* (Aberdeen: Aberdeen University Press 1988). In 1660 Glasgow licensed a school for the teaching of mathematics. See T.M. Devine and G. Jackson, eds., *Glasgow*, vol. 2, *Beginnings to 1830* (Manchester: Manchester University Press 1995), 39.

11 By the early nineteenth century the Scots more or less monopolized the publication of scientific journals. See Richard Hamblyn, *The Invention of Clouds: How an Amateur Meteorologist Forged the Language of the Skies* (Basingstoke and Oxford: Picador 2001), 112–20. A little later the Chambers brothers specialized in the provision of books and magazines on popular science.

12 Captain James Cook (1728–79) was probably the greatest explorer and traveller in world history; his father hailed from the Scottish Borders.

13 The Douglas fir's scientific name, *Pseudotsuga menziesii*, commemorates a fellow countryman, Archibald Menzies from Aberfeldy, another surgeon-naturalist who had accompanied George Vancouver's expedition in 1792. Clive L. Justice, *Mr Menzies' Garden Legacy: Plant Collecting on the Northwest Coast* (Vancouver: Cavendish Books 2000).

14 The following is drawn in part from David Douglas, *Journal Kept by David Douglas during His Travels in North America* (London 1914), and Ann L. Mitchell and Syd House, *David Douglas, Explorer and Botanist* (London: Aurum Press 1999), 49–140. See also John Davies, *Douglas of the Forests: The North American Journals of David Douglas* (Edinburgh: Paul Harris 1979), a much-shortened edition with most of the scientific detail removed.

15 Later in life MacLoughlin became known as the Father of Oregon. He eventually surrendered his British citizenship only to be betrayed by the Americans. See Robert C. Johnson, *John McLoughlin: "Father of Oregon"* (Portland: Binfords & Mort 1958), especially 275–94. The most recent biography is Dorothy N. Morrison, *Outpost: John McLoughlin and the Far Northwest* (Portland: Oregon Historical Society 1999).

16 John Prebble, *The King's Jaunt: George IV in Scotland, August 1822, "One and twenty daft days"* (London: Collins 1988).

17 W. Kaye Lamb, ed., *The Letters and Journals of Simon Fraser 1806–1808* (Toronto: MacMillan Company of Canada 1960).

18 Derek Pethick, *James Douglas: Servant of Two Empires* (Vancouver: Mitchell Press 1969); John Adams, *Old Square-Toes and His Lady: The Life of James and Amelia Douglas* (Victoria, BC: Horsdal and Schubart 2001).

19 On whom see M.J. Ross, *Polar Pioneers: John Ross and James Clark Ross* (Montreal and Kingston: McGill-Queen's University Press 1994).

20 C. Stuart Houston ed., *Arctic Ordeal: The Journal of John Richardson, Surgeon-Naturalist with Franklin, 1820–22* (Kingston and Montreal: McGill-Queen's University Press 1984).

21 Houston, *Arctic Ordeal*, 180n.

22 R.G. Large, ed., *The Journals of William Fraser Tolmie, Physician and Fur Trader* (Vancouver: Mitchell Press 1963).

23 John Galt, *The Autobiography of John Galt*. 2 vols. (Edinburgh 1833), vol. 1, 7.

24 Gilbert Stelter, "John Galt as Town Booster and Builder," *John Galt Reappraisals*, Elizabeth Waterston, ed. (Guelph, ON: University of Guelph 1985), 17–43. Galt, *Autobiography*, vol. 2, is greatly concerned with Galt's treatment by the Canada Company, especially appendix, 295–351.

25 William Dunlop, *Statistical Sketches of Upper Canada, for the Use of Emigrants: By a Backwoodsman* (London 1832). See also David Sinclair and Germaine Warkenstein, eds., *The New World Journal of Alexander Graham Dunlop, 1845* (Edinburgh and Toronto: Paul Harris Publishing 1976). For a list of Dunlop's main publications see "William 'Tiger' Dunlop, Blackwoodian Backwoodsman," in *Essays by and about Dunlop*, ed. Carl F. Klinck (Toronto: Ryerson Press 1958), 179–80.

26 Robina Lizars and Kathleen M. Lizars, *In the Days of the Canada Company: The Story of the Settlement of the Huron Tract and a View of the Social Life of the Period, 1825–1850* (Toronto: William Briggs 1896), 171, 163–4.

27 Catherine Parr Traill, *The Backwoods of Canada* (London: Charles Knight 1836; Toronto: McClelland and Stewart 1989); *The Canadian Settler's Guide* (Toronto 1855; Toronto: McClelland and Stewart 1969). See also Marian Fowler, *The Embroidered Tent: Five Gentlewomen in Early Canada* (Concord: Anansi Press 1982), and Charlotte Gray, *Sisters in the Wilderness: The Lives of Susanna Moodie and Catharine Parr Traill* (Toronto: Penguin Books 1999).

28 Adam Fergusson, *Practical Notes Made during a Tour in Canada, and a Portion of the United States in 1831* (Edinburgh: Blackwood, 1839).

29 William Cattermole, *Emigration: The Advantages of Emigration to Canada, Being the Substance of Two Lectures, Delivered at the Town-Hall, Colchester, and the Mechanics' Institution, Ipswich* (London: Simpkin and Marshall 1831), 194–205. See also Edward J. Cowan, "From the Southern Uplands to Southern Ontario: Nineteenth-Century Emigration from the Scottish Borders," in T.M. Devine, ed., *Scottish Emigration and Scottish Society* (Edinburgh: John Donald 1992), 61–83.

30 Vera Cunliffe, *From Edinburgh to Colborne Township: Daniel Lizars and the Pioneer Collection at Guelph* (Guelph, ON: University of Guelph Library 1984).

31 Lizars and Lizars, *Days of the Canada Company*, 215. The Lizars erroneously associated these remarks with the election meeting at Jedburgh in 1831, at which "the mob were exceedingly vociferous and brutal" towards Scott. In fact they were occasioned by certain proposed innovations in Scots law in 1806. Scott vented his opinion on the Mound, Edinburgh, on his way home, becoming so emotional that tears gushed down his cheek. "Seldom, if ever, in his more advanced age did any feelings obtain such mastery." J.G. Lockhart, *The Life of Sir Walter Scott, Bart.*, 2 vols. (London 1848), vol. 1, 133; for the Jedburgh incident see vol. 2, 228.

32 Kirkcudbright Museum Archives, no. 88, MacTaggart Letters, 25 August 1824.

33 The sense here appears to be "will make a beautiful [English] speaker of my grandmother," who would, of course, in real life have spoken broad Scots.

34 John Howison, *Sketches of Upper Canada, Domestic, Local, and Characteristic: to which are added Practical Details for the Information of Every Class and Some Recollections of the United States of America* (Edinburgh and London: Oliver and Boyd 1821), 175.

35 John Galt, *Lawrie Todd* (London: Walter Scott 1832), 41, 57–8, 160, 184. Galt helpfully included "Yankeyisms" in the novel's glossary.

36 John Galt, *Bogle Corbet*, Elizabeth Waterston, ed. (Toronto: McLelland and Stewart 1977), 2. Unfortunately this edition prints only volume 3 of the novel.

37 John Galt, *Bogle Corbet; or, The Emigrants*, 3 vols. (London: Colburn and Bently 1831), vol. 3, 209–11.

38 Susanna Moodie, *Roughing It in the Bush, or Forest Life in Canada* (London 1852; Toronto: McClelland and Stewart 1962), 92. See also *Life in the Clearings versus the Bush* (London: Richard Bentley 1853; Toronto: McClellend and Stewart 1989) and two volumes edited by C. Ballstadt, E. Hopkins, and M. Peterman, *Susanna Moodie: Letters of a Lifetime* (Toronto:

University of Toronto Press 1985); *Letters of Love and Duty: The Correspondence of Susanna and John Moodie* (Toronto: University of Toronto Press 1993).

39 Robert MacDougall, *The Emigrant's Guide to North America*, ed. Elizabeth Thompson (Toronto: Natural Heritage Books 1998), 66–7.
40 Muirkirk, Ayrshire, owed its existence to the discovery of iron ore in 1787. The population in 1831 was 2,816. Francis H. Groome, ed., *Ordnance Gazetteer of Scotland: A Survey of Scottish Topography, Statistical, Biographical, and Historical*, 3 vols (Edinburgh: Thomas C. Jack 1886), vol. 2, 82.
41 On Glengarry, Ontario, see Rae Fleming, ed., *The Lochaber Emigrants to Glengarry* (Toronto: Natural Heritage Books 1994).
42 The Dumfriesshire village of Dunscore is tiny. In 1831 the population of the parish, as opposed to the village, was 1,488. Groome, *Gazetteer*, vol. 1, 446.
43 Lizars and Lizars, *Days of the Canada Company*, 159–60.
44 All references are from John MacTaggart, *Three Years in Canada: An Account of the Actual State of the Country in 1826–7–8*, 2 vols. (London: H. Colburn 1829), vol. 1, 37, 42, 46, 170; vol. 2, 123, 192–3. On MacTaggart see Julia M. Watt, *Dumfries and Galloway: A Literary Guide* (Dumfries: Dumfries and Galloway Libraries, Information and Archives 2000), 260–3.
45 MacDougall, *Emigrant's Guide*, 48, 41–3, 50, 36–9.
46 David Malcolme, *An Essay on the Antiquities of Great Britain and Ireland ... an attempt to show an affinity between the languages etc of the ancient Britains and the Americans of the Isthmus of Darien* (Edinburgh 1738).
47 MacDougall, *Emigrant's Guide*, 64, 116–19, 69–87, 91–107, 39, 30–40.
48 G. Williams and R. Glover, eds., *Andrew Graham's Observations on Hudson's Bay, 1767–91* (London: The Hudson's Bay Record Society 1969).
49 Alexander Mackenzie, *Voyages from Montreal on the River St Laurence through the Continent of North America to the Frozen and Pacific Oceans in the Years 1789 and 1793, with a Preliminary Account of the Rise, Progress, and Present State of the Fur Trade of That Country* (London 1801; Edmonton: Hurtig 1971).
50 Houston, *Arctic Ordeal*.
51 R.L. Richards, *Dr John Rae* (Whitby: Caedmon of Whitby Publishers 1985); I. Bunyan et al., *No Ordinary Journey: John Rae, Arctic Explorer, 1813–1893* (Edinburgh and Montreal: National Museum of Scotland and McGill-Queen's University Press 1993); Ken McGoogan, *Fatal Passage: The Untold Story of John Rae, The Arctic Adventurer Who Discovered the Fate of Franklin* (Toronto: Harper Flamingo Canada 2001).
52 John Hayman, ed., *Robert Brown and the Vancouver Island Exploring Expedition* (Vancouver: University of British Columbia Press 1989), especially 157–97. Brown was born at Camster, Caithness.
53 George Grant, *Ocean to Ocean: Sandford Fleming's Expedition through Canada in 1872, Being a Diary Kept during a Journey from the Atlantic to the Pacific, with the Expedition of the Engineer-in-Chief of the Canadian Pacific and Intercolonial Railways* (Toronto: James Campbell and Son 1873), 86–7, 106, 118, 175–6. August 12, 'the Glorious Twelfth,' marked the start of the grouse-shooting season in Scotland.

54 Cowan, "Myth of Scotch Canada," 66.
55 Elizabeth Waterston, *Rapt in Plaid: Canadian Literature and Scottish Tradition* (Toronto: University of Toronto Press 2001), 27, and *The Poetical Works of Alexander McLachlan* (Toronto: William Briggs 1900), 205–8, 209–56.
56 Frederick Niven, *Coloured Spectacles* (London: Collins 1938), 351–2.
57 Edward J. Cowan, "The War Rhymes of Robert Service, Folk Poet," *Studies in Scottish Literature* 28 (1993): 12–27.

TWO

Exiles or Entrepreneurs? Snapshots of the Scots in Canada

Marjory Harper

Were Scottish emigrants to Canada unwilling exiles or adventurous entrepreneurs? Was emigration an escape route for the poor and persecuted or an avenue of advancement for the ambitious? While the evidence, not surprisingly, suggests both, it is clear that hope was nearly always a much stronger sentiment than despair or resignation. This study explores various dimensions of emigration from Scotland to Canada – particularly in the nineteenth century – with reference to the inducements that attracted the emigrants, the relationship between their expectations and their experiences, and the impact they made on Canadian society from the Atlantic to the Pacific.

The statistical significance of Canada to Scottish emigrants is evident: until 1847, from 1910 to 1914, and again after the First World War, more Scots went to Canada than to any other country.[1] Even when the United States was absorbing the vast majority of Scottish emigrants to North America, Scottish newspapers and journals still concentrated primarily on Canada in their advertisements, correspondence, and articles. As a result British North America had a consistently high profile in the Scottish media, more so than any other emigrant destination, and Scottish settlers had a similarly high profile in Canada, even though numerically they lagged behind the Irish and the English. Throughout this period parts of Canada exuded a strong Scottish identity, most explicitly in the preservation of Gaelic language and culture in Cape Breton, Quebec's Eastern Townships, Glengarry County, Ontario, and a scattering of Highland crofter settlements on the prairies.

ATTRACTING THE AMBITIOUS

Scots from all corners of the homeland were consistently attracted to North America from the early eighteenth century on, and their motives and aspirations for emigrating during this long period reflect some long-standing continuities.

One of these was the clear focus on acquiring land. Before the American Revolution, Scots had gone further south under the auspices of proprietors, emigration societies, and land companies, but by the beginning of the nineteenth century these approaches to settlement had been transferred to the remaining British territories to the north. In 1803 Thomas Douglas, fifth Earl of Selkirk, managed to secure cheaply a number of lots on Prince Edward Island. To that moribund settlement he brought eight hundred settlers in three ships, in what was to become the most successful of his three colonizing ventures. The settlers, most of whom came from Skye, were attracted by his offer to sell land rather than lease it, and within a few years the area around Orwell had attracted about three thousand Scots. At the heart of the settlement at Belfast the tombstones in the churchyard still bear witness to the West Highland origins of the pioneers and their successors, who were drawn to that Scottish colony until the middle of the nineteenth century, even when most Scots were directing their steps much further west.[2]

It was not only Highlanders who settled in concentrated clusters. In 1820 and 1821 just over three thousand unemployed weavers from Glasgow and the surrounding counties emigrated – with the aid of unprecedented, if limited and short-lived, government funding –

to the Ottawa and Rideau Valleys. Like Selkirk's colonists these emigrants made the voyage to take up farming careers. The tone of their correspondence suggests that the change of location and career direction was generally successful and, as in Prince Edward Island, may have induced chain migration.[3] At the same time, land companies were attracting significant numbers of Scots to the Huron Tract and to Quebec's Eastern Townships. Margaret Bennett has clearly demonstrated how the Eastern Townships – particularly Bury and Lingwick – became an enclave of Gaelic-speaking Scots from the Isle of Lewis, with customs and lifestyles similar to more immediately recognizable Scottish areas like Cape Breton.[4]

The benefits of owning land in Canada were touted ceaselessly in the Scottish press, where the contrast with restricted farming horizons at home was a favourite theme. In Canada emigrants did not have to acquire their land from land companies or speculators; they could buy from the Crown or from private vendors, and after 1872 they could obtain free quarter sections in the prairie provinces. Good farms could be bought for the equivalent of a year's rent at home, held in perpetuity, and bequeathed unencumbered to the next generation.

In Scotland the time was ripe for such encouragement. Not only were Highlanders being forced off their ancestral lands by clearance policies that were replacing people with sheep; lowlanders, too, were facing dislocation as the commercialization of agriculture, involving steeply rising rents and the consolidation of farms, eroded the prospects of both tenant farmers and the large number of farm labourers who aspired to become leaseholders in their own right. These people and others, such as first-generation migrants from the land to the towns, were likely to respond enthusiastically to reports of a country free from interfering landlords, high rents, and crippling taxation, where freehold land was offered in abundance. Much more significant than general press encouragement, however, were personal recommendations from family and friends already in Canada, particularly if the encouragement to emigrate was accompanied by a remittance or prepaid transatlantic ticket.

The significance of this type of chain migration is clearly demonstrated in the settlement of Bon Accord in southern Ontario, founded in the mid-1830s by a contingent of emigrants from Aberdeen and its hinterland. Scottish emigrant and land speculator Adam Fergusson

Memorial to Lord Selkirk's settlement in Belfast,
Prince Edward Island. Courtesy of the Prince Edward
Island Public Archives and Records Office

had established the nearby township of Fergus in 1833, and a year
later a group of friends in Aberdeen, who for some time had been
meeting together to discuss the pros and cons of emigration, sent one
of their number to the area to investigate these claims. The group's
representative, merchant George Elmslie, was instructed to make pur-
chases on their behalf if the land matched up to Fergusson's description. He was impressed enough to buy a large swathe of land – twelve
hundred acres – for himself and his friends and stay on in Canada to

begin clearing the site. The first of Elmslie's fellow townsmen joined him in 1835, and the stream of arrivals from Aberdeen continued throughout the decade, most of the emigrants travelling on timber ships to Quebec before making their way west to the settlement, which they named after the motto of their native city. A handful of Aberdeen-born emigrants already settled elsewhere in Upper Canada chose to move to Bon Accord after hearing of the growing nucleus of Northeast Scots in that vicinity. Contrary to common stereotypes of Scottish emigration, none of these settlers was impoverished; all could afford to pay their passages and purchase farms when they arrived, and several also paid contractors to clear their land.[5]

James Thompson was less well off and an example of an emigrant who worked his way up from wage labouring to independent farming. A journeyman baker, he left Aboyne in Aberdeenshire in 1844, going first to Montreal, where he used a letter of introduction to the minister of St Gabriel Street Presbyterian Church to secure lodgings and employment. For the next seven years he worked at a variety of jobs in Montreal, Ontario, Chicago, and California, until he had saved enough money to buy a farm in Ontario. Throughout that period he regularly sent home remittances, initially to maintain his father and siblings in Scotland. Ultimately, he paid their way to join him – with the exception of his brother Sandy, who had squandered a remittance James had sent home earlier to fund his passage and was not given another chance.[6]

Those without friends or relatives already in Canada to finance a passage or offer encouragement could resort to the advice of an emigration agent. The role of these agents became increasingly significant as the service grew more professionalized and sophisticated, particularly after Confederation. Resident, salaried federal government agents were based in strategic towns across the British Isles, liaising with an army of ticket agents and temporary lecturers, as well as with agents representing the provinces and the transcontinental railway companies. From 1869 to 1907 the whole of Scotland, along with the north of England, was under the control of one federal agent based in Glasgow. In 1907 a second, Gaelic-speaking agent was appointed to cover the north of Scotland, and in 1923 a third office was opened in Inverness.

Emigration agents exploited every promotional tool available to them, very clearly focusing their efforts on the farming community. Written advertising was the easiest and most effective method of blanket publicity. In addition to publishing regular press advertisements, the agents displayed colourful posters and handbills in libraries, post offices, and other public places. They distributed large numbers of government-sponsored pamphlets to these institutions, as well as to individual farmers, clergymen, and teachers, and essay competitions were organized in schools, to which atlases were also distributed. The written word was also reinforced by visual and verbal promotion. Displays of Canadian produce were mounted at agricultural shows and in agents' office windows, and illustrated lectures – delivered in the remotest of places, usually at the most hostile times of year – sometimes attracted audiences of one thousand and more. A particular premium was set on lecture tours, which were often organized by regional booking agents.[7]

In 1924 a delegation of Scottish journalists touring Canada at the invitation of the Canadian National Railways made a stop in Prince Edward Island. There they encountered emigrants whose experience suggested that the agents' efforts were not without their intended effect. One of the delegation, the editor of the *Press & Journal*,[8] visited the farm of Robert Rhynes, a former engine driver from Aberdeen, who related how in 1910 he had decided to emigrate to the Island rather than to the prairies after encountering a persuasive Island agent at an agricultural show in his home city.[9]

UNLOADING THE UNWANTED

Most emigrants therefore looked forward positively to better opportunities in the New World, often inspired by the vision of achieving security and independence through land ownership. But some Scots were clearly pushed rather than pulled to Canada. We cannot ignore the fact that on both sides of the Atlantic, emigration was sometimes perceived as a device for expelling the unwanted from Scotland. Certainly, the thirteen thousand weavers from Central Scotland who joined emigration societies in the late 1810s and early 1820s would not have done so if they had been able to make a living at home. Their

DOES

the present outlook for yourself and family satisfy your aspiration ? If not, the Canadian Government guarantees placement of married couples and experienced and inexperienced men on farms without charge.

CANADA

is urgently calling for farmers and farm workers. The British and Canadian Governments assist to place desirable British families with some farm experience on Canadian farms and help and advise them until established.

Special reduced rates are available for settlers to whom these offers

APPEAL

Emigrate under direct auspices, of the Canadian Government, which guarantees employment and after-care and supervision.

For full information apply to Dept. 73
Canadian Government Emigration Agent,
107, Hope Street, GLASGOW.

Canadian government press advertisement for farmers and farm workers, *Scottish Farmer*, 29 January 1927

petitions to the government were often voiced in terms of prospective starvation or the possibility that they would become a burden on the parish. But images of expulsion are more explicitly and contentiously associated with the Highlands. When the Highland economy went into severe recession after the end of the Napoleonic Wars, landlords' plans for estate redevelopment, which some of them had been constructing for more than half a century, began to crumble. Whereas they had previously viewed and nurtured the densely packed Highland population as an asset – indeed a necessity – they now came to regard it as a millstone around their necks. Having opposed emigration tooth and nail in the optimistic mercantilist era before the wars, the landlords now increasingly came to welcome it as a method of reducing chronic overpopulation on their properties. In the general absence of government funding they began to introduce their own assisted passages to Canada, the nearest and therefore cheapest destination to which to send their unwanted tenants.

It should be noted that the phrase "assisted passage" was often something of a euphemism. The practice began in a Highland context in 1825, when the laird of the island of Rum cleared 300 of his 350 tenants to Cape Breton before leasing the island to a single sheep farmer at a much-enhanced rental. It continued through the potato famines of the 1830s and 1840s, with one newspaper estimating that in the decade to 1849, 20,000 Highlanders had immigrated to Canada.[10] Alexander Buchanan, Canada's chief immigration agent, was less than complimentary about some of the newly arrived Highlanders, who had to be forwarded from Quebec to Upper Canada at government expense. When over 1,600 arrived in August 1849 alone, he observed, "They are respectable, orderly people, but many of them very poor ... Few of them could speak English."[11] He was particularly scathing about parsimonious landlords who made deliberately inadequate provision for their tenants. Most notorious in this respect was John Gordon, proprietor of the Hebridean islands of Barra and South Uist, who in 1851 shipped 1,681 tenants to Quebec, hoping Buchanan's department would pick up the cost of onward transportation.

Gordon was also vilified in the Canadian and Scottish press for the brutal recruitment techniques that he allegedly used in rounding up emigrants, as well as in anticlearance polemics such as Donald MacLeod's *Gloomy Memories of the Highlands of Scotland* and Alexander MacKenzie's *History of the Highland Clearances*.[12] These accounts described how unwilling emigrants were chased across the *machair* by policemen and factors and packed aboard the ships like African slaves, while Canadian newspapers complained about their destitute and distressed state on arrival.[13] The *Quebec Times* pulled no punches:

Many of our readers may not be aware that there lives such a personage as Colonel Gordon, proprietor of large estates, South Uist and Barra, in the Highlands of Scotland; we are sorry to be obliged to introduce him to their notice, under circumstances which will not give them a very favourable opinion of his character and heart.

It appears that tenants on the above mentioned estates were on the verge of starvation, and had probably become an eyesore to the gallant Colonel! He decided on shipping them to America. What they were to do there, was a question he never put to his conscience. Once landed in Canada, he had no further concern about them. Up to last week, 1,100 souls from his estates had landed in Quebec, and begged their way to Upper Canada; when in the summer season, having only a morsel of food to procure, they probably escaped the extreme misery which seems to be the lot of those who followed them.

On their arrival here, they voluntarily made and signed the following statement:

We the undersigned passengers per *Admiral* from Stornaway [*sic*], in the Highlands of Scotland, do solemnly depose to the following facts:– That Colonel Gordon is the proprietor of the estates of South Uist and Barra; that among many hundreds of tenants and cotters whom he has sent this season from his estates to Canada, he gave directions to his factor, Mr. Fleming of Cluny Castle, Aberdeenshire, to ship on board of the above named vessel a number of nearly 450 of said tenants and cotters from the estate in Barra – that accordingly, a great majority of these people, among whom were the undersigned, proceeded voluntarily to embark on board the *Admiral*, at Loch Boysdale, on or about the 11th August 1851; but that several of the people who were intended to be shipped for this port, Quebec, refused to proceed on board, and in fact, absconded from their homes to avoid the embarkation. Whereupon Mr. Fleming gave orders to a policeman, who was accompanied by the ground officer of the estate of Barra, and some constables, to pursue the people who had ran [*sic*] away among the mountains; which they did, and succeeded in capturing about twenty from the mountains and islands in the neighbourhood; but only came with the officers on an attempt being made to handcuff them; and that some who ran away were not brought back, in consequence of which four families, at least, have been divided, some having come in the ships to Quebec, while other members of the same families were left in the Highlands.[14]

Equally uninvolved in the decision to emigrate were the thousands of Home Children sent to Canada between the 1870s and the 1930s – around one hundred thousand in all. Although the institutions that implemented this policy insisted that their schemes were beneficial to donor and recipient countries and children alike, Canadian opinion tended to feel that the Dominion was being burdened with the flotsam and jetsam of Britain's city slums. The main Scottish participant was Quarrier's Orphan Homes of Scotland, which sent to Canada seven thousand of the thirty-five thousand children it took into care from various deprived and depraved backgrounds after it opened its doors in 1871. The children were shipped out to a receiving home built by Quarrier's in Brockville, Ontario, before being placed in private households as farm hands and domestic servants.[15]

IMAGE AND REALITY

Did the experiences of Scottish settlers in Canada confirm or conflict with their expectations? The first area in which image and reality could be compared was the journey itself. Guidebooks bombarded would-be emigrants with advice on how to cope with the Atlantic crossing, particularly in sailing ships. Emigrants were well aware that the voyage was more likely to be a test of endurance than a luxury cruise, but probably nothing prepared them for confinement with three hundred or so fellow passengers in the squalor of the steerage, particularly during bad weather when they were left alone in their seasickness, the hatches battened down and shutting out all light, ventilation, and access to even rudimentary sanitation.

The passengers in the *Hector*, arguably Canada's *Mayflower*, which sailed from Loch Broom to Pictou in 1773, allegedly found the vessel so rotten that they whiled away their time picking the rotten wood out of the hull with their fingers. Food ran low and went mouldy, smallpox and dysentery broke out, and eighteen children died.[16] But the story was not unequivocally negative, for recent research has shown that many of the timber vessels that brought Scottish emigrants across the Atlantic in the nineteenth century were not the leaky coffin ships of legend but were often new, A1-registered vessels with good captains and reputations. News headlines were made by disasters, such as the loss of the *Annie Jane* off the Hebrides en route to Quebec with emigrants and pig iron in 1853, but for most emigrants the experience of the voyage was one of tedium rather than tragedy.[17]

Once emigrants reached their destination they could test the veracity, or otherwise, of all the promises held out by relatives, agents, or guidebooks. While there were few complaints, at least in public, about the advice given by family and friends, there were some bitter complaints about fraudulent agents. The passengers on the *Hector*, having been promised splendid farms, were aghast – coming from the treeless west coast of Scotland – to be set down in a dense forest, where they would clearly have to learn skills of axemanship before they could even begin to cultivate their lands. In frustration they turned on their agent, John Ross. A century later more than seven hundred emigrants from northeast Scotland were enticed 168 miles up the St John River to the depths of the New Brunswick forest by William Brown, an Anchor Line captain, who devised a scheme to transplant a ready-made community from Scotland to a fifty-thousand-acre tract of land granted to him by the New Brunswick government. The emigrants arrived with great fanfare in Saint John, where they were piped ashore by the Saint Andrew's Society, but when they reached the settlement they found a shanty town encased in mud and snow that bore no resemblance to the picture of comfortable houses and good roads painted in advance by Captain Brown. He blamed the New Brunswick government for not fulfilling its part of the bargain, but the colonists, who found that German settlers had already claimed the best land, blamed William Brown.[18]

While some Home Children settled down happily with Canadian families, many who had been led to believe they would be adopted in the new land instead found themselves treated as cheap or unpaid labour, while a number were physically, psychologically, and sexually abused. They were commonly kept out of school to do farm or housework, ridiculed for their accents and their educational backwardness, and accused in the public press of introducing medical and moral pollution into rural Canada.[19] Women who emigrated under the auspices of female emigration societies also had mixed experiences. Encouraged to believe that they were performing a "civilizing mission" for the empire, as well as reducing the surplus of females at home, they were usually carefully chaperoned on the voyage and despatched to jobs from receiving homes in Quebec, Montreal, and Toronto. Many more women were enticed independently by the promises of booking agents that in Canada they would earn more money for less onerous work in a more egalitarian society. Some agents had bonuses revoked for sending unsuitable or incompetent girls, including a recruit sent from Aberdeen to Toronto in 1917 who on her Sunday off did not return until Wednesday and instead of working in domestic service aspired to be a cinema pianist.[20] For their part some of the girls felt that the selection process at the hostels was akin to a cattle market, yet much of the surviving correspondence suggests that the expectations of many were exceeded, rather than disappointed, by their experiences, with central heating and washing machines high on their list of the attractions of Canadian households. "You could have your clothes warm every morning if you chose, for there is a stove that burns all night, and pipes running through the house to keep it warm," enthused Elspet Knowles, an emigrant from Stonehaven in Kincardineshire who went into domestic service in Saint John, New Brunswick, in 1873.[21]

IDENTITIES

Finally, let us consider one of the most intangible issues surrounding the Scots in Canada, namely, the mechanisms by which their ethnic identity was preserved, reinvented, or discarded and the implications of such attitudes for the host country. Emigrants' expectations embraced much more than the practicalities of finding a farm or a job, making a living, and passing on a material inheritance to the next generation. Equally important to many was planting ethnic anchors that bridged the gap between the Old World and the New and allowed them to integrate memories of home into an unfamiliar environment.

It might be assumed that the entrepreneurial Scot, eager to forge a new life overseas, was unlikely to feel the need to remember his or her origins. It is true that some, for various reasons, deliberately sought to put the past behind them. Shortly after Murdo Macleod emigrated from Skye to Prince Edward Island in the 1830s, he received a letter from home expressing pleasure that he had arrived safely. When the correspondent referred to reports that Macleod was about to marry, the tone became somewhat frosty, not surprisingly, as the letter concluded, "Your affectionate wife, Effy Macdonald."[22]

Loss of identity was perhaps most noticed and commented on in Gaelic-speaking communities such as the Eastern Townships, where young Highlanders went off to New England in search of work and English was increasingly perceived as the language of progress. More bitter criticism was levelled at those who turned their backs on their religious heritage, again particularly in Gaelic-speaking communities. But even if the Scots did retain their religious and linguistic identity, it could still be a stumbling block or a source of discord, rather than an asset. A diatribe against the Scots of Pictou described them in 1859 as a "canting, covenanting, oat-eating, money-grabbing tribe of second-hand Scotch Presbyterians; a transplanted, degenerate, barren patch of high cheek bones and red hair, with nothing cleaving to them of the original stock, except covetousness and that peculiar cutaneous eruption for which the mother country is celebrated."[23] Further west on the prairies in the 1880s the sabbatarianism of the Highlanders irritated their less legalistic neighbours, who could not understand why they refused to shave on a Sunday, while the Gaelic language also isolated them from their neighbours, who were more experienced in prairie farming. According to the Killarney merchant who supplied the new arrivals with seed corn, "Gaelic may be a very nice and expressive dialect, but you cannot raise wheat from it."[24]

There were other ways in which emigrants could demonstrate their Scottish identity than by ethnic colonies and monolingualism. The extent to which they wished to remember probably depended, in part, on whether they saw themselves as passive exiles or active adventurers, with those who felt they had been forced out being more likely to cling to their Scottish roots. Yet even if they approached the issue of identity from different angles, exiles and entrepreneurs alike often saw the practical as well as the psychological value of demonstrating their nationality. The mechanisms they used included place-names, as we have seen in Bon Accord, and the dormer-windowed architecture of nearby Fergus, as well as the familiar icons of church, school, and Scottish sporting or cultural associations. Religious symbols were particularly important. Clergymen of all denominations, who were often seen as the keystones of emigrant communities, sometimes accompanied their flocks overseas. While this is evident in the Scottish Catholic communities established in Prince Edward Island and Glengarry County in the late eighteenth century, it is seen most famously in the worldwide wanderings of Norman McLeod, a rusticated Presbyterian cleric from Assynt. Having led four hundred followers from Loch Broom to Pictou in 1817, he relocated them at St Ann's in Cape Breton three years later, then between 1849 and 1851 uprooted them again and led them across the world, first to Australia and ultimately to settle for good as a Gaelic-speaking community at Waipu in New Zealand's North Island.[25]

From time to time clergy and emigrants grumbled about the lack of church provision. An unsigned appeal for a Presbyterian minister made by a group of early settlers in Cape Breton at the end of the eighteenth century asked for "a pastor to take care of our souls – we have none of our way here, only of the church of England and we was never brought up in that way."[26] In the same era Catholic clergy in both Quebec and Nova Scotia were voicing their concern that inadequate provision of Gaelic-speaking priests was encouraging apathy, drift, and loss of religious identity among the Scottish settlers. This refrain recurred throughout the nineteenth century, not just in eastern Canada but much further west too. In 1886 a priest who had recently taken up a charge among Gaelic-speaking crofters in the North West Territories wrote to the Bishop of Oban pleading the need for further help so that his flock would not be proselytised by neighbouring Protestants.[27]

The churches made a huge contribution to the forging of Scottish identity overseas, culturally as well as spiritually. In practical terms, the various denominations provided funds to build and staff churches in emigrant communities. Melville Church, in Captain Brown's Scotch Colony, was built with the aid of a £100 grant from the Free Church of Scotland. The existence of a church was also used to reassure those at home who were thinking of emigrating that their religious identity could be reconstituted overseas. "The greatest blessing of all," wrote Norman Mackenzie, of Lake Megantic, to his brother in Lewis in 1866, "is that we have the gospel preached to us in our own tongue."[28] The Highlanders who continued to flock to the Earl of Selkirk's colony in Prince Edward Island well into the nineteenth century were attracted partly by the clear religious dimension of the area's Scottish identity. This is highlighted in Sir Andrew MacPhail's autobiographical novel of life in Orwell, where, even among second- and third-generation settlers in the 1860s, "the way of life, religious customs and hierarchy of values were those of the old country."[29]

Closely allied with the church, of course, was the school. The Scotch Colony boasted four schools by 1877, and many ministers were also teachers. Emigrants could equally demonstrate their identity and their solidarity through a range of Scottish institutions, including Burns Clubs and Saint Andrew's Societies, some of which, through their charitable function, helped to turn exiles into entrepreneurs. According to Alexander MacKenzie it was only thanks to financial help from the Montreal Saint Andrew's Society that a group of 229 Lewis emigrants to the Eastern Townships in 1841 was saved from starvation and death, and the Scotch colonists in New Brunswick had to be assisted by the Saint Andrew's Society in Fredericton after their first, disastrous winter.[30]

But ethnic identity could also be spurious, and it is possible that the Scots in Canada, deliberately or subconsciously, filtered out images of home that did not fit the picture they wanted to create. Inevitably, memories of home became more divorced from reality as the years passed, but in some cases the image and the reality had never coincided. Perhaps those who were entrepreneurial but possessed a guilty conscience about their ambition and success could justify their emigration to themselves and others only if they painted a somewhat distorted picture of the land from which they had been exiled. There was of course a commercial dimension to such attitudes. Just as Scotland's tourist industry in the nineteenth century owed much to the romantic lure of an invented Highland landscape, so tourism in parts of Canada has been built on "tartanization," with the attendant proliferation of Highland games and Scottish heritage sites. Nowhere is this exemplified more clearly than in Nova Scotia. Deep in the forest of the Cape Breton Highlands National Park on the most northerly stretch of the Cabot Trail we find the "lone sheiling," a completely spurious 1930s replica of a Highland settler's home. More recently, Pictou's waterfront has been rejuvenated through the reconstruction of the pioneer ship *Hector* and the associated museum complex.[31] But perhaps this is simply another demonstration of how the Scots and their descendants have successfully turned exile into entrepreneurship.

NOTES

1 For statistical details, see N.H. Carrier and J.R. Jeffrey, *External Migration: A Study of the Available Statistics, 1815–1950* (London: HMSO 1953).

2 Selkirk's ideas of colonization are discussed in *The Collected Writings of Lord Selkirk, 1799–1809*, edited by J.M. Bumsted (Winnipeg: The Manitoba Record Society 1984). See also Lucille Campey, *"A Very Fine Class of Immigrants": Prince Edward Island's Scottish Pioneers, 1770–1850* (Toronto: Natural Heritage 2001).

3 Robert Lamond, A Narrative of the Rise and Progress of Emigration from the Counties of Lanark and Renfrew to the New Settlements in Upper Canada (Glasgow 1821); Carol Bennett, The Lanark Society Settlers, 1820–1821 (Renfrew, ON: Juniper 1991).

4 Margaret Bennett, *Oatmeal and the Catechism: Scottish Gaelic Settlers in Quebec* (Edinburgh and Montreal: John Donald/McGill-Queen's University Press 1998).

5 The Bon Accord settlement is described in Marjory Harper, *Emigration from North-East Scotland*, vol. 1, *Willing Exiles* (Aberdeen: Aberdeen University Press 1988), 215–24.

6 James Thompson, *For Friends at Home: A Scottish Emigrant's Letters from Canada, California and the Cariboo, 1844–1864*, edited by Richard A. Preston (Montreal and London: McGill-Queen's University Press 1974).

7 For further discussion of emigration agents, see Marjory Harper, *Emigration from North-East Scotland*, vol. 2, *Beyond the Broad Atlantic* (Aberdeen: Aberdeen University Press 1988), 12–32; and *Emigration from Scotland between the Wars: Opportunity or Exile?* (Manchester: Manchester University Press 1998), 41–70.

8 The north of Scotland's main newspaper.

9 Harper, *Emigration from Scotland*, 126–7.

10 *The Scotsman*, 25 August 1849.

11 PP 1851 (173) 40, *Papers Relative to Emigration to the North American Colonies*, extracts from notes appended to the periodical reports of arrivals of passenger ships at the ports of Quebec and Montreal in the season of 1849, no. 5, 1–31 August.

12 Donald Macleod, *Gloomy Memories in the Highlands of Scotland: versus Mrs Harriet Beecher Stowe's Sunny Memories: a faithful picture of the extirpation of the Celtic race from the highlands of Scotland* (Toronto: McLeod 1857); Alexander MacKenzie, *The History of the Highland Clearances* (Inverness: A. & W. Mackenzie 1883).

13 Machair is a distinctive type of coastal grassland found in the north and west of Scotland, and in western Ireland.

14 *Quebec Times*, n.d., quoted in MacKenzie, *Highland Clearances*, 257–8.

15 There are numerous studies of the Home Children phenomenon, some of which are sensational rather than substantial. One of the best is Joy Parr, *Labouring Children: British Immigrant Apprentices to Canada, 1869–1924* (London and Montreal: Croom Helm/McGill-Queen's University Press 1980).

16 Donald MacKay, *Scotland Farewell. The People of the* Hector (Toronto: Natural Heritage 1996).

17 For discussion of the qualities of timber ships, see Lucille Campey, *"Fast Sailing and Copper Bottomed": Aberdeen Sailing Ships and the Emigrant Scots They Carried to Canada, 1774–1855* (Toronto: Natural Heritage 2002). The wreck of the *Annie Jane* is described in Robert Charnley, *Shipwrecked on Vatersay!* (Portree: Maclean Press 1992).

18 Marjory Harper, "A Family Affair: The Colonisation of New Kincardineshire," *History Today*, 37 (October 1987): 42–8.

19 See, for instance, Phyllis Harrison, *The Home Children* (Winnipeg: Watson and Dwyer 1979); Philip Bean and Joy Melville, *Lost Children of the Empire* (London: Unwin Hyman 1989).

20 Harper, *Beyond the Broad Atlantic*, 241.

21 Harper, *Willing Exiles*, 226.

22 Rusty Bitterman, "On Remembering and Forgetting: Highland Memories within the Maritime Diaspora," in Marjory Harper and Michael Vance, eds., *Myth, Migration and the Making of Memory: Scotia and Nova Scotia, c. 1700–1990* (Halifax and Edinburgh: Fernwood Press/John Donald 1999, 2000), 256. Others who had good reason not to remember Scotland included emigrants who had fled from the consequences of financial or moral misdemeanours committed back home. Many others, however, maintained their links with Scotland by receiving newspapers, magazines, and correspondence from home, and by associating with fellow Scots in clubs and societies. See Marjory Harper, *Adventurers and Exiles: The Great Scottish Exodus* (London: Profile 2003), 35–6, 326–72; E.J. Cowan, "The Myth of Scotch Canada," in Harper and Vance, *Memory*, 49–72.

23 Frederick S. Cozzens, *Acadia: Or a Month with the Blue Noses* (New York 1859), 150, 199, quoted in Harper and Vance, *Myth, Migration and the Making of Memory*, 29.

24 Wayne Norton, *Help Us to a Better Land: Crofter Colonies in the Prairie West* (Regina: Canadian Plains Research Center 1994), 36, from National Archives of Scotland, AF51/198/514, Lawlor to Sir George Trevelyan, 21 January 1895.

25 Flora McPherson, *Watchman against the World* (London: Hale 1962).

26 Public Archives of Nova Scotia, RG1, vol. 326, no. 171, "Miscellaneous Papers relating to Cape Breton, 1780–1809," quoted in Laurie Stanley, *The Well-Watered Garden: The Presbyterian Church in Cape Breton, 1798–1860* (Sydney, Cape Breton: University College of Cape Breton Press 1983), 44.

27 Scottish Catholic Archives, DA9/44/1, Rev. George Corbett, parish priest, St Andrews, Ontario, to Bishop Angus MacDonald, Oban, 19 March 1884.

28 PP 1884, 32–36, *Report of HM Commissioners of Inquiry into the Condition of the Crofters and Cottars in the Highlands and Islands of Scotland* (Napier Commission), Norman Mackenzie to his brother, 1 February 1866.

29 Sir Andrew MacPhail, *The Master's Wife* (Toronto: McClelland and Stewart 1977), 101–2.
30 MacKenzie, *Highland Clearances*, 313; Harper, *Willing Exiles*, 231.
31 For more on the tartanization of tourism in Nova Scotia, see Ian McKay, *The Quest of the Folk: Antimodernism and Cultural Selection in Twentieth-Century Nova Scotia* (Montreal: McGill-Queen's University Press 1994).

THREE

A Man's a Man because of That:
The Scots in the Canadian
Military Experience

H.P. Klepak

To most observers the influence of the Scots in Canada is so pervasive and obvious that it seems unnecessary to insist very much on the fact, even if time has diffused this influence as Canada's link to Scotland has become less direct. Nowhere is this reality more visible than in the Canadian Armed Forces. The Scottish fact in the Canadian military has continued despite the loss of the regular force's key Scottish symbol when the two regular battalions of the Black Watch (Royal Highland Regiment) of Canada were disbanded in the massive defence cuts of 1970. Reserve force Highland and Scottish regiments, air force pipe bands, the navy's special links with Nova Scotia and the Maritime provinces, and much else in the regular armed forces have helped to preserve the Scottish fact in the Canadian military, with no need to "insist" in order to make that preservation stick.

THE FIRST MILITARY LINKS

As is apparent from many of the other essays in this volume, there was a clear and powerful Scottish connection from the very beginning of ties between northern North America and the British Isles. In the military sphere, Scottish regiments were sent to North America from the outset of serious imperial efforts to unseat the French and render the continent British from Florida to the Arctic Circle.[1]

Scottish regiments existed in the British Army soon after the joining of the two Crowns. The Royal Scots, deemed "Pontius Pilate's Bodyguard" because of their long service, are one of the senior regiments in British service. The Black Watch, founded in 1729 as a Protestant group of companies and joined together as a full-scale regiment in 1742, became the first permanent Highland regiment in the British army. Both served in North America, the Black Watch (42nd Foot) arriving alongside Montgomery's (Montgomerie's) Highlanders (77th Foot) and Fraser Highlanders (78th Foot) in 1757 to fight the French in the Seven Years' War (1756–63) and the Royal Scots taking part in the seizure of Louisbourg the next year.

This was all part of Prime Minister Pitt's (Pitt the Elder's) famous plan to take North America finally from France and to defeat Versailles through strikes at its empire. It is interesting to note, given the future extent of Highland and Scottish regiments in the British North American colonies and then in the Dominion, that they were considered from the beginning well suited for warfare in the region. One historian's comments serve as an example: "When the Highland regiments landed in that continent their garb and appearance attracted much notice. The Indians in particular were delighted to see a European regiment in a dress so similar to their own."[2] However, it was not merely their uniforms that attracted attention. Their fieldcraft (or *woodcraft*, as it was then called) was far more impressive than that of line regiments, a state of affairs usually, and surely with fairness, attributed to their hunting needs at home in the Highlands. As elsewhere at this time, Scottish soldiers in British North America soon gained a reputation for being good shots, as well as patient, sober, and hardy.[3]

D Company, Royal Scots, QC, 1884, composite photograph, Wm Notman and Son. Courtesy of the Notman Photographic Archives, McCord Museum of Canadian History (N-1993.14)

Over the next century or more, that hardiness would be necessary not only for Scottish soldiers but also for other immigrants from "home." For the moment, however, most initial links between the Old Country and the New were through the army.[4] A long tradition of North American service, impressive in the Seven Years' War, was given an even firmer foundation with the American War of Independence (1775–83) and the War of 1812 (1812–14), particularly with the long years of imperial garrisoning that preceded and followed these events. Indeed, further Highland regiments were raised in Scotland in large part as a result of loyal and successful service in North America. Doubts about Highland military loyalties were squashed in these years not only by the relatively rapid demise of the Jacobite cause but also by the clear keenness so many Highlanders exhibited for serving in the army. Military service was made all the more popular by harsh conditions at home. In addition, several prominent clan and local leaders came forward to champion loyal military service. Such personal linkages were important to Highland men making decisions about their future.

The Highland regiments at this time were very different from their English counterparts. To an extraordinary extent different values prevailed. The harsh discipline of the English infantry was unnecessary with troops from the Far North, for whom military service tended to be considered an honour. There were disciplinary troubles, and even some mutinies, but the reasons for such events tended to be honour-related, rather than the classic type of soldier misbehaviour. In essence, the Highlander liked military service, a state of affairs remarkable in the desertion-ridden armies of eighteenth-century Europe.[5]

With the end of the Seven Years' War in 1763, some Highlanders were given land owned previously by *seigneurs* in the former New France. The Fraser Highlanders, disbanded at the end of hostilities, settled between 150 and 300 of their veterans in the Quebec region.[6] This settlement occurred in the five *seigneuries* acquired by General James Murray, upon the reassembling of the regiment after its duties along the St Lawrence and in the retaking of Newfoundland from the French at the end of the war. A first and major Highland settlement scheme thus began that introduced the "Scottish fact" to what would become the province of Quebec. Men from other regiments retired in other parts of British North America, and these loyal military settlements would prove highly useful in the not-too-distant future. A dozen years later, during the period between the end of the Seven Years' War and the beginning of the American Revolution, Scottish civilian settlement began in earnest in Prince Edward Island, Nova Scotia, and Newfoundland, and to some extent in Quebec. These settlements represented a pool of support for the Crown when the rebellion in the South began, especially when added to the soldiers already established throughout. A first battalion of the Royal Highland Emigrant Regiment was quickly raised as the war progressed. Most volunteers were men who had retired from Highland regiments, such as the 42nd Black Watch, Montgomery's Highlanders, or the Fraser's themselves, and many of the rest were civilians recently arrived from Scotland.[7] The Royal Highland Emigrant Regiment was the first Highland regiment ever to be recruited in North America or, indeed, outside Scotland and was modelled on the 42nd Black Watch.

At the end of the American Revolution this regiment and others were disbanded, and many of the troops settled alongside Loyalists in what are now Eastern Ontario, Quebec, and the Maritime Provinces.[8] The country was being settled anew, and the Scottish fact, along with its military dimension, was central to prevailing trends in that settlement. Conditions at home, both political and social, added to the Scottish numbers in the arriving population. The slow death of the Jacobite movement motivated many of its followers to leave the British Isles, and the steady impact of capitalist and industrialist revolution at home also ensured that the exit of highlanders from their native home grew apace as the years passed.[9]

The first half of the nineteenth century saw the continuation and strengthening of almost all these trends. The Highland Clearances produced many thousands of immigrants for Canada under circumstances that stain the history of England, Britain, and capitalism to this day. Highlanders no doubt often chose to leave, but it would appear that, often as not, they were driven to abandon their homes and seek their futures in the great cities of Britain or the "wilds of Canada."[10] Be that as it may, Canada was becoming populated, and the Scots and their Highlands were the source of a huge percentage of that immigration. Scottish officers were in the majority in the scruffy British sedentary militia of the early post-Conquest years, which was a pale successor to the impressive militia system the French had been forced to establish in order to face the asymmetries of population and power in North America.[11] When the War of 1812 saw the British North American colonies invaded over and over, Scots were prominent not only among the British regulars sent to help the defence but in the fencible and other units raised to stop the invasions and even counterattack the South.

During the Rebellions of 1837 one company of the Montreal Light Infantry wore tartan stripes on their uniform trousers, probably the first material Scottish reference in a Montreal military unit. However, the American Civil War would be the real spur to the organization of a Canadian military force of some substance and efficiency. As before, Scottish units made up a significant part of that force.

THE NEW DOMINION

In the prelude to the Civil War, Washington viewed Britain and the Canadian colonies as meddling and pro-Confederacy, and there was some reason for this sentiment. The dramatic Confederate raid on the northern city of St Alban's in 1864 was carried out from Canada, the main economic partner of the South was Britain, and some real pro-Southern sentiment existed in both the United Kingdom and Canada, despite the power and effective action of the abolitionist movement. In addition, a number of Confederate officials, including President Jefferson Davis himself, found refuge in Canada at the end of the war.

Under these conditions the Reciprocity Treaty of 1854 had little chance of lasting when the war ended in 1865, even though it was viewed by most as highly favourable to the British North American economy. Indeed, the next year it was denounced by the United States, and, given the importance of Fenianism at the time, this action was fittingly taken on St Patrick's Day, 1866.[12] In this context were born ideas of a Canadian Dominion. The need for increased intercolonial trade, more efficient defence in case of American invasion, and a new imperial arrangement in the face of waning enthusiasm for the Empire and its commitments in Britain all pointed in the direction of a new political experiment for northern North America. Perhaps most dramatically, the United States was filled to overflowing with anti-British veterans of the war and Irish Fenian sympathizers – all manner of schemes were being hatched, one of which was to seize Canada and trade it for Ireland – which gave even more urgency to the Dominion idea.

The military threat meant that in 1861–62 further measures were taken to put the colonies into a defensive posture not entirely dependent on the mother country. The seizure of Confederate officials from the British ship *Trent* in 1861 nearly led to war, but in spite of this the next May the Canadian Parliament threw out the Militia Bill, a bill authorizing the creation of a large trained militia to provide security during the American Civil War. The British were furious with what they saw as endless demands on the imperial treasury; it seemed they were being asked to provide a defence system to which the citizens most affected by the threat were unwilling to contribute. North America was the only portion of the entire British Empire where there existed a land border with a significant land power. Thus the strength of the Royal Navy was less decisive in Canadian defence than it was in that of other parts of the imperial family. It therefore behooved Canadians to contribute to an effort on land, where they would be the principal beneficiaries. A sharp rebuke in the *Times* suggested that "Canada has learned to trust others for the performance of services for which weaker and less wealthy populations are wont to rely exclusively on themselves."[13] Successive British politicians expressed the same sentiments at a time when procolonial sentiment was already on the wane.[14]

The defeat of the Militia Bill did not mean that nothing at all was done. A fledgling combined reserve force was reinforced, as it had been in 1855 at the height of the Crimean War. Several new militia units were raised in a far more serious manner than had been shown to the sedentary militia to date. One of these was the 5th Battalion, Royal Light Infantry, in Montreal, which went through several name changes before becoming formally the Black Watch (Royal Highland Regiment) of Canada.[15] In 1862 people considered as traditional chieftains raised six companies. This manner of raising companies was not so different from the practice with their namesakes in Scotland before them. In the absence of clan chiefs, prominent citizens of Montreal took over the role of chieftains, and the list of officers read like a *Who's Who* of Scottish Montreal. A further two companies were quickly added, as recruiting proved to be no difficulty in the context of an almost constant threat of war with the United States.

A Highland company was authorized as No. 9 of the battalion in 1863, being transferred from the strength of another Montreal unit. That company was to wear the trews and tartan of the Black Watch, as well as the famous Red Hackle of that imperial regiment, which was clearly already taken as the model for the development of the Canadian unit.[16] Officially this Montreal regiment was the only formal unit with a Scottish basis in the army at this time, even if there was plenty of informal reflection of the Scottish fact elsewhere.

At the time of the founding of the Dominion just under two-thirds of the total population (as measured by the Dominion census of 1871) reported itself as being of British origin and slightly under one-third French. Of the British figure the Irish were the largest group with 846,414; the English placed second and the Scottish third. It is important to note that a number of the Irish were in fact Scots-Irish and Protestant.[17] The Scots soon dominated much of the commercial and financial world in the country, a role in which they are still very prominent. Montreal was the financial capital of the new Dominion at this time, and it is hardly a surprise that its first full-scale *modern* militia unit should be Scottish. However, all segments of the Montreal elite were determined to be well represented in the militia of the new country, and this was shown to be true when the Fusiliers Mont-Royal were founded later in the decade.[18] It is clear, as well, that many foot soldiers in the Royals (as the 5th Royal Battalion was soon to be called) had seen service in the past, usually in Scottish regiments in the mother country. This proved useful in the preparations for the Fenian Raids of 1866, 1870, and 1871.

The Royals regiment steadily "improved" on its Scottish connection over time. In the first seventeen years of its existence the officers and troops who could afford it could by gradual stages wear Highland uniform off parade (the great expense of Highland dress is not a recent phenomenon). By the early 1880s the whole regiment (in 1884 the Royal Scots of Canada) was fully kitted out in proper fashion with authority to wear the highly prized Red Hackle coming from militia headquarters in 1895.[19]

It should be noted that the popularity of British garrisons in the country often stood in stark contrast to their level of popularity in the United Kingdom. In general, Canadian towns were happy to host British regulars, which was far from automatically the case in Britain, although it was largely so in Scotland. This doubtless had an effect on the option of making a militia regiment Highland in dress and traditions. In Britain volunteer forces often did everything possible to distinguish themselves from their regular counterparts. In Canada, however, militiamen wanted to model themselves as closely as possible on the imperial regular army. The difference between British and Canadian volunteer forces is particularly noticeable with respect to uniforms. The scarlet tunic of the infantry was much sought after by patriotic Canadians, while their cousins in Britain contrived every colour of uniform imaginable in order to look different from those whom they considered to be loutish regulars. After the Napoleonic Wars, the Crimea, the colonial wars, and the Boer War the prestige of Highland regiments was considerable, and the call of blood, history, and name was doubtless central to so many units choosing to become their imitators despite the often ferocious cost of such a choice.[20]

Scottish immigration continued apace in the years before the First World War, with the ups and downs one expects in changing economic and political circumstances. Imperial sentiment, at such a low ebb when the Royals in Montreal were founded, was now firmly on the rise.[21] On the military front, the success of Montreal's Royals combined with this situation to bring forth requests by a number of communities for militia regiments based on Scottish, and overwhelmingly Highland, models. The most famous of these were doubtless the 48th Highlanders of Canada in Toronto, formed in 1891 as the 48th Battalion (Highlanders) and thus Highland from their beginnings. The 48th were not, however, the first to join the Black Watch as *Canadian* Highland regiments. Many regiments of older lineage were to become Highland after 1891. And even before that date the Pictou infantry unit became the Pictou Highlanders in 1879, and the Cape Breton infantry militia battalion was renamed the Cape Breton Highlanders in 1885. The Perth Regiment, not surprisingly, was thoroughly Highland in all but official designation virtually from its founding in 1866. Many other regiments had Highland companies on their strength, even though they were not fully Highland. This was even true in the early years of Quebec City's justly famous

Voltigeurs de Québec.[22] Pre-World War I militia popularity also stimulated the founding of many new units, and some of these began life as Highland regiments. The Argyll and Sutherland Highlanders of Canada (Princess Louise's) were founded in Hamilton in 1903 and were designated as Highland from their beginnings. In 1910 the Queen's Own Cameron Highlanders of Canada were founded in Winnipeg. The next year the Seaforth Highlanders of Canada were founded in Vancouver, yet another regiment with Highland status from its foundation.[23]

During these years, informally and then formally, there began to grow the practice of allying Canadian militia regiments with regular regiments of the British army. It is important to remember that the Canadian regular army, despite its beginnings in the early 1870s, remained a force aimed essentially at militia training until the eve of the Second World War; before then it was in no sense a field force meant to fight as configured.[24] Canadian units also saw press reports of the British regulars in action everywhere, and many worked with them in South Africa in the Boer War of century's end. The prestige associated with being "allied" with a British unit was considered likely to help recruiting. It was also a way to connect with something more serious than the rag-tag organization the militia occasionally seemed to be, despite its growing efficiency in the years before 1914. The romance of the kilt and the pipes, as well as the call of tradition, and even homeland, continued to suggest that alliances with Highland regiments were somehow even more special. It was in this period that Montreal's 5th Royal Scots cemented their connection with the Black Watch of Scotland by becoming officially allied with this senior Highland Regiment of the British forces in 1905. The Canadian unit changed its name once more, in 1907, to conform with the Scottish parent regiment, becoming the 5th Regiment the Royal Highlanders of Canada (Black Watch).[25]

THE FIRST WORLD WAR

It would be impossible in any way to cover the massive effort of Canadian Highland regiments in World War I. That effort would beggar description, such would be its scope. Suffice it to say that those regiments were seen in all the Canadian Expeditionary Force's

Captian Bovey and Officers of the 5th Royal Highlanders, Montreal, QC, 1914, Wm Notman and Son. Courtesy of the Notman Photographic Archives, McCord Museum of Canadian History (II-206458)

divisions and took almost untold casualties. Whether accurately or not, Highland and Canadian Highland troops gained a reputation as shock troops able to overcome firm opposition and rarely failing in pressing home their attacks. Thus the press added greatly to the lustre of these units. At least one new Scottish regiment was added to the list when the Waterloo Regiment opted to become allied to the Highland Light Infantry and in 1915 changed its title to the Highland Light Infantry of Canada.

After the war there was an explosion of Canadian units that elected to become Scottish or Highland. In the 1920s and 1930s, depressing times for the militia, all manner of means were sought to recruit and retain personnel, and the popularity and prestige of Highland regiments and traditions, sustained now by a Canadian war record of unparalleled importance, seemed one more way to try to gild the lily of militia service.[26] Units from across the country reflected this trend, which did honour to Scottish and Highland prestige and potentially served a practical purpose. Dating from this period is the "Highland" or "Scottish" status of regiments now known as the Cameron Highlanders of Ottawa, the Lorne Scots (Peel, Dufferin, and Halton Regiment), the Stormont, Dundas, and Glengarry Highlanders, the Essex and Kent Scottish, the Calgary Highlanders, the Toronto Scottish, and the Lanark and Renfrew Scottish.[27] The Canadian Army had never been more "Scottish," and while the continuing arrival of large numbers of new Canadians from the Old Country no doubt helped to bolster this fact, by now the vast majority of recruits had been born in Canada.

WORLD WAR II

Canadian Scottish regiments mobilized again when war came again in September 1939, as did the rest of the militia. Units prepared for service overseas, and if they did so without the same enthusiasm as was seen in 1914, nonetheless headquarters had little reason to complain when the troops were asked to volunteer for active service. For the special Highland nature of many units, there was an unpleasant surprise waiting. Early in 1940 a general prohibition of the wearing of the kilt was issued throughout the Commonwealth armies. The reason was fear of the use by the Germans of gases that would attack exposed skin. With great reluctance the kilt was thus removed from active service, although, as many photographs show, the new regulation was flouted on a number of occasions. For the first time the famed kilt of the Highland soldier was not to be worn in battle. It was a major blow, but one from which the "jocks" soon recovered.

The war saw many units and individuals serve at one time or another in Scotland, a state of affairs that further cemented links between regiments in the Dominion and those at "home." Service elsewhere had the same effect, as did the Canloan program of temporary officer postings that sent many Canadian Highland officers to serve in Scottish regiments.

THE POSTWAR ERA

The postwar era saw a number of regiments disband but this time did not produce such a large number of name changes. The prestige of Highland regiments, while in no way declining in those years, did not gain particularly. After the war, only one reserve infantry regiment asked to become Scottish (the Lake Superior Scottish Regiment). As the years went on, successive army reorganizations sent different messages to the infantry. After the usual cuts associated with demobilization in the months succeeding victory, mobilization began again only five years after the end of the second Great War. Canada needed to increase its forces tremendously to face the double challenge of war in Korea (beginning in 1950) and the buildup of conventional forces in Europe occasioned by the decision to provide real muscle to the North Atlantic Treaty Organisation (the alliance was entered into in 1949).

In the postwar world – where Canada was now a significant player on the international scene and Britain was quickly losing its status as a front-rank power – the decision was finally made to abandon the tradition of a regular army whose main role was militia training. Instead, a small but real army was set up during the years 1947–50. Nonetheless, when faced with Cold War crises in Europe and Asia, Ottawa was forced to call on the militia yet again to provide a mobilization base for the enormous expansion of the forces at hand in the early fifties. The Highland regiments of the militia were expected to field up to four battalions of infantry from current serving personnel, returning men who had served in World War II, and new recruits. At first grouped in the 1st and 2nd Canadian Highland Battalions (companies being drawn from the Black Watch, the 48th Highlanders, the Seaforths, the Canadian Scottish, and the North Nova Scotia Highlanders), by late 1953 the two units were dubbed the 1st and 2nd Battalions, the Black Watch (Royal Highland Regiment) of Canada. The militia battalion in Montreal was then renamed the 3rd Battalion.[28]

Thus began a remarkable period in the history of Highland regiments in Canada. From 1953 until 1970, and for the first time in peacetime history, the Canadian regular force included two battalions of Highlanders. The Royal Canadian Regiment, the Princess Patricia's Canadian Light Infantry, and Le Royal 22e Régiment, all of which had existed in the interwar period or even before, were joined not only by the Highlanders but also by Rifle and Guards battalions. It was an extraordinary display of just how seriously Canada was taking its commitments as an active and important member of the international community and NATO. That active and important membership began to wane, however, by the late 1960s. The government of Prime Minister Pierre Trudeau had other priorities than defence, and the foreign policy and defence review conducted after his landslide election victory in 1968 called for massive cuts in the regular army. The Canadian Black Watch lost both its regular battalions, while many reserve Highland regiments across the country saw their strength cut by significant margins.[29] Today, reduced again to reserve status, the militia Highland units have fallen on hard times. Used increasingly as a resource for the regular battalions (of whom none are any longer Highland), these units in some senses have less opportunity than ever before to contribute to the traditional Highland fact within the armed forces.

On the other hand, these regiments can be proud of their exceptional role in providing absolutely essential personnel to an over-stretched regular force that has been faced with multiple tasks in peace support operations over much of the world since the end of the Cold War. With thousands of forces personnel abroad all the time, reserve soldiers, to a significant extent drawn from the Highlanders, are virtually a sine qua non of continued Canadian participation in such operations. As in the past, reserve service in Highland regiments provides a way for thousands of Canadians to serve in units with great traditions and provides Canadian governments with the means to further Canadian objectives abroad and at home.

At the present time almost one-third of the Canadian reserve infantry is "Highland," and many personnel whose ancestors never saw the "green hills of home" represent, in today's multicultural Canada, well over half the troops in those regiments. It is fair to say that anyone accusing such people of not being good "Highlanders" will land themselves in a scuffle.

WHAT OF THE NONINFANTRY?

In spite of the emphasis this overview places upon the infantry, it is essential to note that the historic Highland presence in the Canadian Forces went far beyond.

The Royal Canadian Air Force (RCAF) was created in the years after World War I, in which Canadians had served with great distinction in the Royal Flying Corps. From the beginning the RCAF latched on to Highland and Scottish traditions, which it found well anchored in Canadian society and culture. The air force obtained its own tartan and, despite defence penury over most of the interwar years, several squadrons fitted out pipe bands in these early years. The extraordinary role of the Royal Canadian Air Force in World War II, suffering a staggering seventeen thousand combat deaths (40 percent of the Dominion's total war dead), saw the force come of age.[30] Pipe bands abounded, and during this conflict many thousands of RCAF personnel served in Scotland and with Scots around the world.[31] After the war the traditions were more than maintained. During the great expansion of the peacetime service as a result of NATO and the Korean War there were few RCAF stations that did not form a pipe band, often more than one. The service's central pipe band became a famous part of the Ottawa military musical scene. Through the cuts of the 1960s, 1970s, 1980s, and 1990s, the RCAF and then the Canadian Air Force tried, usually successfully, to hold on to its pipe bands and traditions.

The Royal Canadian Navy has shared fewer of these traditions. Reflecting the situation in the United Kingdom, there appears to be little that is "Scottish" about the navy. There are no formal pipe bands in the service, nor is there a naval tartan. However, here, as well, a different reality lies just beneath the surface. In fact, many naval ships leave port and return to the sound of Highland pipes being played by a member of the ship's company, and troops leaving or returning home are frequently accompanied on their way "up the brow" by the pipes.[32] This is at least partially because the Canadian navy is closely tied to Nova Scotia and the Maritime provinces, arguably the heart of Scottish Canada. These provinces give it the largest group of its personnel, and in the Maritimes the Scottish fact is simply taken for granted as an anchor of Canadian nationality, one of the characteristics that make up Canada's unique identity.

The Royal Military College of Canada respects a number of Scottish traditions, most notably in the form of a large pipe band and a Highland dance group wherein the percentage of francophones is larger than that in the college population as a whole. They wear the Mackenzie tartan in honour of the prime minister (Alexander Mackenzie) who authorized the foundation of the college in 1876. Furthermore, noninfantry units with Scottish traditions abound. Many artillery units, for example, have a pipe band. Few people in or outside the regiment seem to find this out of the ordinary, itself evidence that the Scottish fact is rarely considered foreign in this country's military. Almost all the other "corps" have units that have adopted Scottish traditions, especially pipe bands or, at the very least, pipers.

Supposedly Welsh and English militia regiments also have or have had pipe bands and many other Scottish traditions. The 2nd Battalion of the Royal Canadian Regiment, a regular-force product of the disbanding of the 1st and 2nd Battalions of Canada's Black Watch in 1970, still has a pipe band going back to the days of its ancestor organization. And pipe bands, some official but many unofficial and paid for by the troops, have the principal role of ensuring that the public continues to associate the Canadian military with the country's Scottish heritage.

CONCLUSION

Much more could be said on this subject, but this short chapter has shown that the Scottish, and especially the Highland, fact has long been part and parcel of Canada's military history. Since the British conquest, whose last act – Montreal's surrender – was witnessed by all three Highland regiments of the British army in North America, only a few years have passed in which this country has lacked a Highland military presence of some kind. With time, that Scottish presence has been so closely linked with Canadian military identity that one rarely hears any suggestion that such traditions are in any way "not Canadian." Rather, personnel from all ethnic backgrounds appear to join the armed forces' units of Scottish origin with alacrity and become full members of them with no loss of their own pride of ancestry.

To be certain, there is more room for research on this last point. But the experience of this author, which amounts to a lifetime of observation of the Scottish fact in the Canadian army, has led him to such conclusions in dramatic fashion. Scottish immigration has declined markedly in the years since the Second World War, and the Scottish and Highland reality in the Canadian armed forces has almost certainly been damaged by defence cuts, a weakening of the Commonwealth connection, fewer connections with the British army, and other trends. Canada has, however, remained a remarkably Scottish country through all of this, and as this paper has tried to show, the Scottish military influence in the Canadian army has continued to thrive even in adversity.

NOTES

1 For a discussion of the participation of Highland Regiments during the Seven Years' War in North America, see George F.G. Stanley, "The Scottish Military Tradition," in W. Stanford Reid, ed., *The Scottish Tradition in Canada* (Toronto: McClelland and Stewart 1976), 141–5.

2 Quoted in Michael Brander, *The Scottish Highlanders and their Regiments* (London: Baylis 1971), 161. It should be noted that Highlanders had been recruited into the British army as early as 1690–92, when two regiments of such troops were raised from Whig clans. See Robert Clyde, *From Rebel to Hero: The Image of the Highlander, 1745–1830* (East Linton, Scotland: Tuckwell 1995), 150.

3 Brander, *The Scottish Highlanders.* See also John Prebble's pungent comments in *The Highland Clearances* (London: Penguin 1980), 296–302, as well as R. Money Barnes, *The Uniforms and History of the Scottish Regiments* (London: Seeley 1969), 64–5.

4 This is not to say that the connection was only military. Nova Scotia (minus Cape Breton Island) was yielded to Britain after the War of the Spanish

Succession in 1713, and the island was finally captured and retained after Wolfe took it in 1758. Scottish settlement in the colony, although very limited, had already begun by the time cousins of those settlers arrived in the more southerly colonies. In 1749 some arrived as part of the Earl of Halifax's scheme to settle veterans of the War of the Austrian Succession. The process was a slow one. See James A. Williamson, *A Short History of British Expansion*, vol. 1 (London: Macmillan 1961), 392–3.

5 Clyde, *Rebel to Hero*, 151–9. The title of this paper reflects the sense, common in the Highlands over so many years, that military service is part and parcel of being a complete man.

6 The discrepancy in the figure arises from the difference between the traditional figure, usually given as some three hundred such settler veterans, and the figures resulting from the research of J.R. Harper for his book *The Fraser Highlanders* (Montreal: Society of the Military and Maritime Museum 1979), 122–3.

7 While the first battalion of this regiment included many personnel from the Southern colonies, the 2nd (each was about a thousand men) was recruited in Nova Scotia, Prince Edward Island, and Newfoundland, and largely from veterans of the Fraser's, Montgomery's, or the Royal Highland Regiment (Black Watch). See Harper, *Fraser Highlanders*, 154–5.

8 Some fifty thousand Loyalists had actually served under arms for the Crown during the conflict. Thus, many of those coming north did so within formed units or having recently left such units. Many of these had strong Scottish links. See North Callahan, *Royal Raiders: The Tories of the American Revolution* (Indianapolis: Bobbs-Merrill 1963), 9. See also the sections on Loyalism in John Shy, *A People Numerous and Armed: Reflections on the Military Struggle for American Independence* (New York: Oxford University Press 1976).

9 The evictions from the Highlands began early to affect settlement patterns in Canada. Some five hundred Macdonnells were thus treated as early as 1782, being displaced from Glengarry in Inverness to make way for sheep. They soon founded Glengarry in what was to be Ontario. That these same people should prove so astoundingly loyal to the Crown in the years to come should give us pause. See Brander, *Scottish Highlanders*, 172.

10 See Prebble, *Highland Clearances*, especially 265, for this depressing story.

11 Paul P. Hutchison, *Canada's Black Watch: The First Hundred Years, 1862–1962* (Toronto: Best Publishers 1962), 7.

12 Charles P. Stacey, *Canada and the Age of Conflict*, vol. 1, (Toronto: University of Toronto Press 1984), 13–15.

13 Quoted in Desmond Morton, *A Military History of Canada* (Toronto: McClelland and Stewart 1992), 82.

14 Bernard Porter, *The Lion's Share: A Short History of British Imperialism, 1850–1983* (London: Longman 1984), 48–9.

15 Because a regiment in the British/Canadian tradition is composed of one or more battalions, a regiment and a battalion may, if manpower numbers dictate, be one and the same, as it was with the Royal Light Infantry at this time. Thus the terms "battalion" and "regiment" can be applied to the

unit. It was the fifth battalion to be raised under the new system, hence the number 5.

16 Hutchison, *Canada's Black Watch*, 9–10. Note that an infantry battalion is composed of several companies.

17 Ibid., 6–7.

18 Elinor Kyte Senior, *Roots of the Canadian Army: Montreal District, 1846–1870* (Montreal: Society of the Montreal Military and Maritime Museum 1981), 44–6.

19 Ibid., 25–8.

20 Clyde, *Rebel to Hero*, 176–7.

21 R.G. Moyles and Doug Owram, *Imperial Dreams and Colonial Realities* (Toronto: University of Toronto Press 1988), 15–26.

22 Jacques Castonguay, *Les Voltigeurs de Québec: Premier régiment canadien-français* (Québec: Voltigeurs de Québec 1987), 225.

23 Barnes, *Uniforms and History*, 167, 319–31.

24 See the first chapters of John A. English, *The Canadian Army and the Normandy Campaign* (New York: Praeger 1991).

25 Hutchison, *Canada's Black Watch*, 44.

26 Even in Newfoundland, still two decades from joining Canada, the Scottish military fact flourished. The United Kingdom government had doubtless been wise in ensuring that this much-blooded regiment of World War I, soon named the Royal Newfoundland Regiment, served in a division, the 9th, made up of Scottish regiments. See Michael Mitchell, *Ducimus: The Regiments of the Canadian Infantry* (Ottawa: Canadian War Museum 1996), 228–9.

27 Barnes, *Uniforms and History*, 320–8.

28 It is interesting to note that when three years later, in 1956, the Imperials (the Canadian Black Watch's term for the Parent Regiment in Scotland) were reduced to only one battalion, the Canadian Black Watch became the biggest regiment of the family of Black Watch regiments around the Commonwealth. See Hutchison, *Canada's Black Watch*, 268–9. The family still included member regiments in Australia, New Zealand, South Africa, and, of course, Britain, as well as Canada, and historically had reached even farther abroad.

29 It should be said that by then it was increasingly difficult to maintain the strengths allocated to those regiments in the indifferent or even hostile conditions for army recruitment of the 1960s. See Morton, *Military History of Canada*, 254–60.

30 See Allan D. English, *The Cream of the Crop: Canadian Aircrew, 1939–45* (Montreal: McGill-Queen's University Press 1996), 4–5.

31 This extraordinary personal connection with Great Britain is studied in Charles P. Stacey and Barbara Wilson, *The Half Million: The Canadians in Britain, 1939–1946* (Toronto: University of Toronto Press 1987).

32 "Up the brow" is an old term for the gang-board or plank.

FOUR

The Curious Tale of the Scots and the Fur Trade: An Historiographical Account

J.M. Bumsted

One might have thought that one of the central verities of the ethnic history of Canada would be the central role played in the British fur trade by the Scots, particularly between 1790 and 1850.[1] An examination of historical writing on that fur trade reveals, however, that the place of the Scots is much more problematic than might otherwise be expected. Indeed, in most nineteenth-century historical surveys and analyses (as opposed to personal memoirs of fur trade participants) the Scots presence either went unacknowledged or was mentioned only in passing. This lack of acknowledgment continued in the mainstream historiography of the fur trade until well into the twentieth century and was often combined with an approach to ethnicity that turned the Scots into "the English" or "the British," or even into "the Canadians." Meanwhile, occasional ethnic writing on the Scot in Canada emphasized the importance of Scots in the trade but typically did not attempt to argue a particular Scottish influence in it. That is to say, the Scots presence in the fur trade was important to Scottish ethnicity but not to the fur trade itself. Not until the 1970s – and the beginning of modern ethnic study – did a literature begin to emerge that suggested that the dominant role of the Scots in the fur trade may have had some significant effect on the trade itself.

This chapter comes in two parts. In the first part I will explore the pre-1970 fur trade historiography to illustrate its failure either to acknowledge the importance of Scots in the fur trade or to regard their dominance as a matter that had some influence on the trade. In the second I will discuss briefly some of the possible explanations for this curious treatment. Explaining why things do not happen, of course, is much harder than explaining why they do, and this is particularly true with historical interpretation.

Perhaps the first serious effort to deal with the history of the post-French fur trade came just over two hundred years ago, in the introductory chapter to Alexander Mackenzie's *Voyages from Montreal through the Continent of North America to the Frozen and Pacific Oceans in 1789 and 1793 with an account of the rise and state of the fur trade,* published in London at the close of 1801. Most scholars credit "A General History of the Fur Trade from Canada to the North-West" to Mackenzie's cousin Roderick, who was known in the trade as a collector of manuscript material on the subject.[2] Much of Roderick's collected material was reprinted in 1889 and 1890 by L.R. Masson as *Les Bourgeois de la Compagnie du Nord-Ouest récits de voyages, lettres et rapports inédits relatifs au Nord-Ouest Canadien.*[3] The tendency to base historical accounts on such manuscripts – which seldom recognized ethnicity – was perhaps, as we shall see, part of the reason why the Scots received less notice than one might otherwise have anticipated. There were other reasons as well.

"A General History" begins in the French period and speaks of a suspension in the trade after the Conquest of Canada until traders of unspecified ethnicity coming from Canada resumed it in the 1770s. These traders founded the North West Company (NWC) over the winter of 1783–84, and the enterprise expanded in July of 1787. No mention is made of the ethnicity of the members of this company, but their base in Canada, particularly at Montreal, is emphasized. A discussion of the personnel of the concern, "fifty clerks, seventy-one interpreters and clerks, and one thousand one hundred and twenty canoe-men, and thirty-five guides," equally avoids any discussion of the ethnic origins of these workers, although we know that the bulk of them were French-Canadians.[4] A good deal of attention is paid to a detailed description of communication and transportation routes to the West, and the First Nations tribes along the route are distinguished in some detail. On the other hand, throughout a description of the inland route and the ultimate Athabascan trade with the First Nations the fur traders are simply called "the people from Montreal."[5] Special sections are devoted to the Knisteneaux (Cree) and Chepewyan (Dene) Indians – including lists of vocabulary – but the European fur traders are not similarly described or categorized. This lack of specificity about the backgrounds of the fur traders continues in the actual narratives of Mackenzie's voyages that follow this introduction and serve as the basis of the text. We are barely told that Alexander Mackenzie was a Highlander.

A similar unwillingness to label the leadership of the Nor'Westers in terms of their ethnicity characterizes the Earl of Selkirk's *A Sketch of the British Fur Trade in North America; with Observations relative to the North-West Company of Montreal*, published in London in 1816. A Scottish lord from the Lowlands, Selkirk had been involved in a number of colonial ventures that sought to transplant Scots Highlanders to British North America. The chief opposition to his attempt to recruit Highland servants for the Hudson's Bay Company (HBC) in 1811 came from a writer who called himself "Highlander." In his book Selkirk labelled the partners of the NWC as "the merchants in Canada," a usage he pursued throughout. In terms of his discussion of the relationship between the Nor'Westers and the HBC, he wrote of the former as "the Canadians" and the latter as those "trading directly from England." His major thesis was that the NWC carried on its business beyond the reach of law and government, behaving with utter ruthlessness in this enterprise, particularly with regard to the First Nations but also with regard to their fur trading opponents. As one of his illustrations of behaviour toward the competition, for example, Selkirk wrote of "a party of Canadians in two canoes, commanded by Mr. Alexander MacDonell, then a clerk of the North-West Company."[6]

The Earl of Selkirk was prepared to acknowledge that the servants of the NWC were drawn from "the peasantry of Lower Canada," and that the servants of the HBC were recruited from "chiefly Orkney and the North of Scotland," but he did not complete the process by identifying the origins of the NWC partners, who were, of course, almost without exception from Scotland, mainly the northern regions.[7] One of the major reasons for this curious omission may well have been Selkirk's desire to portray the furtrade conflict as one between an English company (which he and his family, all Scots, controlled) and a Canadian one, with the further suggestion that the Canadian company was able to control the administration of justice in the colonial courts and thus thwart the intentions of the mother country. This description of the fundamental nature of the fur trade war as one between the English and the Canadians rather than two rival groupings of Scots would characterize a good bit of the subsequent historical treatment of the fur trade itself.

Early histories of the fur trade were written for various purposes. Roderick Mackenzie's effort was designed to provide context for the narrative of his kinsman's adventures, while Lord Selkirk's account was a masterful polemic intended to indict the NWC for its brutalities. Washington Irving's *Astoria* was designed to provide a picturesque North American subject for an author just returned from seventeen years of exile in polite Europe. Irving was encouraged by his good friend John Jacob Astor to write about the men "who had passed years remote from civilized society, among distant and savage tribes, and who had wonders to recount of their wide and wild peregrinations, their hunting exploits, and the perilous adventures and hair-breadth escapes among the Indians."[8] By his own account, Irving had long been fascinated by the fur trade, and at one point on a visit to Canada in his youth had contemplated accompanying one of the canoe brigades westward. John Jacob Astor's particular interest was in a history of his own attempt to establish the fur trade on the West Coast, and he offered to furnish an "abundance of materials in letters, journals, and verbal narratives," as well as to subsidize the writing of the work.[9] We do not have any information on the precise nature of the material Astor made available, but much of that on the early NWC undoubtedly came in the form of Astor's own memories

– he was, after all, one of the Nor'Westers' keenest competitors –
supplemented by Irving's recollections of "the Magnates of the
North West Company" from his youth.[10] In his introduction Irving
wrote of the journals and business papers on which he had relied,
commenting that "they were often meagre in their details, furnishing
hints to provoke rather than narratives to satisfy inquiry."[11] As a literary man, what Irving would chiefly supply, of course, was an imag-
inative way of looking at this material.

The section on the early Canadian fur trade is relatively brief. Irving's task, after all, was basically to recount the story of the thrust
onto the Pacific Slope, although it is true that the NWC would represent Astor's chief competition, in the end successful in controlling
both the trade and the territory. Irving began with the French trade
and then followed it as it transmuted into the "famous 'Northwest
Company,' which for a time held a lordly sway over the wintry lakes
and boundless forests of the Canadas, almost equal to that of the
East India Company over the voluptuous climes and magnificent
realms of the Orient."[12] The very introduction of this simile elevat-
ed Irving's work well above its predecessors, and he proceeded to
outdo it by his description of the leading traders. "Most of the
clerks," Irving wrote, "were young men of good families, from the
Highlands of Scotland, characterized by the perseverance, thrift, and
fidelity of their country, and fitted by their native hardihood to encounter the rigorous climate of the North, and to endure the trials
and privations of their lot."[13] Irving then turned to a description of
the principal partners, who lived in "lordly and hospitable style," ex-
hibiting a "gorgeous prodigality, such as was often to be noticed in
former times in Southern planters and West India creoles, when flush
with the profits of their plantations."[14] He then turned to annual
meetings at Fort William and to the exemplification of his main simile, "the feudal spirit of the Highlander." In a brilliantly evocative
passage, Irving wrote:

They ascended the rivers in great state, like sovereigns making a
progress: or rather like Highland chieftains navigating their subject
lakes. They were wrapped in rich furs, their huge canoes freighted with
every convenience and luxury, and manned by Canadian voyageurs, as

obedient as Highland clansmen ... The councils were held in great state
... alternated by huge feasts and revels, like some of the old feasts described in Highland castles ... was the Northwest Company in its powerful and prosperous days, when it held a kind of feudal sway over a vast
domain of lake and forest.[15]

For the first time, the Highland Scottish origins of the Nor'Westers
were made an important matter, inextricably interwoven with the
trade they dominated. Unfortunately, Irving's achievement was not
often followed up over the ensuing years.

In 1841, a young Scotsman from Edinburgh named Robert Michael
Ballantyne joined the HBC and spent six years as a clerk in British
North America. His first book, *Every-day Life in the Wilds of North
America, During Six Years' Residence in the Territories of the Hon.
Hudson* [sic] *Bay Company*, was autobiographical, assembled from
his letters home and his journals. It was also a superb introduction
to the Western fur trade in the middle of the nineteenth century. Despite its contemporary focus, Ballantyne's book inevitably strayed
into the past. This was one author who knew perfectly well how important the Scots were numerically in the trade, and in his chapter
on the HBC, he wrote: "It is a strange fact that three-fourths of the
Company's servants are Scotch Highlanders and Orkneymen. There
are very few Irishmen and still fewer English. A great number, however, are half-breeds and French Canadians, especially among the
labourers and *voyageurs*."[16] The author left this strange fact hang-
ing, and in the very next paragraph moved on to discuss the food on
which the traders subsisted. A few pages later, in the chapter on the
Red River Settlement, Ballantyne observed that its "motley crew"
consisted of "Norwegians, Danes, Scotch, and Irish," adding that
"the great bulk of the colonists then, as at the present time, consisted of Scotchmen and Canadians."[17] Ensuing paragraphs describe the
battle of Seven Oaks and the violence between the two furtrading
companies: "Personal conflicts with fists between the men – and, not
unfrequently, the gentlemen – of the opposing parties were of the
commonest occurrence, and frequently more deadly weapons were
resorted to." But the ethnicity of these "gentlemen" was not mentioned. Ballantyne was not prepared to use the "Scottish fact" as a

literary or interpretive device, and his book makes clear that the Scots' dominance was merely a "strange fact" that did not enter into his interpretation of the fur trade.

Ballantyne subsequently returned to the fur trade in one of his most popular novels, *Snowflakes and Sunbeams; or the young fur traders*, originally published in 1856. The novel was in many ways a curious production. It featured, for example, a young mixed-blood hero and heroine (how many of these do we find in nineteenth-century literature?). Charley and Kate Kennedy, we are told at the outset, were the son and daughter of old Frank Kennedy, who had run away from school in Scotland and had entered the HBC service, "in which he obtained an insight into savage life, a comfortable fortune, besides a half-breed wife and a large family."[18] In the second chapter, the author takes his reader to the counting room at Fort Garry, inhabited by three clerks. The senior was a Scotchman, as was the second clerk. Ballantyne observed that it "is curious to note how numerous Scotchmen are in the wilds of North America," but again made nothing more of this ethnic identification.[19]

In one of the later chapters, Ballantyne introduced a character described as "a native of Orkney, a country from which, and the neighbouring islands, the Fur Company almost exclusively recruits its staff of labourers. These men are steady, useful servants, although inclined to be slow and lazy *at first*; but they soon get used to the country, and rapidly improve under the example of the active Canadians and half-breeds with whom they associate; some of them are the best servants the Company possess."[20] This one was "a very bad specimen of the race," however. Ballantyne subsequently described a fight between the Orkneyman and a Métis named Baptiste, in the course of which he wrote:

Every nation has its own peculiar method of fighting, and its own ideas of what is honourable and dishonourable in combat. The English, as everyone knows, have particularly stringent rules governing the part of the body which may or may not be hit with propriety, and count it foul disgrace to strike a man when he is down; although, by some strange perversity of reasoning, they deem it right and fair to *fall* upon him while in this helpless condition, and burst him if possible. The Scotchman has less of the science, and we are half inclined to believe that he would go the length of kicking a fallen opponent; but on this point we are not quite positive.[21]

In the comic scene that follows, the Orkneyman is thoroughly beaten by the Métis, who fights with "no reference to rules at all."[22] Throughout this novel Ballantyne took full advantage of racial stereotypes, particularly of the mixed bloods and of the peculiar ethnic mix of Red River. His description of a wedding dance in the concluding pages demonstrated his talents. But he nowhere attempted to associate Scottishness with any particular characteristics of the fur trade.

Serious historical study of the British fur trade, particularly of the great trading companies, did not begin until the last years of the nineteenth century. Masson's documents appeared in 1889–90, and in 1900 appeared *The Remarkable History of the Hudson's Bay Company including that of the French Traders of North-Western Canada and of the North-West, XY, and Astor Fur Companies,* by George Bryce. One of those early Canadian historians whose work has fallen through the historiographical cracks – he was not one of the national historians favoured by Professor Berger (although he wrote a pioneering social history of Canada entitled *A Short History of the Canadian People,* 1887, rev. 1914) and was not considered by Professor Taylor because he was from the West – Bryce deserves to be taken more seriously. Born in Canada, he was a Presbyterian clergyman who helped found Manitoba College and the University of Manitoba, as well as the Manitoba Historical Society and the Manitoba Historical and Scientific Society. He was the first to attempt to demythologize the early history of Manitoba, doing considerable research in the Selkirk family papers in Scotland in preparation for his study of Lord Selkirk.

In his book on the HBC Bryce clearly accepted the prominence of Scots in the fur trade. One of his early chapters is entitled "The Scottish Merchants of Montreal," and in the pages that follow most of the Scottish figures are identified as such. Nevertheless, Bryce did not see the presence of so many Scots as particularly significant. In his chapter entitled "The Lords of the Lakes and Forests" – a deliberate reference to Washington Irving – he sought, in his own words, "to sketch, from their own writings, pictures of the lords of the fur trade."[23] Bryce continued: "They were a remarkable body of men. Great as financiers, marvellous as explorers, facile as traders, brave in their spirits, firm and yet tactful in their management of the Indians, and, except during the short period from 1800–1814, anxious for the welfare of the Red men." He concluded with a quote from Washington Irving: "The feudal state of Fort William is at an end; its council chamber is silent and desolate; its banquet hall no longer echoes to the auld world ditty; the lords of the lakes and forests have passed away." But curiously, nowhere in this chapter does Bryce emphasize that the men he has been describing were Scots or Highland Scots. The major point of Irving's epitaph about feudal Fort William – that it was part of a feudal Highlands recreated in North America – is totally lost in Bryce's text.

As if to emphasize his recognition of the ubiquitous furtrading Scot, in 1911 George Bryce contributed to one of the first ethnic histories, the multivolume *The Scotsman in Canada*. Bryce's volume was devoted to Western Canada and dedicated to Lord Strathcona; it touched on "Nations and Tribes of the Scottish Motherland," "The Men of Orkney in Rupert's Land," and so on, for a total of thirty-five chapters. Notable Scots are listed according to their fields of endeavour, and biographical sketches abound. According to Bryce these men did great honour to their Scottish blood, but there is no attempt to argue that their influence or impact was distinctively Scottish in nature.

The history of the fur trade became increasingly dominated by academics in the first half of the twentieth century. One of the chief characteristics of mainstream fur trade history in this period was utter disdain for either culture or ethnicity as important determinants of development. Occasionally a cultural question unexpectedly intruded into the analysis, as in the revised edition of Harold Innis's *Fur Trade in Canada*. Innis described the way in which the HBC became dependent on Orkney Islanders and quoted an 1812 memorandum from Colin Robertson that points out why, in his judgment, Canadians were better employees than Orkneymen.[24] But Innis never really pursued this insight, either in the particular or especially in the larger sense. One searches in vain in these histories – Davidson's on the NWC, Innis's on the fur trade, J.S. Galbraith's on the HBC, E.E.

Rich's massive work on the HBC or his briefer one on the fur trade and the Northwest – for much mention of the presence of ethnically labelled Scots, much less any serious discussion of how their involvement in the fur trade might have influenced it.[25] All these historians were interested in business and economic history and would have found cultural complexity an alien affair.

In a collection of documents on the NWC he published in 1934, William Stewart Wallace missed an opportunity to correct the already standard interpretation of the fur trade as an economic enterprise with vague and shifting ethnic overtones. Not until the close of his historical introduction did Wallace address the question of ethnic participation in the trade. Some of the Nor'Westers were French-Canadians, he noted, and others were American frontiersmen. "Most of them," he added,

were Scottish Highlanders, the sons of those who had come to Canada in Wolfe's army or as United Empire Loyalists in the American Revolution. The number of them who were connected with that gallant regiment, the 78th or Fraser's Highlanders, is remarkable; and it is no less remarkable that the numerous Frasers, McTavishes, and McGillivrays, who played such an important part in the history of the North West Company, nearly all came from Lord Lovat's estates. The names of the North West Company partners sound like a roll-call of the clans at Culloden. These men were hardy, courageous, shrewd, and proud.[26]

Wallace further noted that it was a Scot, Lord Selkirk, who "ruined the first great industry that Canadians, by means of fortitude and foresight, had developed."[27] This subtle shift on a single page, from characterizing the Nor'Westers as Highlanders to seeing them as Canadians, perhaps helps account for Wallace's failure to explore fully the possible meanings of his ethnic insights. His subsequent book on the Nor'Westers was entitled, of course, *The Pedlars from Quebec*, not *The Traders from Lord Lovat's Estates*, and it virtually ignored the Scottish dimension.[28]

The breakthrough book in the study of Scottish ethnicity in the fur trade ought to have been Marjorie Wilkins Campbell's *North West Company*.[29] Skillfully written, it manages to suggest an important Scottish influence on the company without actually arguing it or documenting it. The clearest statement of a Scottish interpretation comes, not in Campbell's own words, but in Hugh MacLennan's 1983 foreword to a reprint edition, which characterized the book as

the story of a wonderful body of men, Highland Scots who had been driven to Canada by the ruination of the Highland way of life after the '45. It is the story of Montreal's most important business company; it is the story of the Highlander in Canada, without whom the Loyalists and Canadiens could never have united politically, because in the early days it was the Highlander who provided the social cement. And finally it is the story – so pathetically true to the Highlander's life style – of the absorption of their efforts by calculating Anglo-Saxons whose greatness, I truly believe in my more Hebridean moods, has always consisted in their capacity to appropriate to themselves with a free conscience not only the labours of other men, but the credit won by other men's genius and courage.[30]

The reference to others is to the HBC, "in absorbing them, appropriating their superior methods, and claiming most of the credit for what other men had done." MacLennan quoted the "Canadian Boat Song" – "From the lone sheiling in the misty island / Mountains divide us and a waste of seas / But still the blood runs strong, the Heart is Highland / And we in dreams behold the Hebrides" – and described Campbell's study as one approached with "controlled emotion."

The control is certainly apparent. The dominance of the Highlanders in the NWC is never clearly stated by Campbell, and we get only veiled references to the "clannishness" of the company, instead of a detailed analysis of how this clannishness was manifested or what it possibly meant. Perhaps symptomatically, Campbell treats George Landemann's descriptions of monumental Highlander drinking bouts at the Beaver Club as evidence of the camaraderie and companionship of Alexander Mackenzie and his mates, rather than as major ethnic blowouts. Landemann described one occasion in 1798 when a collection of soldiers and fur traders, "all of them, I believe, natives of the Highlands of Scotland ... sat down, and without loss of time expedited the lunch intended to supersede a dinner, during which time the bottle had freely circulated, raising the old Highland

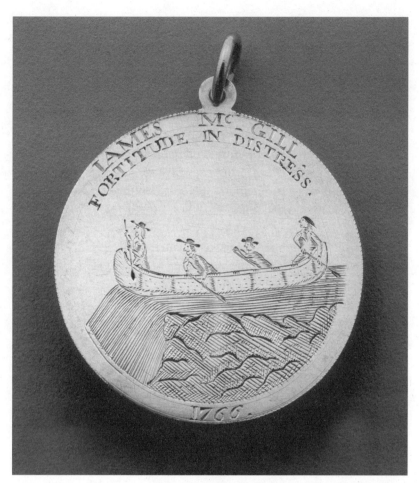

Beaver Club medal belonging to James McGill, founder of McGill University. Courtesy of the McCord Museum of Canadian History (M1149). This medal dates from about 1785 and signifies McGill's membership in the Beaver Club, a social club for North West Company merchants and traders who had spent at least one winter in the *pays d'en haut*. Members were largely Scottish or of Scots descent, and meetings were known to turn into raucous drinking bouts.

drinking propensity, so that there was no stopping it; Highland speeches and sayings, Highland reminiscences, and Highland farewells, with the *dioch* and *dorich*, over and over again, was kept up with great energy."[31] Campbell characterized this occasion as "another of the glorious Bacchanals by which the lives of the Nor'Westers offset some of the toils of their arduous lives," which certainly shifted Landemann's ethnic emphasis.[32] The only part of Landemann's quite explicit ethnic reference Campbell retained was to the sharing of the "boisterous '*dioche* and *dorichs*,'" a reference probably quite mysterious to any reader without knowledge of the original Landemann account.[33]

Why did historians fail to engage adequately the question of the dominance of the Scots in the fur trade? There are several possible explanations:

1 They were unaware of it. But since most of the authors were of Scottish background, ignorance seems a most unlikely explanation.
2 They took it for granted. This is more possible, especially for the early writers. For them, there may have been no point in belabouring the obvious.
3 They didn't want to acknowledge it. This seems likely for several authors. Some may have sought to avoid complicating the classic confrontations of the fur trade – English (or British) v. Canadian, Montreal v. the Bay, North America v. Europe – the simplicity of which is undermined if the traders' Scots origins are acknowledged. Other authors may have adopted a typically Scottish reticence. Acknowledgment did not automatically imply importance but might resulted in a need for further explanations. Why were the Scots so dominant? Or how did Scots dominance play out in the development of the fur trade?
4 They thought it interesting but did not think it important. This is a perfectly plausible explanation, certainly suggested by the writings of Robert Ballantyne. In Canada before 1960, ethnicity was a nationalistic boast, not an analytical tool. Moreover, the Scots represented not a single ethnic group but a collection of at least four quite distinguishable groups – Orkneymen, Shetlanders,

Highlanders and Islanders, and Lowland Scots – who did not necessarily have much in common. Indeed, the best argument against a serious ethnic interpretation of the fur trade may well be that there was no homogeneous group of Scots engaged in it.

5 They thought it both interesting and significant, but hesitated to make too much of the point for fear of accusations of racial stereotyping.

Attempting to establish definitively why early historians – especially those whose papers have not been preserved – failed to include certain material or provide particular interpretations is, of course, a thankless task. But we can certainly speculate on it. It seems to me that all but the first possible explanation offered above were operative with one or more of the early historians of the fur trade. An early writer like Roderick Mackenzie, approaching the subject from the inside, quite likely took Scottish involvement for granted. Lord Selkirk, on the other hand, probably did not want to call attention to the ethnic background of the Nor'Westers for political reasons. Several authors, like Robert Ballantyne, found the role of Scots interesting but not particularly important. But the chief reason for the failure to treat Scottishness as an explanatory factor in the fur trade has to do with the way in which ethnicity was viewed by scholars before the 1970s. For those historians who concentrated on what was regarded as mainstream constitutional, political, and military affairs, ethnicity beyond the French-English conflict simply was not important. Many other scholars in the twentieth century, reacting against the fierce racial stereotyping of the public debate over immigration in Canada, deliberately chose to ignore ethnicity as a factor in their explanations of many things, including the fur trade.[34] Pretending that ethnicity did not exist in Canada was, of course, a political statement in its own right. Old habits did not change until ethnicity ceased to be conceived in racial terms and was seen instead as a cultural construct. When Elaine Mitchell wrote on the Scot in the fur trade in the mid-1970s, she did so in a work that was part of a revival of ethnic studies in Canada connected with the rise of multiculturalism.[35] The sort of analysis offered by a modern scholar like Ferenc Szasz in his *Scots in the North American West, 1790–1917* would have been quite unthinkable before 1970.[36]

NOTES

1 According to Michael Payne, in *The Most Respectable Place in the Territory: Everyday Life in Hudson's Bay Company Service* (Ottawa: National Historic Parks and Sites, 1989), 34–5, the percentage distribution of all HBC employees by place of origin for the period 1824–70 was

All Scotland	63.5
England	5.7
The Canadas	11.5
Rupert's Land	17.9
Other	1.5

Of the Scots, 41.1 percent came from Orkney, 6.0 percent from Shetland, 8.3 percent from the Hebrides, and 8.1 percent from mainland Scotland. John Nicks observes that in 1800, 390 of the HBC's 498 officers and servants were Orkneymen (78 percent), although the proportion had declined to 40 percent by union. John Nicks, "Orkneymen in the HBC, 1780–1821," in Carol Judd and Arthur Ray, eds., *Old Trails and New Directions: Papers of the Third North American Fur Trade Conference* (Toronto: University of Toronto Press 1980), 102. In 1911, in his book *The Scotsman in Canada*, George Bryce listed the names of the partners of the North West Company and the New North-West Company at the time of their merger in 1804, observing that "of the forty-six prominent men of the fur trade in the two companies there seem to be only six who are known not to be Scotsmen." *The Scotsman in Canada* (Toronto: Musson 1911), 52.

2 *Dictionary of Canadian Biography*, vol. 7, (Toronto: University of Toronto Press 1988), 565–7.

3 Reprinted (New York: Antiquarian Press 1960).

4 Alexander Mackenzie, *Voyages from Montreal through the Continent of North America to the Frozen and Pacific Oceans in 1789 and 1793 with an Account of the Rise and State of the Fur trade*, 2 vols. (Toronto: George N. Morang & Company 1902), liii–liv.

5 Ibid., lxxvii.

6 Selkirk, "A Sketch of the British Fur Trade," in Bumsted, ed., *The Collected Writings of Lord Selkirk*, vol. 2, 1810–1820 (Winnipeg: Manitoba Record Society 1988), 76.

7 Ibid., 81.

8 Washington Irving, *Astoria, or Anecdotes of an Enterprise beyond the Rocky Mountains*, edited and with an Introduction by Edgeley W. Todd (Norman, OK: University of Oklahoma Press 1964), xlv.

9 Pierre Munro Irving, *Life and Letters of Washington Irving* (Waterloo: Wilfrid Laurier University Press 1977), vol. 3, 60–2.

10 Irving, *Astoria*, xlvn.

11 Ibid., xlvii.

12 Ibid., 9.

13 Ibid., 10–11.

14 Ibid., 12.

15 Ibid., 13.

16 Robert Ballantyne, *Hudson Bay; or, Everyday Life in North America*, 4th ed. (London, Edinburgh, and New York: T. Nelson n.d.), 27.

17 Ibid., 62.

18 R.M. Ballantyne, *The Coral Island and the Young Fur Traders* (London: Collins 1979), 255.

19 Ibid., 268.

20 Ibid., 305.

21 Ibid., 306.

22 Ibid., 306

23 George Bryce, *The Remarkable History of the Hudson's Bay Company* (Toronto: William Briggs 1900), 187.

24 Harold Innis, *The Fur Trade in Canada*, rev. ed. (Toronto: University of Toronto Press 1956), 160–2.

25 G.C. Davidson, *The North West Company* (Berkeley 1918); Harold Innis, *The Fur Trade in Canada*; J.S. Galbraith, *The Hudson's Bay Company as an Imperial Factor, 1821–69* (Toronto: University of Toronto Press 1957); E.E. Rich, *The Hudson's Bay Company, 1660–1870*, 3 vols. (Toronto: McClelland and Stewart 1960); E.E. Rich, *The Fur Trade and the Northwest to 1857* (Toronto: McClelland and Stewart 1967).

26 W. Stewart Wallace, ed., *Documents Relating to the North West Company* (Toronto: Champlain Society 1934), 34–5.

27 Ibid., 35–6.

28 W. Stewart Wallace, *The Pedlars from Quebec and Other Papers on the Nor'Westers* (Toronto: Ryerson Press 1954).

29 Macmillan, 1957.

30 Vancouver: Douglas & McIntyre 1983, n.p.

31 Quoted in Roy Daniells, *Alexander Mackenzie and the North West* (London: Faber & Faber 1969), 166.

32 Campbell, *North West Company*, 120.

33 Ibid.

34 The existence of such a situation is implicit in the several studies of the historiography of ethnic studies in Canada, especially Howard Palmer, "Canadian Immigration and Ethnic History in the 1970s and 1980s," *Journal of Canadian Studies*, 17 (1982), 35–50, and his "History and Present State of Ethnic Studies in Canada," in Wsevolod Isajiw, ed., *Identities: The Impact of Ethnicity on Canadian Society* (Toronto: P. Martin 1977), 167–83; see also Dirk Hoerder, "Ethnic Studies in Canada from the 1880s to 1962: A Historiographical Perspective and Critique," *Canadian Ethnic Studies*, 26: no. 1 (1994): 1–18.

35 Mitchell's "The Scot in the Fur Trade" was published in W. Stanford Reid, ed., *The Scottish Tradition in Canada* (Toronto: McClelland & Stewart 1976), a volume in the series sponsored by the Multiculturalism Branch of the government of Canada.

36 Norman, OK, 2000.

FIVE

Sojourners in the Snow? The Scots in Business in Nineteenth-Century Canada

Douglas McCalla

Enterprising Scottish businessmen are familiar figures in Canadian history, their influence an essential element in the standard story. The image is nicely caught by Michael Bliss in *Northern Enterprise*, his sweeping account of the history of Canadian business:

In 1759, 1760, and 1761 [Glasgow] merchants shipped thirty-three full shiploads of provisions for the conquering armies. Soon the Scots merchants began shipping out clerks and apprentices to represent them and start up new ventures in the new colony. The adventurers who came from the south and from the British Isles after the Conquest were of several nationalities, including an important Jewish group. But the Scots became strikingly dominant ... The trading networks created by the first generations of Scotsmen established a grip on the commanding heights of Canadian business that lingered well into the twentieth century.[1]

Such prominence did not go without criticism. For example, not long after he arrived in Upper Canada in 1805, the Irish-born judge Robert Thorpe virulently denounced the baneful power of the "Scotch pedlars" who formed a "chain ... from Halifax to Quebec, Montreal, Kingston, York, Niagara and so on to Detroit ... [a] Shop-keeper Aristocracy [that] stunted the Province and goaded the people until they ... turned from the greatest loyalty to the utmost disaffection."[2]

This story begins with the fur trade and its leaders, including Simon McTavish, James McGill, William McGillivray, Alexander Mackenzie, and, later, George Simpson.[3] It goes on to the Bank of Montreal and the development of canals and railways, including such leading figures associated with the Pacific railway projects as Hugh Allan, George Stephen, and Donald Smith. To them can be added key Confederation-era political figures – themselves active participants in the business world – such as John A. Macdonald and Alexander Tilloch Galt. Notwithstanding various criticisms, the story of enterprising Scots remains one of the absolutely central narratives of Canadian history: self-made men from humble beginnings led in making a transcontinental nation, with the Canadian Pacific Railway (CPR) and its close ally, the Bank of Montreal, replacing the old fur trade links.[4] "[T]he most famous photograph in Canadian history," according to the book accompanying the recent television series *Canada: A People's History*, is of Donald Smith driving the last spike on the CPR.[5] "Smith's life ... closely mirrors Canada's passage to nationhood," writes one recent biographer.[6] Another concludes that he "remains the foremost example of the Canadian rags-to-riches story."[7] The narrative of the enterprising, nation-building Scot is central even to critical, muckraking accounts of Canadian history.[8]

This is an explicitly Laurentian, Montreal-based story. But elsewhere, too, Scots were present in business communities in numbers disproportionate to their overall share of local populations. As late as 1910 more members of the Canadian "industrial elite" (as identified by T.W. Acheson) had fathers born in Scotland than in Canada.[9] This paper examines how this situation came to be. It argues for a wider, more complex narrative of the Scots in Canadian business. For example, as the title suggests, a number of leading figures, including

Mackenzie, Smith, and Stephen, crowned their careers by returning
to Scotland (and London). Is there anything to be learned by seeing
such businessmen as sojourners whose greatest dream was to return
home in triumph?

BACKGROUND

The Union of 1707 was just one factor in Scotland's eighteenth-century economic development. Nonetheless it was a crucial development, as Scots became increasingly full participants in a British
Empire run on mercantilist policies.[10] One of the ways Glasgow firms
made places for themselves in the Empire was through their readi-
ness to seek opportunities in regions not yet settled into established
structures. Thus, in the Chesapeake they captured a growing share
of the fast-expanding trade in a major grocery staple, tobacco, by
sending young men to establish stores in newly opening areas on the
frontier. There they sold imported goods on long credit to relatively
modest planters. Glasgow firms sold Scottish products and were an
element in Scotland's industrialization, which paralleled that of England. Still, much trans-Atlantic trade in both directions was of an entrepôt character; 85 percent of all tobacco imported to Britain, for
example, was reexported.[11] When Scots clerks and apprentices arrived in Canada between 1759 and 1761 they were part of a much
wider process that carried Scots to the farthest British trading fron-
tiers – and to the heart of the Empire in London.

If Scotland was now within the imperial system, it nevertheless
continued to have distinctive institutional patterns, including Europe's most advanced banking system.[12] However modern the banks,
it is essential to recall that one did not lend directly to strangers. The
visible flow of trade was founded on underlying personal and community networks that structured payments and credit. Overseas
trading firms were typically organized as interlocking but formally
distinct partnerships extending from London and Glasgow to overseas ports and sometimes, as in the Chesapeake, inland. As trade
grew it tended to deepen and reinforce the main channels; transportation and flows of information, funds, goods, and people were
organized around a few focal points, notably for the North Atlantic
trades, Glasgow and Liverpool. Both within and among ports the

Donald Smith Driving the Last Spike, CPR, Craigellachie,
BC, 1885, Alexander Ross, gift of Mr Stanley G. Triggs.
Courtesy of the Notman Photographic Archives, McCord
Museum of Canadian History (MP-0000.25.971)

business world was highly competitive, with many participants and would-be participants. To create places for themselves in the commercial system, the Scots who went overseas had to be nimble, adaptable, and connected at home.

DIFFERENTIATION

Describing Scottish towns early in the process of expansion, T.M. Devine writes, "It is important to recognise at the outset that the merchant communities of these towns were far from homogeneous."[13] Within any port on either side of the Atlantic, business communities were hierarchical, and there were numerous trading circles. Similarly, in the partnerships that linked metropolis and frontier, those at the centre generally had the greatest power in the firm. The leading mercantile and banking families of Glasgow were far above the level of the individual shopkeeper on the Piedmont frontier. Compared to the Caribbean and the Chesapeake, as Tom Wien and James Pritchard note, "Canada's commerce [was] relatively small, accounting ... for less than 5% of British trade with North America in the 1770s."[14] That trade may not have been attractive to well-established traders in major markets such as New York, but the opportunities in the north were surely equivalent to those in many smaller Caribbean, American, or Latin American markets. They permitted those who succeeded in the Canadian trades to accumulate wealth far beyond that of the country retailers with whom they dealt. In the Hudson's Bay Company there was also a large gap, effectively a class divide, between the ordinary workers, many of them Orkneymen, and the leading Scots in the organization.[15]

Scots were prominent in the business world everywhere in early- and mid-nineteenth-century British North America. Yet nowhere were they more than a minority, as selected data on the ethnic identity of various business groups indicate. The classifications in table 5.1 range from forty "great merchants" of Saint John between 1820 and 1850 to all the merchants in Halifax from the late eighteenth century to 1850 and to all the "self-employed" in Brantford in 1852. In Quebec and Montreal the Scottish-born ranked as the leading group, although they did not have an absolute majority. In Saint John and

TABLE 5.1
SCOTS IN CANADIAN BUSINESS CIRCLES, SELECTED EVIDENCE

Place	Years	Group	Number in Group	Born in Scotland %	Rank of Scots Born	Number of Categories	Origins Highest Rank
Halifax	to 1850	Merchants	370[1]	18	2	6	Nova Scotia
Quebec	1800–30	Marchands	34[2]	32	1	4	
Saint John	1820–50	Great merchants	40	n.a.	2	4	Loyalist
Saint John	1851	High-status positions	66[3]	15	2, tied	8	New Brunswick
Montreal	1837–53	Business community	n.a.	n.a.	1	6	
Hamilton	1851–52	Entrepreneurial class	143[4]	23	2	6	England
Brantford	1852	Self-employed	237	11	5	5	England
				Father Born in Scotland			
Canada	1885	Industrial elite	151	28	1	8	7
Canada	1910	Industrial elite	175	30	1	9	7

Sources: David Sutherland, "The Merchants of Halifax, 1815–1850: A Commercial Class in Pursuit of Metropolitan Status," PhD diss., University of Toronto, 1975, 470–81 (Halifax); George Bervin, Québec au XIXe siècle: L'activité économique des grands marchands (Sillery: Septentrion 1991), 263–4 (Quebec); T.W. Acheson, Saint John: The Making of a Colonial Urban Community (Toronto: University of Toronto Press 1985), 50, 261; (Saint John); Gerald Tulchinsky, The River Barons: Montreal Businessmen and the Growth of Industry and Transportation, 1837–53 (Toronto: University of Toronto Press 1977), 19–20 (Montreal); Michael B. Katz, The People of Hamilton, Canada West: Family and Class in a Mid-Nineteenth-Century City (Cambridge, MA: Harvard University Press 1975), 180 (Hamilton); David Burley, A Particular Condition in Life: Self-Employment and Social Mobility in Mid-Victorian Brantford, Ontario (Kingston and Montreal: McGill-Queen's University Press 1994), 79 (Brantford); T.W. Acheson, "Changing Social Origins of the Canadian Industrial Elite, 1880–1910," in Glenn Porter and Robert Cuff, eds., Enterprise and National Development: Essays in Canadian Business and Economic History (Toronto: Hakkert 1973), 57 (Canada).

1 Number for which the birthplace is known.
2 Number for which the birthplace is known.
3 Sample, class 1.
4 Number for which the birthplace is known.

Halifax men born in Scotland ranked second behind locally born merchants. In Brantford, on the other hand, the Scottish-born ranked last (fifth), at 11 percent of the more than two hundred men who were self-employed in 1852. Scots were often particularly prominent in the higher circles of business, as Acheson's study of the late-nineteenth- and early-twentieth-century Canadian "industrial elite" suggests. By one test of ethnic background – father's birthplace – Scots were the leading group in both 1885 and 1910, at about 30 percent. By comparison, 16 percent of the Canadian population was of Scottish ancestry in 1881 and 14 percent in 1911.[16] Thus, depending on definition and place, Scots represented up to one-third of the leading local business group, however defined. Other groups, such as those of Loyalist background in New Brunswick, often ranked higher. Finally, the total numbers in even the largest of the business groupings reported in the table are very modest. This reminds us that "Scot" and "businessman" were not synonyms, and most Scots, like most other people in Canada, were not members of the leading business circles.

DEFINITIONS

In the material summarized in the table, the authors defined Scottish identity in terms of place of birth or father's place of birth; emigrants and the sons of emigrants obviously had the most immediate and recent ties to Scotland. These criteria include someone like Galt, who was born in London and grew up in England, Scotland, and Canada; to contemporaries, his identity would have been audible in his "slight Scottish accent."[17] Prominent figures in early-twentieth-century Canadian business with Scottish-born fathers included Edward Clouston of the Bank of Montreal, born at Moose Factory; William Mackenzie, born in Eldon Township, northeast of Toronto; and Max Aitken, born in Ontario and brought up in New Brunswick. Beginning in 1871 the Canadian census also sought to record ancestry, however remote; it precluded categories such as "American" and "Canadian" and divided the "British" into separate groups.[18] In the process, it greatly simplified actual lineages, which after even a few generations could be very complex.[19] Of course, ethnic identity was not simply a matter of birth and biology; it was made and remade. Families with long histories in the New World could readily see themselves as Scots, as has been well documented, for example, in Nova Scotia. Such people are missed in the classifications used here, and the Scottish presence may therefore be somewhat underestimated.[20] Still, it is not unreasonable to see someone two generations removed from Scotland as part of the general Canadian population. After two generations, the Scotland claimed by those who identified themselves as Scots was often an imagined place, effectively made in Canada (as Edward Cowan observes elsewhere in this volume).

Setting the limits of a business community, whether locally or on a wider scale, is also a matter of definition, as the variety of categorizations in the table suggests. Thus, in his study of Saint John, Acheson distinguished great merchants from more modest shopkeepers and from those who passed through quickly. He was interested in leaders, men who "played important roles in the commercial and public life of [New Brunswick] over a number of years," combining "a variety of commercial interests" with participation "in vital shipping and financial concerns" of Saint John.[21] Michael B. Katz's entrepreneurial class was "an overlapping elite governing economic, political, and associational life" in Hamilton.[22] David Burley's self-employed worked on their own account, holding "through ownership or tenancy, the means of producing and distributing goods and services;"[23] his grouping included a wide range of occupations, everyone from leading merchants and manufacturers to ordinary carters and cab men. On the other hand, his grouping does not include self-employed professionals or anyone employed on a salaried basis in a business.

Business itself also requires definition. One important issue is whether professionals are included. Lawyers, in particular, were often deeply engaged in business. Law was inaccessible for most first-generation Scottish immigrants because it was locally controlled and based on English or French law. It was, however, very much open to their sons. Whether engineers were professionals was contested, but in any case many of them were necessarily entrepreneurs. A second issue is hierarchy. Between the highest and the lowest ranks in many sectors there might in fact be distinctions of class rather than status. A single job title could span the ranks of ordinary artisans and the community's most substantial business figures. Contracting, for example, encompassed everyone from the carpenter who built houses one at a time to the men who organized the country's biggest works projects; for some, in fact, it provided an avenue for dramatic social ascent. Thus, Thomas McKay began as a mason and ultimately became one of most eminent business figures in Bytown; and future prime minister Alexander Mackenzie, once a stonemason, became a successful general contractor before entering politics. A third issue is choice of category. Newspapers, for example, combined craft, business, and politics. Would we call William Lyon Mackenzie a businessman? Or George Brown? Should we call Montreal's William Notman a businessman or a photographer? The latter carries implications of art and technology that the former, in itself, does not. As all these examples show, definition and categorization are fundamental to understanding the groupings in the table, or in any alternative table we might devise.

Business was largely a male sphere, which is why men are the main focus of this paper. Especially at higher levels, it was uncommon for a woman to play an autonomous, direct, visible business role in her own name over a long term. However, it is important to recall that here, too, definition affects categorizations.[24] Women had various business roles, sometimes on their own but most often in a family context, as wives, widows, mothers, and agents for absent husbands. Moreover, family dynamics were at the heart of many business decisions.

It has been common, and in some respects reasonable, to see development as transforming the economy from "simple" to complex. But this understanding of change can lead to an underestimation of the actual complexity of doing business in earlier historical contexts, a failure to differentiate adequately within business circles, and a misunderstanding of the specific circumstances that gave the Scots their opportunities. For example, the standard text in Canadian economic history speaks of Isaac Buchanan, a Scot whose fortune was made primarily by exporting British goods to the Upper Canadian frontier, as a "grain forwarder."[25] That does not begin to explain why he, rather than a local descendant of a Loyalist family, quickly became the leading wholesaler in Upper Canada. Like Buchanan many Scots made their places in the international aspects of the Canadian business world. Having a base or connections in Britain was a fundamental advantage over men whose associations were mainly local. What the leading merchants, those Acheson calls "great," did was to organize the international flow of British exports and re-exports and of Canadian exports, including the flow of transactions necessary to finance and complete these processes.

MIGRATION

Scottish clerks and apprentices came to the colonies essentially one at a time, often with a position already established in the overseas operations of a business based in Scotland or England. Although there are exceptions – such as the fur trader-explorer Alexander Mackenzie, who came to New York at the age of ten with his father – most were single and young, between fifteen and twenty-five years old, when they first crossed the Atlantic. The youngest were just beginning a commercial apprenticeship, while older ones might be sent with more responsibility. Writing of young Scots who went in similar circumstances to Jamaica and Virginia in the eighteenth century, Alan Karras notes that they "hoped to emulate those who had already returned ... with handsome fortunes."[26] Their ambitions were thus to be sojourners, not permanent emigrants. As noted earlier, it seems at least possible that those taking ship for the northern colonies had similar dreams.

Later, perhaps, they would remember themselves as starting from nothing. But without underestimating their achievements, we can note that starting in the New World with limited means was normal – on the whole, the wealthy did not emigrate. And even those who began in modest circumstances came with valuable assets, such as contacts with or an initial position within established commercial networks. William McGillivray's biographer notes that although he "came from a poor family," he had a powerful uncle, Simon McTavish, who opened the path for him into the fur trade and ultimately to the head of the North West Company.[27] George Simpson, although born out of wedlock, grew up with the support of his father's family and connections; when he first crossed the Atlantic, it was to take charge of North American operations for the Hudson's Bay

Company. Family connections opened doors at the HBC for Donald Smith as well. (That Smith's older brother qualified in medicine at the University of Edinburgh also suggests that he did not begin his life in rags.) Indeed, speaking of the "prominent members of the Montreal commercial fraternity" in the period from 1837 to 1853, Gerald Tulchinsky writes: "This cadre of leaders were not men of poor or modest beginnings ... [Most] had been favoured with considerable advantages ... Their recruitment to the largest or best established firms was not ... a result of upward mobility – though this was true for a few – but of a transference of wealth and advantage within Montreal families, or the transmigration of capital and skills, entrepreneurial and technical, from Britain and the United States."[28]

A second strand of Scottish trans-Atlantic migration was family-based, especially during the waves of emigration from Britain to British North America between 1815 and the 1850s. Contacts and connections could also be crucial in directing this type of migration, but when whole families moved, the strategy clearly focused on a permanent stay, reestablishing the family in the New World. Some came with business in mind; often, the head of the family had fared badly in business at home. Thus, Adam Ferrie had lost much of his fortune in other overseas trades, and William Notman's family business had gone bankrupt. Many more of the Scottish families who emigrated came in search of land, seeking the independence that a successful farm provided. Others included artisans and their families, retired military officers, clergy, and teachers. It was family emigration that brought men like John McDougall and Donald McInnes, later prominent as manufacturers in Montreal and Hamilton, to Canada. The former was seven years old when his parents came to Lower Canada, and the latter was a teenager when his parents began to farm in nearby Beverly Township. Acheson notes that there were many such men in the Canadian industrial elite of 1885. Discussing upward mobility, he writes, the "most characteristic Canadian success stories were those of the large group of young sons of Scottish farmers who, armed with little more than a traditional craftsman's training, descended upon the Canadas in the 1840's and '50's, and by dint of industry and frugal living rose in middle age to the proprietorships of substantial manufacturing establishments."[29]

A FAMILY AFFAIR

Both individual and family-based migration reminds us that family and business were deeply interconnected. Business networks were based on trust and interest, in both of which ties of family and community were essential. Of course, not all family members were equal. It was not uncommon for positions in Glasgow or London to be reserved for immediate family members of the senior partners and, within families, for older sons to be given preference over younger ones. Success at home would, however, depend on the overseas efforts of others, and disputes over power, shares, and position could readily arise, leading to the disruption of a partnership. Moreover, in a culture of enterprise, heading a business of one's own was normally the ultimate objective. If an existing business did not offer adequate advancement, setting up a separate firm was always an option.

In a quick note written in 1859, Peter Buchanan, Glasgow partner of a large firm in the Canadian trade, reminded himself that "A Canadian business such as B[uchanan] H[arris] & Cos never intended to be wound up. Should have people coming forward to continue it & relieve me. This is the only & true Policy. Better late than never."[30] He already knew this, but the urgency of the issue had never been greater. Having barely been able to sustain payments during and after the 1857 financial crisis, despite apparently enormous assets, he was planning a complete reorganization of the firm, to be effected on a trip to Canada in 1860. His avowed aim had long been to retire in prosperity, free of the burdens and worries of active business. Yet most of the assets of the business consisted of accounts due to it in Canada. An ongoing business could manage and collect these even as it generated new business, but a business in liquidation lost much of the leverage needed to keep funds flowing in. Buchanan himself could hardly be called a sojourner, though he had been a regular visitor to Canada and between 1838 and 1843 had twice managed the business there for relatively extended periods. Nevertheless, his predicament was a characteristic one for sojourners, as Karras's work on Jamaica highlights: "colonial residents frequently found themselves entangled in endless webs of debt. Though they intended to return home, and though they accrued capital in their books, fear of losing that cash in the transition from Jamaica to Britain prevented them from leaving the island permanently ... even the most carefully earned fortune would not easily cross the Atlantic."[31]

The problem of succession required that someone able and trustworthy would be prepared to take over. In this case Peter Buchanan, aged fifty-four, had never married, nor had his partner, Robert W. Harris, who was also fifty-four. Buchanan did not trust the other main partner in the business, his younger brother Isaac, now forty-nine, to manage the entire business and their joint fortune on his own. As the will he prepared at this time makes clear, he was also anxious to preserve the wealth they had built up together for the next generation, Isaac's children. At the age of thirty-three and after thirteen years in Canadian business, Isaac Buchanan had married seventeen-year-old Agnes Jarvie of Glasgow. In 1859 their family was large, relatively young, and still growing. The oldest boy (who, not coincidently, was named Peter) was just fifteen and the next boy was only eight. If Isaac died in the next ten or twelve years, they would not be old enough to take over sole control; besides, the firm's main creditors in Glasgow and London would not readily accept young colonials. The number of heirs also complicated the succession. This is a familiar business story – many factors had to coincide for a father-to-son transition to succeed. The standard case in Canadian business history is that of Robert Hamilton, whose older sons (the eldest was twenty when he died) were not able to manage a complex and challenging transition.[32]

Important in shaping business succession and structures, family making was also important in the context of identity. For a sojourner, returning home to marry might be the ultimate goal of his business in the colonies. It took time to make one's way in business even under ideal circumstances; this contributed to the often-protracted interval between trans-Atlantic migration and marriage and to the fact that a number of successful businessmen never married at all. On the other hand, marrying overseas and having children there were signs that a man had ceased to be a sojourner and was becoming rooted in his new land. This was an important factor in the fur trade – hence the frustration felt by many historians at Peter Newman's account of it, which seemed unduly to emphasize the casual character of sexual relations between HBC men and Native women.[33]

INSECURITY AND COMPETITION

One standard account of Montreal's business elite includes a picture of Peter McGill, a member of "the close-knit group of Scots whose leaders wielded great power in the city's commerce and English-speaking social life."[34] McGill's biographer, Robert Sweeny, does not disagree, but he emphasizes the failure of Peter McGill to foresee the city's industrial future as the Redpath and Molson families did, and he comments that the "*ex officio* head of the Montreal business community failed to establish a fortune that would ensure the continuance of the McGills as a leading bourgeois family in the city."[35] Indeed, this was by no means an uncommon story among the prominent Scottish-Canadian businessmen whose lives are recounted in the *Dictionary of Canadian Biography*. Businesses did not last, sometimes because of family succession issues or schisms among partners but also because business was highly competitive – taking risks with others' funds and one's own was unavoidable. Every decade produced a financial crisis that tested each firm's ability to maintain payments when suddenly called upon to do so. However close-knit the Scottish businessmen may have seemed to others, there were limits to their mutual interests and support. They were also rivals jostling in the marketplace.

In addition to the challenges of making, keeping, and extracting funds from a business, anyone thinking of returning home faced a decision on how best to invest his wealth securely and remuneratively. If funds were left overseas, someone trustworthy was required to attend to them. Investments in land (rural or urban) were a possibility, but required attentive – and thus costly – management. Moreover, the British-style landed estate did not become a normal mode of agriculture anywhere in British North America, although there were some experiments in estate-making and the seigneurial system offered some analogous opportunities to generate revenue from a large land-holding. Bank shares were another possibility, but it is likely that the leading merchants connected to the first chartered banks were interested less in a return on the shares they held than in access to credit for their main businesses. In their core businesses, the merchants who headed local business communities were typically generalists, importing and exporting a wide range of products. Often they diversified even more widely: from opportunity, as their connections and access to information and credit allowed them to exploit opportunities that came their way; from necessity, for example as they accumulated illiquid but potentially valuable assets (such as land) in the course of collecting debts; for strategy, as they adapted to changes in the business climate and sought to provide places or secure assets for the next generation; and for community-building, as they combined with other leading businessmen to promote local development. Many of these investments were linked to a particular place; once he was committed there, the merchant could not easily transfer his wealth elsewhere.

ECONOMIC AND INSTITUTIONAL CHANGE IN THE NINETEENTH CENTURY

By the mid-1850s the mass migration that had brought so many Scottish families to British North America was coming to an end. Throughout the next forty years there would be substantial net emigration from every part of Eastern Canada. At the same time economic development, marked by technological and institutional change, would add new layers to the Canadian business world. The process was general, but its net effects were selective, fostering the dramatic growth of a handful of Canadian cities, notably Montreal and Toronto. In the same period, Glasgow's economy was fundamentally reoriented. Britain's adoption of free trade had explicitly undercut policy-created entrepôt trades, but a more significant change was the rise of heavy engineering and shipbuilding on the Clyde. By 1870 the transatlantic cable was affecting the dynamics of trade and foreign exchange. By permitting almost simultaneous knowledge of prices on both sides of the Atlantic, for example, it allowed successful firms to better manage the risks associated with handling much larger volumes of bulk commodities than had earlier been the case. London's role in world finance was reinforced in the process, while the relative advantage of a Scottish base for Canadian trade was reduced.

The period was also marked by sustained institutional development. The establishment of a corporation had once required a special charter and, in principle, a purpose beyond a single family's grasp. This form had been used for banks and other financial institutions and for railways, and the Hudson's Bay Company remained

as a representative of the earlier era of chartered companies. By the
end of the nineteenth century, however, the corporation had become
the principal institutional form of business, both through the development of big, capital-intensive enterprises that would have been
difficult to shape without the formal separation of businessman and
business that corporations embodied and because the corporate form
proved useful to many families in the management of firms of many
kinds. Wealth increasingly took the form of paper – certificates of
ownership or credit that brought a flow of funds to their owners and
that could be bought and sold. Information remained vital to invest-
ing, but the new forms of wealth allowed a hitherto unimaginable
divorce between fortune and place. Donald Smith's investments, un-
representative though they were in their scale, indicate the change.
Some of his fortune took the form of property, mortgages, and debts
owed to him personally, but most of it was in stocks and bonds representing every kind of late-nineteenth-century enterprise: railways,
shipping companies, land companies, banks, insurance companies,
mortgage companies, industrial companies (textiles, steel, sugar, paper,
milling, foundries), utility companies (telephone, cable, telegraph, etc.),
urban transit, newspapers and publishers, natural resources (coal,
oil, mining, quarries), and government bonds (municipal, provincial/
state, national).[36]

Both in recruitment and advancement of personnel, larger corporations tended to create bureaucratic processes. Even so, their rules
and routines were seldom neutral or impersonal. Links to powerful
figures in the directorate or the administration were advantageous,
and recruiting could be selective in other ways. Hence, despite London's place at the centre of the financial universe, Canadian banking
retained a strongly Scottish tone. "Well into the twentieth century,"
Duncan McDowall writes, "Canada imported Scottish bank clerks
in the belief that they contained the seeds of 'the sternest frugality
and industry.' They also came as well-trained practitioners of the
Scottish branch-banking system that seemed so well suited to Canada's vast expanses. As a consequence, Canadian banking is shot
through with nostalgia for its Scottish connection."[37] Corporations
might thus continue older practices in recruitment. As long as there
were family and business ties between Canada and Scotland, some
young Scots continued to cross the Atlantic as had so many earlier.

Still, even in the banks the proportion of Scottish-born men was much lower than it had been in international trading firms earlier. As McDowall demonstrates, that did not necessarily inhibit identification with Scotland. The Scottish tone to Canadian business faded much more slowly than did the processes that had first created it.

CONCLUSION: SOJOURNERS IN THE SNOW?

How the rich lived, what they bought, what values they sought to live up to, whom they emulated and patronized are all crucial to understanding the artifacts they have left us. Interpreting that artistic and material legacy is not primarily the task of the business historian, but the business context can be vital in thinking about the artifacts. With this in mind, let us return to the story of the prominence of Scots in Montreal business, this time as told by the respected popular historian, Donald MacKay, writing about Montreal's affluent Square Mile:

Generation after generation, Scots were the single most powerful group in the Montreal business community, which meant they were the most powerful in Canada. Many were officers or directors of the Bank of Montreal. Tradition and motivation undoubtedly had something to do with their success, for most were Protestants, with a Calvinist appetite for hard work. English conquest and social upheaval had driven them out of Scotland, and they made Canada their home with no thought of going back. Unlike the French, however, they had strong commercial ties with the United Kingdom. Unlike the English, they were not hampered by a class system that discouraged initiative by people of modest beginnings.[38]

To attribute Scottish prominence, in Montreal and nationally, to specifically Scottish experience and character is, however, much too general. As MacKay himself shows, the Scots had no monopoly on business success. Nor did most of the Scots who came to British North America (even most Protestant Scots) achieve, or even seek, the kind of success attained by the builders of the great houses that are MacKay's focus. In any case, "hard work" was normal and essential to anyone's success in settlement society, for Catholics as much as for Protestants.

Obviously ethnic identity mattered, but as a structuring element of communities and networks rather than as a direct explanation of business success. In his study of the Scots in the eighteenth century, Karras argues for the "fundamental ... Scottishness" of the Scots' business networks. Underlying that, however, was a hierarchy of factors: "location within Scotland ... personal acquaintances, business links, and kinship (in ascending order of importance) increasingly differentiated the ranks of Scottish networks."[39] In essence, this analysis shifts the emphasis away from a distinct Scottish character to a story of family and community. Similar stories can be told for entrepreneurs of other backgrounds. For example, discussing Horace Dickinson, the American operator of stages and steamboats between Montreal and Upper Canada, Frank Mackey notes how "family, church, and business affairs were closely interwoven" in his life.[40]

Imagining many of the young single Scots clerks and apprentices as sojourners situates them within their families and in a business world centred in Glasgow and London. From this perspective it is clear that MacKay's depiction of the affluent Montreal merchants as refugees "driven" from Scotland is fundamentally wrong. And while it is not unreasonable to speak of "modest beginnings," those who attained the pinnacle of success had often arrived with a substantial advantage – namely, direct access to the business sector offering the greatest possibility of future wealth. Many immigrants began with much less.

If most of those we have sought to imagine as sojourners did not return home, that was true elsewhere too. What made them Canadian, eventually? Contributing factors were the accumulation of overseas assets, a realization that they were unlikely to attain the headship of their firm in Glasgow or London, marriage to a local woman, and the growth of a Canadian family. It is not inappropriate to speak as MacKay does of generations, but a better term might be cohorts or waves. Some families did entrench and perpetuate themselves at the head of the business world, but many firms disappeared through failure, the dynamics and adjustments of partnerships and families, and the continuing evolution of the business world. The traditional account of enterprising Scots, the fur trade, and the "national dream" privileges a single strand among all these business stories – and greatly simplifies the actual processes by which Canadian business and

Canadian society developed. Moreover, Canadian business was never just or uniquely Scottish. Rather, the Scottish stories, which highlight family and the importance of linkages to the centre of the business world, are in many ways representative of the larger making and remaking of the Canadian business world and of Canadian elites. Today, as in the past, family is a strikingly prominent motif in Canadian capitalism.[41]

NOTES

This paper is part of a research program supported by a Killam Research Fellowship from the Canada Council and by the Canada Research Chairs program. In thinking about the issues discussed here, I am, as always, much indebted to my late colleague and friend, David S. Macmillan. My title is adapted from Alan L. Karras, *Sojourners in the Sun: Scottish Migrants in Jamaica and the Chesapeake, 1740–1800*. An earlier version of this paper was presented at the colloquium Character and Circumstance: The Scots in Montreal and Canada, held at the McCord Museum of Canadian History, 9–11 May 2002; this revision has benefited greatly from the advice and encouragement of other participants and of Kris Inwood.

1 Michael Bliss, *Northern Enterprise: Five Centuries of Canadian Business* (Toronto: McClelland & Stewart 1987), 110.

2 Quoted in Bruce Wilson, *The Enterprises of Robert Hamilton: A Study of Wealth and Influence in Early Upper Canada, 1776–1812* (Ottawa: Carleton University Press 1983), 2.

3 Discussions of individuals, except where otherwise noted, are drawn from their biographies in the *Dictionary of Canadian Biography* (hereafter DCB), vols. 4–14. Articles are specifically cited only when directly quoted.

4 For the criticisms, see, e.g., Bliss, *Northern Enterprise*, 119, 285–6, 297–300.

5 Don Gillmor, with Achille Michaud and Pierre Turgeon, *Canada: A People's History*, vol. 2 (Toronto: McClelland & Stewart 2001), 47. The photograph is at 22.

6 Donna McDonald, *Lord Strathcona: A Biography of Donald Alexander Smith* (Toronto and Oxford: Dundurn 1996), 7.

7 Alexander Reford, "Smith, Donald Alexander, First Baron Strathcona and Mount Royal," DCB, vol. 14, 947.

8 Gustavus Myers, *A History of Canadian Wealth*, vol. 1 (Toronto: James Lewis & Samuel 1972 [first published 1914]), e.g., 69–72 for use of Thorpe's critique.

9 T.W. Acheson, "Changing Social Origins of the Canadian Industrial Elite, 1880–1910," in Glenn Porter and Robert Cuff, eds., *Enterprise and National Development: Essays in Canadian Business and Economic History* (Toronto: Hakkert 1973), 57. However, only 7 percent of the elite had themselves been born in Scotland.

10 Richard Saville, "Scottish Modernisation prior to the Industrial Revolution, 1688–1763," in T.M. Devine and J.R. Young, eds., *Eighteenth Century Scotland: New Perspectives* (East Linton: Tuckwell Press 1999), 6–23.

11 Jacob M. Price, *Capital and Credit in British Overseas Trade: The View from the Chesapeake, 1700–1776* (Cambridge, MA: Harvard University Press 1980), 96. For the system close up, see Michael L. Nicholls, "Competition, Credit and Crisis: Merchant-Planter Relations in Southside Virginia," in Rosemary Ommer, ed., *Merchant Credit and Labour Strategies in Historical Perspective* (Fredericton: Acadiensis Press 1990), 273–89.

12 See S.G. Checkland, *Scottish Banking: A History, 1695–1973* (Glasgow: Collins 1975), xvii–xviii.

13 T.M. Devine, "The Social Composition of the Business Class in the Larger Scottish Towns, 1680–1740," in T.M. Devine and David Dickson, eds., *Ireland and Scotland, 1600–1850: Parallels and Contrasts in Economic and Social Development* (Edinburgh: John Donald 1983), 164.

14 Thomas Wien and James Pritchard, "Canadian North Atlantic Trade," in R. Cole Harris, ed., *Historical Atlas of Canada*, vol. 1, *From the Beginning to 1800* (Toronto: University of Toronto Press 1987), plate 48.

15 See Edith I. Burley, *Servants of the Honourable Company: Work, Discipline, and Conflict in the Hudson's Bay Company, 1770–1870* (Toronto: Oxford University Press 1997).

16 In 1851–52, the census counted 1,376 people born in Scotland in Hamilton, 10 percent of the city's population. The Scots-born were 8 percent of the Upper Canadian population and were outnumbered by both the English- and the Irish-born. See Canada, *Census*, 1871, vol. 4 (Ottawa 1875), 182.

17 Jean-Pierre Kesteman, "Galt, Sir Alexander Tilloch," DCB, vol. 12, 355.

18 It also divided Scots from the Protestant Irish, but this was evidently a distinction that people themselves made at the time.

19 See Bruce Curtis, *The Politics of Population: State Formation, Statistics, and the Census of Canada, 1840–1875* (Toronto: University of Toronto Press 2001), 250–1.

20 By father's ethnic origin, the proportion of Scots in Acheson's industrial elite was slightly higher: 32 percent (rather than 28 percent) in 1885 and 34 percent (rather than 30 percent) in 1910. Acheson, "Changing Social Origins," 59.

21 T.W. Acheson, "The Great Merchants and Economic Development in Saint John," *Acadiensis* 8, no. 2 (spring 1979): 7.

22 Michael B. Katz, *The People of Hamilton, Canada West: Family and Class in a Mid-Nineteenth-Century City* (Cambridge, MA: Harvard University Press 1975), 177.

23 David Burley, *A Particular Condition in Life: Self-Employment and Social Mobility in Mid-Victorian Brantford, Ontario* (Kingston and Montreal: McGill-Queen's University Press 1994), 6; see 241–3 for occupations.

24 For example, defining ethnicity by maternal rather than paternal birthplace would produce a less "Scottish" group, given the frequency with which Scottish businessmen who had come as bachelors married younger women they met in Canada. In the fur trade, indeed, this would produce a Native group.

25 See Kenneth Norrie, Douglas Owram, and J.C. Herbert Emery, *A History of*

the Canadian Economy, 3d ed. (Toronto: Thomson Nelson 2002), 96, 117. On Buchanan, see Douglas McCalla, *The Upper Canada Trade, 1834–1872: A Study of the Buchanans' Business* (Toronto: University of Toronto Press 1979).

26 Alan L. Karras, *Sojourners in the Sun: Scottish Migrants in Jamaica and the Chesapeake, 1740–1800* (Ithaca and London: Cornell University Press 1992), 49.

27 Fernand Ouellet, "McGillivray, William," DCB, vol. 6, 454.

28 Gerald Tulchinsky, *The River Barons: Montreal Businessmen and the Growth of Industry and Transportation, 1837–53* (Toronto: University of Toronto Press 1977), 25.

29 T.W. Acheson, "The Social Origins of the Canadian Industrial Elite, 1880–1885" in David S. Macmillan, ed., *Canadian Business History: Selected Studies, 1497–1971* (Toronto: McClelland & Stewart 1972), 152.

30 Peter Buchanan business memo, n.d. [1859], Buchanan Papers, 90/63509, MG24 D 16, Library and Archives Canada.

31 Karras, *Sojourners in the Sun*, 52.

32 Wilson, *The Enterprises of Robert Hamilton*, 164–76.

33 See Jennifer S.H. Brown, "Newman's *Company of Adventurers* in Two Solitudes: A Look at Reviews and Responses," *Canadian Historical Review* 67, no. 4 (December 1986): 562–71, and Peter C. Newman, "Response to Jennifer Brown," *Canadian Historical Review* 67, no. 4 (December 1986): 572–8. Brown's *Strangers in Blood: Fur Trade Company Families in Indian Country* (Vancouver: University of British Columbia Press 1980) offers a rich account of family and business in the fur trade.

34 Donald MacKay, *The Square Mile: Merchant Princes of Montreal* (Vancouver and Toronto: Douglas & McIntyre 1987), 26.

35 Robert Sweeny, "McGill, Peter" in DCB, vol. 8, 544.

36 McDonald, *Lord Strathcona*, 527–34.

37 Duncan McDowall, *Quick to the Frontier: Canada's Royal Bank* (Toronto: McClelland & Stewart 1993), 95. Internal quotation from the *Monetary Times*.

38 MacKay, *The Square Mile*, 28.

39 Karras, *Sojourners in the Sun*, 141. See also 119–20.

40 Frank Mackey, *Steamboat Connections: Montreal to Upper Canada, 1816–1843* (Montreal and Kingston: McGill-Queen's University Press 2000), 78. For other networks, see, e.g., Gerald Tulchinsky, *Taking Root: The Origins of the Canadian Jewish Community* (Toronto: Lester 1992), 61–3; and Rosemary Ommer, *From Outpost to Outport: A Structural Analysis of the Jersey-Gaspé Cod Fishery, 1767–1886* (Montreal and Kingston: McGill-Queen's University Press 1991).

41 See, for example, Konrad Yakabuski, "The Extended Family," *R.O.B. Magazine*, July 2001, 55–6.

PART TWO
Creating

Thistles in the North: The Direct and Indirect Scottish Influence on James Bay Cree Material Culture

Cath Oberholtzer

The material culture of a particular group documents both its internal and its external influences. In the case of the James Bay Cree in the nineteenth century, material culture allows a glimpse of the direct and indirect influence of the Scots, who, as Hudson's Bay Company (HBC) officers and servants, were stationed at fur trade posts throughout the region. Indeed, this influence is demonstrated by artifacts collected from the Cree who lived on the east coast of James Bay, in what is now Quebec, and at Moose Factory, which functioned historically as an important hub for both the fur trade and missionary endeavours. From the conspicuous incorporation of thistles in floral beadwork and silk embroidery to the wearing of tartan clothing, the impact of the Scots on Cree material culture appears to have been direct cause and effect. Less obvious, however, is the relation between Scots influence in the region and the increased production of Cree objects as souvenirs and trade items.

A recent breakthrough in my ongoing research to determine the locations and dates for the origin of Cree items held by museums in North America and Europe established that a small, eclectic collection of Cree material in the Royal Ontario Museum was most likely acquired by Dr John Rae, a Hudson's Bay Company surgeon stationed at Moose Factory.[1] This finding holds significant implications for identifying the sources of objects, but in particular it allows us to make connections between certain aspects of those items and the Scots involved in the fur trade.

From Rae's first arrival in 1833 and throughout the ensuing ten-year contract that lasted until 1844, this young Scot gained the respect and admiration of both the Cree and the fur trade personnel. Enthusiastic about life in the Bay and adept at virtually everything he tried, Rae's interests motivated him to rig up "a handy little work bench [which he] found convenient to make up odds and ends, such as canoe paddles, snowshoe frames for his own use as well as [making] hooks and eyes, patterns for bead and silk work for the women and repairing watches for others."[2] Unfortunately, Rae does not note in his autobiography if these "patterns for bead and silk work" were created as templates or as designs. Nor do we know to what degree his pattern-making influenced the overall iconography of Cree material culture. However, it is probable that, through his engagement with these producers of fine handiwork, Rae introduced the stylized thistle motif seen on a silk-embroidered caribou-hide octopus bag that was made expressly for him.[3]

Here it must be emphasized that Rae's friendship and long-term involvement with Cree men and women were vital to his ability to introduce new patterns or designs.[4] His position among the Cree was unique and experienced by few other European men involved in the fur trade, even those married to Cree women. Indeed, other collectors of this period noted the difficulties they encountered trying to obtain Native goods during their brief stays in Native communities. A good example is John Lefroy's efforts to collect while conducting a magnetic survey of the Canadian northwest in 1842–44. On one occasion he wrote to his sister: "Curiosities are not so easily procured by one who travels hastily, as you would suppose – if made at all it is usually by the daughters of the traders, from whom we cannot buy them, and one does not like to ask them; and in my case almost every

Silk-embroidered caribou-hide octopus bag with stylized thistles from the Rae Collection, National Museums of Scotland. Courtesy of the Trustees of the National Museums of Scotland (L304.128).

moment that I passed at the different forts was occupied, so that I have very little time or opportunity to get them by indirect means."[5]

Thus, Rae's interest, combined with a ten-year sojourn in one community, afforded him the time and opportunity to have an impact on Cree material culture. Furthermore, as Dale Idiens points out in her discussion of Rae as a collector and an ethnographer, while "a student in Edinburgh Rae had been exposed to the emerging recognition of the importance of non-European ethnography in the early nineteenth century, views which were in turn endorsed by his superior Sir George Simpson."[6] This predisposition towards the ethnographic aspects of Native culture, coupled with Rae's innate curiosity, consequently placed him in a prime position to be an active participant in cultural exchange – both to learn from the Cree and to share his own knowledge with them.

THISTLES

With regard to the use of thistle motifs in Cree material culture, it should be noted that both indigenous and introduced varieties of this plant grow in the lower regions of the James Bay area.[7] A survey conducted by this author confirms that the thistle was used as a decorative element on Cree-made items but also indicates that it did not appear in Cree iconography before Rae's sojourn in the area.[8] Of the twenty or so examples in the survey, which date from Rae's time at Moose Factory into the early twentieth century, the majority can be associated directly with the southern and southeastern areas of James Bay. For example, in addition to the octopus bag mentioned above, both a double-peaked beaded cloth hood[9] and a silk embroidered "wall pocket"[10] dating from the early period bear stylized thistle motifs and can be directly associated with Rae. Similar stylized thistles are embroidered on a roll-up sewing bag,[11] a beaded panel bag (illustrated here),[12] a very old piece of embroidered caribou hide,[13] and an octopus bag.[14] Cree moccasins with more naturalistic thistles embroidered on them (as in the illustration) were collected by, or presented to, Donald A. Smith.[15] The single representational thistle embroidered on an "eared" (or double-peaked) cloth hood in the Pitt Rivers Museum is so strikingly similar to the single thistles beaded on a pair of moccasins collected during the same time period[16] that

Beaded panel bag from the Grant Collection
(969.11.2). Courtesy of the Nor'Westers and
Loyalist Museum. Note the thistle.

it also may have originated in this area.[17] Later in the early twentieth century a few pairs of moccasins decorated with beaded thistles
also were collected from this southeastern area.[18] All this evidence
suggests that the thistle – at least in this stylized form – was introduced to the Cree by Rae while he was at Moose Factory.

Moccasins collected by Donald A. Smith
(Lord Strathcona). Courtesy of the British
Museum (1936.10-20.33(2))

HEARTS AND OTHER DESIGNS

Rae may have influenced Cree iconography further by introducing designs using a compass and ruler and through a coincidental appearance of hearts cut into the backboards of infants' *tikanagans* (also known as cradleboards). Interesting correlations develop when the geometric designs painted on the back of a model cradleboard (illustrated here)[19] and beaded on a cloth hood[20] – both collected by Rae – are compared with a similar design painted on another model cradleboard made around thirty years later at Moose Factory for Alice Malloch (also illustrated here). Somewhat simplified, the later design continues to reflect the earlier mathematical technique, a technique that in all probability came from the Scotsman John Rae.[21]

These same two tiny *tikanagans* are further decorated with a heart-shaped cutout on the upper portion of the backboard. As with the thistle motif, hearts do not appear to have been used by the James Bay Cree before the one found on the model collected by Rae. While it is tempting to speculate that this heart motif was incorporated as an adoption and an adaptation of Scottish folk beliefs, which viewed the heart as a protective device for young children, there is no evidence to substantiate this speculation.[22] These two examples and an additional one housed at the Cranbrook Institute of Science (the illustration shows a similar one photographed at the time by Ben East) all originated at Moose Factory, and so provides a basis for linking other cradleboards bearing a similar heart motif to this area.[23] However, three *tikanagans* in the Nor'Westers and Loyalist Museum, all part of the Grant collection, are not from Moose Factory (this fact is determined by the shape of the face protector, or bow), and so the source area broadens only slightly. This definitive provenance, combined with the fact that heart-shaped motifs were used only on cradleboards, indicates that great importance was attached to the heart motif. The extended period of usage – ranging from Rae's circa 1835 model through Malloch's 1875 example to the full-sized cradleboard collected by East in 1937 – further supports this idea. And altogether the tight provenance, the association with Rae, and the continued usage reflect a probable Scottish influence.

TARTAN

From ethnohistoric accounts and a handful of dolls, we know much about the clothing and accessories the Cree wore during the 1700s and early 1800s. With the introduction of trade goods the materials used in making some of these items were replaced, as with cloth for hide, beads for porcupine quills, and thread for sinew. With these changes came a concomitant blossoming of floral designs in the early years of the nineteenth century. However, from about the mid-1800s onward the clothing changed again, this time quite dramatically. As

Left: Back of a model cradleboard collected by Dr John Rae, in the collection of the National Museums of Scotland (L304.126). Courtesy of the Trustees of the National Museums of Scotland

Above: Back of a model cradleboard made for Alice Malloch, from the Malloch Collection. (M18538). Courtesy of the McCord Museum of Canadian History.

sparse evidence exists in museum collections,[24] we must turn to photographs for the recording of this change. In photograph after photograph the Cree are shown dressed in "tartan": the women are in tartan skirts, blouses and/or shawls, the men in tartan shirts and ready-made trousers, and infants, once laced into beautifully decorated cradleboard covers, are now wrapped in tartan.[25] Ironically, this most obvious symbol of the stereotypical Scottish presence, while first introduced by the Scots, gained greater popularity only through the promotion of it by English missionaries.

Before the arrival of missionaries the Cree used tiny scraps of tartan in specific places, such as around the opening of a bag, as the binding on the tops of hide mittens, or to wrap a treasured amulet. They would have been aware of tartans through their encounters with Scots employed in the fur trade and by the distinctive cloth's

Infant in a cradleboard, photographed by Ben East.
Courtesy of the Cranbrook Institute of Science

Short Neck's Wife and Daughter. Courtesy of the
Archives of Ontario (F 2179-1-0-0-23). Note the
woman's tartan dress and the girl's tartan under-
blouse and beaded hood in this image of a Cree
woman and her daughter at Rupert's House, c. 1869.

presence at some trading posts,[26] it having been introduced as an experiment in the 1690s by the Hudson's Bay Company.[27] But we must
credit Queen Victoria's passion for the Scottish Highlands as a major
stimulus for the wearing of tartan by people outside Scotland, including the Cree.[28]

The conspicuous adoption of tartans suggests the Cree readily accepted this new clothing style, probably through a combination of
desire and necessity.[29] Certainly, the Cree exhibited overt pleasure in
the bright primary colours of the square patterns. However, it was

the protective symbolism of the interwoven lines, directly applicable to the traditional Cree belief system, which gave tartan its cachet. Lines, and by extension, knots, connect and entwine the Cree with each other, with the animals, and with the spiritual world. These same lines and knots serve to protect them from the negative forces of their world, enabling an easy ideological transition from painted hide to decorated trade cloth to tartan fabrics, shawls, and clothing.

Ordered by the yard and in the form of shawls,[30] these "tartans" were given to the Cree by the missionaries as payments for "tripping, missionary journeys, work, fishing, hunting, or for an occasional article of food," according to the Reverend Edwin A. Watkins.[31] The extent of these exchanges pressed Watkins into lamenting that he was nothing but a "preaching trader."[32] The bales of garments made and collected through the "kind liberality of dear Christian friends" in England were another source of clothing.[33] These items were given as gifts to the poor but were distributed mostly to those Cree who showed signs of progress in religious training and in becoming "civilized." Although there is little indication of what precisely these bales contained, they were largely comprised of used clothing collected by women's work parties throughout England. Responses to one missionary's request for "Capots, Trousers, and Frocks made of something strong, course [sic], and warm,"[34] would have included worn, but usable, tartan items made popular by the effect of Balmorality. As a result we have a wealth of photographs of the Cree clothed after a Scottish fashion.

SCOTTISH ENCOURAGEMENT TO PRODUCTION

When I undertook this research, I had long suspected that a number of nineteenth-century Cree women produced exquisite artwork for sale. A letter from Rae to HBC governor Sir George Simpson confirmed my suspicion. In this private letter addressed to Simpson and dated at Moose Factory 19 August 1844, Rae itemizes the contents of two cases he was sending to Simpson, who was in London at that time. The contents consisted mainly of birchbark containers, or *rogans* of various sizes and shapes, with specific mention of "nests of Rogans" (increasingly smaller rogans nestled inside each other), which show up today in a number of British museums.[35] Regrettably, no silk embroidery or beadwork is mentioned. Rae does mention, however, that the three women who made these items – Mrs Gladman, Mrs Vincent, and Mrs Flett – were paid through the "Sale Shop Accts" debited from Simpson's account.[36] Mrs Gladman, widow of George Gladman Sr, lived with Mrs Vincent (also known as Jane Renton) at the edge of Moose Factory.[37] Due to the large number of Flett men working for the HBC, the identity of Mrs Flett has yet to be determined. All these women were of Cree heritage, all lived in communities associated with HBC posts, and all had greater access to European trade goods than their relatives who lived inland.

In fact, Rae seems to have recognized the potential inherent in this combination of factors, for fairly early on in his career he acknowledged that "[m]ost of the women – who are of mixed Indian and English, scotch [sic] or French blood – are neat and excellent seamstresses and washers, earning a great deal of money by this last occupation, and in making clothes, and moccasins, besides netting snowshoes at which they are very expert – They also do handsome silk and bead-work on cloth and leather, and porcupine quill-work on birch bark."[38]

That these women, who were mentioned by name, were making items specifically for sale on a scale measurably larger than for casual buyers and that this appears to be merely one of a number of transactions, suggests that Simpson and Rae were not only encouraging these women – and possibly others – to supply them with Native curios but also enjoining other HBC personnel to do the same. Although other women and their products cannot specifically be identified, there are three avenues of evidence supporting the idea that a cottage industry was operating in this southeastern corner of James Bay.

The first avenue of evidence is compiled from sparse archival documentation, in the form of requests for sewing materials and in private letters between HBC personnel. An assessment of the private accounts for HBC officers and servants, such as "Servants Commissions 1787–1897," yields names and lists of items ordered by specific men for their own use.[39] Many of these requests were for quantities of fabric, silk ribbon, needles, thread, and "Ladys Magazines"[40] ordered for Cree wives and daughters – daughters who later became the wives of other HBC personnel. These details imply that not only were these Cree women engaged in producing finery for themselves and training their daughters in the intricacies of working with these materials, they may also have been producing items for sale. The 1848 request by Mr Gladman for 20 bunches[41] of white, pink, light blue, and glass (clear) seed beads from the Moose Factory sales shop appears to be more than coincidental in the light of several exquisitely beaded women's hoods decorated predominately with beads of those very colours.[42] Further notations in the sales shop accounts record several orders for birchbark baskets and children's silkwork moccasins.[43]

Even wider perspective is gained from the letters of HBC personnel. A letter from James Clouston at Moose Factory (1870) to Charles Stuart at Timiskaming notes tersely, "We have sent a case of Moccassins [sic] by this canoe, an invoice of which you will find in the packet."[44] As postmaster and trader it was Stuart's responsibility to see that letters and parcels sent to his post were forwarded to the parties concerned, although this particular letter does not indicate the moccasins' final destination. Two years later Clouston again wrote to Stuart expressing some concern that "You don't say whether you want any more mocassins [sic] from us. We could easily get them made of a smaller size if you wanted them."[45] Not everyone seemed to appreciate this industry, for in 1875 Chief Factor Alexander Mac-Donald, at Moose Factory, wrote a letter to Colin Rankin, Esquire at Timiskaming in which he grumbles, "The silk work that has been supplied to the frontier posts for the last few years ... only increase[s] the scarcity of beaver – I therefore discourage the work."[46] At least some production must have continued, however, as a letter written in 1891 to the Hudson's Bay House in London concerns an item missing from "the collection of curiosities sent home in 1889," apparently purchased through the sales shop at Moose Factory.[47]

A second avenue towards substantiating the deliberate production of Native items for sale to a large foreign market is the examination of scholarly research providing comparative information from other regions of the fur trade. Judy Thompson, Western Subarctic curator at the Canadian Museum of Civilization, has meticulously documented that Gwich'in women in the Mackenzie Valley of northwestern Canada were sewing for this market as early as 1860, when Bernard Rogan Ross and his colleagues were collecting for Scottish and American national museums.[48] Thompson arrived at this conclusion once she began to understand that while archival photographs showed these Athapaskan speakers wearing European clothing, the Gwich'in material collected in the same time period consisted of traditional summer clothing. Thompson has proven that, while favouring European clothes, Gwich'in women who were particularly skilled in making and decorating caribou-hide clothing in the old ways continued to supply indigenous outfits for the souvenir market at home and abroad. For the Colonial and Indian Exhibition held in London in 1886 these women produced eight porcupine-quill-trimmed caribou hide outfits consisting of shirt, leggings, hood, mittens, and knife sheath. It was a prodigious undertaking that also had implications for the production of Cree artistic traditions.

A third approach is to consider extant material held in museums. Since I have already considered his introduction of thistles into the repertoire of Cree floral images, a logical place to start is with Rae and a comparison of the items he collected with other identified pieces. Most notable is the similarity between a beaded-cloth woman's hood collected by Rae and one that C.G. Gladman donated to the Royal Ontario Museum.[49] Even more noteworthy is the greater similarity between motifs used on the Gladman hood and those found on woman's leggings collected by Rae. As well, painted caribou-hide coats obtained by both Rae and Gladman are, according to Dorothy Burnham, similar enough as to have been made by the same woman.[50] A third coat featuring a very similar cut belonged to Sir John Lefroy, the geographer, who coincidentally spent the winter of 1844–45 instructing Rae in the fine arts of surveying. These and other similarities suggest – but do not necessarily confirm – that only a few women were producing a surplus of certain items for sale outside the community.

The strongest evidence for an organized production of indigenous goods destined for the souvenir market is the combined material of two relatively small collections, one in the Canadian Museum of Civilization (CMC) and the other in the Nor'Westers and Loyalist Museum in Williamstown, Ontario. Several beaded hoods, leggings, and bags demonstrate meticulous needlework and an aesthetic that bridges Native and non-Native cultures, and comparisons with examples in other venues increase the numbers actually produced. For

Beaded hood from the Grant Collection. Courtesy
of the Canadian Museum of Civilization (III-D-606).
Note the heart-shaped leaves.

example, motifs on the Nor'Westers' bags are identical to those found on a hood in the National Museum of the American Indian,[51] which in turn shares similar motifs with a hood at the CMC, illustrated here.

Both the CMC and the Nor'Westers collections were donated by the late Dorothy Grant of Port Hope, Ontario. Documentation provided by Grant indicates that her great-grandfather, George Gladman, was appointed chief factor at Eastmain in 1805 and that her grandfather, Charles Stuart, was a factor in the Moose Factory–Temiskaming area, circa 1840–65. While the career details of these two men need to be corrected and expanded, it is their family connections that are important here. As noted above, the "Mrs Gladman" mentioned in Rae's letter to George Simpson was the widow of George Gladman Sr. Jane Renton Vincent's daughter Harriet was married to George Gladman Jr and his brother Joseph's daughter Margaret married the Scot Charles Stuart, who we know to have been involved in the distribution of Cree handiwork. Later, the Stuarts' only daughter Josephine married Albert Grant. Josephine bore three daughters, including the donor mentioned above. Therefore, it is more probable from the genealogical connections that many of the items were handed down through the generations, than that all of this material was collected by either Gladman or Stuart. The distinctive floral iconography – including the depiction of a thistle – suggests that it is possible that a few of these items were produced under the "encouragement" of Rae and Simpson.

The long-term impact of Scottish influence is also reflected in the Malloch collection, held at the McCord Museum of Canadian History. This ethnographic material consists primarily of a Cree-made outfit for a little girl, as well as pairs of moccasins, a floral embroidered bible-cover, snowshoes, and other small objects originally acquired by Dr William Bell Malloch, a Scots-Canadian, McGill-trained physician who served in the dual capacity of physician and trader at Moose Factory from 1870 to 1878. The Malloch collection is one of the most significant sources of identifiable and datable James Bay Cree material, and associated photographs and archival documents further enrich its value.[52] The blending of skills, techniques and aesthetics of two cultures is best exemplified by an outfit made specifically for young Alice Malloch: the fine quality of the

Alice Malloch wearing a Cree-made outfit with a model cradleboard at her feet. Courtesy of the Notman Photographic Archives, McCord Museum of Canadian History (MP-0000.391.36).

brain-tanned caribou hide transformed into a tunic using traditional British sewing techniques, the traditional Cree style of the moccasins, and the fur trim and embroidered flowers all point to Cree decorative expression. Most significant, however, is the tiny *tikana-gan*[53] – resplendent with its floral beaded outer bag laced over a tartan moss bag – an exact but diminutive version of those made to hold Cree infants. A tiny heart was carved out of the backboard, and the reverse painted with a simplified version of the rayed figure first noted on the double-peaked hood and the geometrical design on the model *tikanagan*. Altogether, it speaks volumes about the continuity of Scottish influence.

Model cradleboard. Courtesy of the McCord
Museum of Canadian History (M18538). Note the
tartan moss bag inside the floral beaded cover.

SUMMARY

The influence of Scottish-born Dr John Rae during his years at
Moose Factory is evident in his impact on Cree iconography. The introduction of thistles in the rendering of floral handiwork, the addition of hearts carved out of the backboards of *tikanagans*, and the
use of geometric figures all testify to this influence. The wearing of
Scottish tartans, while first introduced by Scots and a traditional sig-
nifier of Scottish identity, actually gained greater popularity through
English missionary endeavours. The greatest influence engendered by
Scots was not only their encouragement of the Cree women to produce items for sale but also their establishment of a market for these
goods. From these few examples it is evident that the Scots – most
notably, Dr John Rae – had a marked influence on the material culture of the James Bay Cree.

NOTES

ABBREVIATIONS

AMNH	American Museum of Natural History
AO	Archives of Ontario
BM	British Museum
CIS	Cranbrook Institute of Science
CMC	Canadian Museum of Civilization
CMS	Church Missionary Society
HBC	Hudson's Bay Company
HBCA	Hudson's Bay Company Archives
MMCH	McCord Museum of Canadian History
NLM	Nor'Westers and Loyalist Museum
NMAI	National Museum of the American Indian
NMS	National Museums of Scotland
PRM	Pitt Rivers Museum
ROM	Royal Ontario Museum
SPRI	Scott Polar Research Institute

1 For details of this breakthrough, see my article "Six Degrees of Separation: Connecting Dr John Rae to James Bay Cree Objects in the Royal Ontario Museum," in *Selected Papers of Rupert's Land Colloquium 2002*, compiled by David G. Malaher (Winnipeg: The Centre for Rupert's Land Studies 2002), 211–25.

2 SPRI MS787/1-2, *John Rae's Autobiography*, 188.

3 NMS L304.128. The term "octopus" is used to indicate the four pairs of tabs or "eight legs" on the lower edge of this form of bag.

4 The strength of this relationship was most evident in Rae's efforts to learn both the language and the survival skills of the Cree.

5 George F.G. Stanley, ed., *John Henry Lefroy: In Search of the Magnetic North: A Soldier-Surveyor's Letters from the North-West, 1843–1844* (Toronto: Macmillan 1955), 160.

6 Dale Idiens, "Rae as Collector and Ethnographer," in *No Ordinary Journey: John Rae – Arctic Explorer 1813–1893*, Ian Bunyan, Jenni Calder, Dale Idiens, and Bryce Wilson, eds. (Edinburgh: National Museums of Scotland 1993), 97. As a student Rae had been exposed "to the emerging recognition of the importance of non-European ethnography," which was further endorsed by Simpson. In 1857, "scientific collections" which included "finished products" were requested by means of a list of instructions circulated to the HBC officers by George Wilson in Edinburgh. The ensuing material collected by Scots in the Arctic and the Subarctic formed important museum collections in Edinburgh (see Idiens, "Rae as Collector," 96–7). See also Debra Lindsay, *Science in the Subarctic: Trappers, Traders and the Smithsonian Institution* (Washington, DC: Smithsonian Institution 1993), 77–9.

7 For example, bull thistle (*Cirsium vulgare*, introduced), swamp thistle (*Cirsium arvense*, indigenous), and sow thistle (*Sonchus arvensis*, introduced). Of these, the bull thistle is the most similar in appearance to the Scotch

thistle (*Onopordon acanthium*). Although Henry Youle Hind, in *Explorations in the Interior of the Labrador Peninsula: The Country of the Montagnais and Nasquapee Indians*, records that among the linguistically related Montagnais the "roots of the thistle are all employed medicinally," he does not identify the species. (London: Longman, Green, Roberts & Green 1863), 190.

8 This survey entailed perusing illustrations in some seventy publications that focus on aboriginal ethnographic art and in my extensive photographic collection of Cree material in more than sixty European and North American museums.

9 ROM 916.22.1.

10 ROM 916.22.8.

11 Glenbow Museum AR 235. At one time this bag belonged to Emily McTavish who, as George Simpson McTavish's sister, had connections to Moose Factory, Rupert's House, and Eastmain (email communication from Judith Hudson Beattie, keeper, Hudson's Bay Archives, 9 July 2001).

12 NLM 969.11.2; part of the Grant collection, possibly from Rupert's House.

13 AMNH 50.2-2060; collected at Mistassini. Possibly cut from a shot pouch.

14 Peabody Museum of Archaeology and Ethnology, Harvard University 10/62487. Collected by Father Arnaud at Mistassini.

15 BM 1936.10-20.33(2). Smith, a Scot, who was raised later to the peerage as Baron Strathcona and Mount Royal, was married to Isabella Hardisty. His father-in-law, Richard Hardisty, was active as an HBC officer at various posts in the southeast region of James Bay before taking up positions in Labrador and, ultimately, at Albany (HBCA biography). If we are to take Charles Stuart's personal letter to Donald Smith at face value, it establishes a connection between the two men and establishes Stuart as a possible source for moccasins and other items for Smith (HBCA B.134/c/117; cf. AO MU1399; box 7; H.B.Co. Papers – Timiskaming District no. 6541; envelope 11 Moose Factory. Fur Trade Records C-7-11, "Moose Factory Sep.13/1870").

16 CMC III-L-284a,b. These moccasins were collected at Moose Factory or Timiskaming, circa 1840–1865, by Charles Stuart, whose wife's family was active in producing quantities of items for sale.

17 PRM 1893.67.181. According to Pitt Rivers Museum catalogue documentation, this hood was sold to the museum in 1893 by the widow of Edward Martin Hopkins, who had served as secretary to Sir George Simpson on the latter's global tour in 1842. The assumption is that the hood was collected during that journey. However, since memories tend to fade over the years, especially when coupled with second-hand information, there is a strong possibility that portions of this information may be inaccurate. Hopkins spent the years 1847 through to 1870 employed by the HBC, first at Lachine and later in charge of the Montreal District, with duties that took him to Moose Factory and the Timiskaming district (Margaret Arnett MacLeod, *The Letters of Letitia Hargrave* (Toronto: The Champlain Society 1947), 123, 123n), and so his period of collecting in that particular area can be extended. Conversely, the hood may have actually been intended for Sir George Simpson. The single, representational thistle motif is similar to that used by the St Andrew's Society of the City of Montreal, an organization to which

Simpson belonged (Sir Hugh Allan, *The St Andrew's Society of the City of Montreal* [Montreal 1844], 14, 42). Without precise documentation, these possibilities remain speculative.

18 For example, AMNH 50-7084, collected by Alanson Skinner in 1909 on the east coast of James Bay.

19 NMS L304.126.

20 ROM 916.22.1.

21 An embroidered sampler created by a young Scottish girl who immigrated to Cape Breton with her parents in 1831 corroborates the use of rayed figures made with compass and ruler by Scots. The designs on the sampler include two circles filled with geometrically determined rayed "petals" and several stylized thistles. Illustrated in Deborah A. Young, *A Record for Time* (Halifax: Art Gallery of Nova Scotia 1985), figure 18.

22 See, however, Raymond Lamont-Brown, *Scottish Superstitions* (Edinburgh: Chambers 1990), 77–8; Cath Oberholtzer, "Algonquian Net Baby Charms: Metaphors of Protection and Provision," in *Papers of the Twenty-fourth Algonquian Conference*, William Cowan, ed. (Ottawa: Carleton University 1993), 318–31 and "'Womb with A View': Cree Moss Bags and Cradle Boards," in *Papers of the Twenty-eighth Algonquian Conference*, David Pentland, ed. (Winnipeg: University of Manitoba 1997), 258–73; and George Dalgleish's chapter in this volume.

23 Such as one in the Manchester University Museum and another at the Pitt Rivers Museum.

24 I have encountered only one shawl, one child's dress, and two baby bonnets of tartan in American museums.

25 Scott Thompson, in "Scottish Traders: An Opportunity for Cultural Exchange" (*Whispering Wind* 27, no. 3 (1995): 16) provides a chart indicating the regions served by the Hudson's Bay and North West Companies and the coincidental areas where "photographs or artifacts show more than incidental use of plaid material," but the chart does not take into consideration the prevalence of tartan shawls worn by the women. Although the overlapping areas on Thompson's map do not include the James Bay area, my research results indicate that this region should be included as well.

26 This may very well have been Shepherd's Check, which was used as plaids of that time; however, many North Americans refer to tartan as "plaid."

27 Elizabeth Mancke, *A Company of Businessmen: The Hudson's Bay Company and Long Distance Trade, 1670–1730* (Winnipeg: Rupert's Land Research Centre 1988), 45. HBC Officers' private orders often requested several yards of "Highland plaid" (for example, in 1792 Donald McKay ordered "12 yd highland plaid best quality cold blue, black, & green" (HBCA A.16/111–113), "gala plaid" for a dressing gown (HBCA B.135/z/3 fol. 292), 15 yards of "common tartan" (HBCA B.186/z/2 fols. 11–12), and an "Indian silk blue tartan piece" (ordered by Wm Yorkstone at Albany in 1804: HBCA A.16/111–113 fol. 15). For the year 1851–52, bolts of authentic woollen tartans – Argyle, Clan Ranald, McDuff, Rob Roy and Royal Stuart – were shipped to posts by the HBC (see Lester Ross, *Hudson's Bay Company Suppliers*, vol. 1 [1979], 208). By the 1890s the yardage had increased considerably as a single invoice for goods sent internally from Rupert's

House to Fort George itemizes "156 yards hard tartan" (HBCA B.186/z/2 fol. 30). On some of the early orders it is not clear whether the request for "plaid" fabric is actually for tartan or the shepherd's check noted above.

28 Hugh Cheape, *Tartan* (Edinburgh: National Museums of Scotland 1991), 61; Georgina O'Hara, *The Encyclopædia of Fashion* (New York: Harry N. Abrams 1986), 238. It must also be noted that repeal of the ban on wearing Highland dress prompted a fashion trend in Scotland at the end of the eighteenth century whereby no costume was complete without a tartan plaid or shawl (see T.A. Stillie, "The Evolution of Pattern Design in the Scottish Woollen Textile Industry in the Nineteenth Century," in *Textile History 1968–70*, K.G. Ponting, ed. (Newton Abbot: David & Charles 1971), 327, and Eileen Stack's chapter in this volume.).

29 Cath Oberholtzer, "Wrap Us in Tartan: Native Choice or Limited Selection?" paper read at the Northeastern Anthropological Association, Lake Placid, New York, April 1995.

30 For example, four missionaries from one mission station ordered a total of 115 yards of tartan and 32 tartan shawls between 1847 and 1856 (CMS C C1/019/22B, 34B, 50B; CC1/035/8B, 12, 24C, 24D, 30A, 32, 46B). The 1848 order also requested "18 Highland caps for Boys," to be worn by the boys attending the mission school.

31 Rev. Edwin A. Watkins, CMS C C1/071/21.

32 Rev. Edwin A. Watkins, CMS C C1/071/22.

33 See numerous citations in Watkins' annual letters (CMS C C1/071/ 43–52).

34 Rev. Henry Budd, 1851. CMS C C1/012/3.

35 Two wonderful examples of these "nests of rogans" are held by the British Museum in London, England, and in the Thaw Collection of the Fenimore House Museum, Cooperstown, New York. A less pristine and incomplete set is held by the Manchester Museum, University of Manchester, in England. Single baskets are scattered among several other museums.

36 Letter from John Rae to George Simpson HBCA E.15/3; published in E.E. Rich, *Rae's Arctic Correspondence 1844–55* (London: The Publications of the Hudson Bay Record Society 1963), 1–3.

37 In a letter to her mother in 1840 Letitia Hargrave relates a brief history of Mrs Gladman, who mentioned that her mother (Jane Renton Vincent) "went & lived with Mr Gladman's mother, widow of one in the same Coy" (MacLeod, *Letters of Letitia Hargrave,* 82). When Mr Hargrave visited the two women at Moose Factory on his way to England in 1837, he declared that they were "without flattery two of the most respectable Ladies I have met in this land" (Ibid., 82n). On his visit to Moose Factory in the early 1850s, Bishop David Anderson reported: "Later in the day, I went with Mr Horden to see many of his flock. One cottage, at the extreme end, was occupied by two aged widows, and it is quite a little model. God has spared them to a very advanced age, but they are still able to tread the way that leads to his house: they can make out the measured half mile from their cottage to the church, the one supported by a staff; but it is the very limit of their strength." David Anderson, *The Net in the Bay* (London: Thomas Hatchard 1854), 108.

38 Rae's Autobiography, SPRI MS/787/1-2, 69.

39 HBCA A.16/111-113.

40 For example, in 1800 Robert Goodwin ordered "Ladys Magazines ... new with fashionable dresses" (HBCA A.16/111-113 fol. 66). From 1802 to 1805, Thomas Vincent – Jane Renton Vincent's "husband" – ordered eighty yards plus two pieces of fabric (a piece being a number of yards according to fabric type), several pieces of ribbon and silk, "silk of colours" (silk thread) and four hundred White Chapel needles (HBCA A.16/111-113, fols. 5, 16, 29). The daughters of other men ordering similar items during this period appear later as the wives of HBC personnel in the 1830s, 1840s, and 1850s.

41 A bunch consisted of several thousand beads on a thread.

42 HBCA B.135/z/3, page 301. In particular, see Cree hoods in the Birmingham Art Gallery and Museum (England) 242, 60, the CMC III-D-605, and in private collections.

43 E.M. Hopkins ordered baskets and moccasins (HBCA B.135/z/3 fol. 306), Mr Cameron also ordered baskets and moccasins (HBCA B.135/z/3 fols. 302, 306). From these same sources the women employed in producing these items were Nancy Taylor and Mrs Hurvey [sic].

44 AO MU 1399, box 7, HBC papers, Timiskaming District, no. 6541; envelope 11, Moose Factory fur trade records, C-7-11: "Moose Factory Sep 13/1870."

45 AO MU 1399, box 7, HBC papers, Timiskaming District, no. 6541; envelope 11 Moose Factory fur trade records C-7-11. "Moose Factory Feb. 26/1872."

46 AO MU 1392 box 1, envelope 8 HBC fur trade records (C-1-8). MacDonald was referring to the number of beaver skins coming in for the fur trade.

47 HBCA A.11/48, fol. 63.

48 Judy Thompson, "Marketing Tradition: Late Nineteenth-Century Gwich'in Clothing Ensembles," in *American Indian Art Magazine* 24, no. 4 (1999): 48–59.

49 Although C.G. Gladman was originally believed to have been Charles George Gladman, the son of George Gladman Jr, according to genealogical information provided by Upper Canada Genealogy he "died young." It is more likely that this donor was Charles Gilbert Gladman, son of Joseph Gladman, who was the son of George Gladman Jr.

50 Dorothy Burnham, *To Please the Caribou* (Toronto: Royal Ontario Museum 1992), 210.

51 NMAI 20/8126.

52 Formal studio prints as well as photographs taken by Dr Malloch are held by the Notman Photographic Archives (MMCH), and documents pertaining to Malloch are in the MMCH Archives

53 MMCH M18538.

SEVEN

Aspects of Scottish-Canadian
Material Culture: Heart Brooches
and Scottish Pottery

George R. Dalgleish

This chapter investigates two very specific aspects of the intricate web of connections between Scottish and Canadian material culture. Heart-shaped brooches, popularly known as "luckenbooths," and Scottish pottery are two excellent examples of the vigorous way in which Scots businessmen pursued commercial opportunities in Canada. Both will be examined in terms of their Scottish roots and the particular way they thrived in the Canadian market. This paper also represents a museum curator's plea for increased appreciation of material culture and its ability to illuminate migration studies by providing additional strands of historical evidence.

HEART BROOCHES

In Scotland, heart-shaped "luckenbooth" brooches were popular as love tokens from at least the late seventeenth century. As an increasing number of Scots made their home in the New World, many such

brooches must have made the journey across the Atlantic as heirlooms. Once in North America, their designs were adapted by European silversmiths, who made silver ornaments for exchange as trade
goods with some of the indigenous peoples – a fascinating example
of cultural transference.[1]

The Scottish origins of these brooches have a long history. Heart-
shaped brooches have been worn in Scotland for more than four hundred years, but the heart shape itself is not peculiarly Scottish; it has
been common throughout Europe and beyond for centuries. In the
medieval period it appeared in the *Arma Christi*, and it has a long
history in heraldry.[2] However, it is as a symbol of love that the heart
appears most frequently in Scotland. Hearts are found on marriage
lintels, carved chair backs, and samplers, but especially in the form
of brooches. Although there are fifteenth- and sixteenth-century doc-
umentary references to heart brooches in Scotland, no surviving examples can safely be dated much before 1700.

Eighteenth-century brooches were usually made of silver, although
gold and base metal examples are known. They have long been
known as Luckenbooth brooches, possibly because they were apparently sold in the luckenbooths, or small shops, which clustered
round the High Kirk of St Giles in Edinburgh's High Street. This is
likely true, since this section of the High Street was the traditional
goldsmiths' and jewellers' quarter, but the name luckenbooth cannot
be traced before the late nineteenth century. Thus, a more accurate
name for them is simply heart brooches, although they have also
been known as Queen Mary, Witches, and Johnny Faa brooches. Inscriptions on early examples prove that they were love tokens, probably given as engagement or marriage presents: for example, "My
[heart] ye have and thine I crave." The placing of two hearts together also shows they were love tokens, and the resultant M-like shape
may explain the name Queen Mary brooch – although there is absolutely no proven historical connection with Mary, Queen of Scots.

Heart brooches also seem to have been credited with supernatural
powers. In the eighteenth century they were worn as protection
against witches, and one given to the National Museum in 1893
"was worn on the breast of the chemise by the grandmother of the
donor, to prevent the witches from taking away her milk." Children,
boys as well as girls, had heart brooches pinned to their petticoats
(or rather under them, for keeping the charm hidden seems to have

made it more powerful) "for ... averting the evil eye and keeping away witches."[3]

Towards the end of the eighteenth century, heart brooches became larger and more complicated in shape. Most now had crowns above the hearts, and twin hearts were common. Some of the crowns resembled two birds' heads, a design that may have been introduced from Norway, where heart brooches remained popular into the nineteenth century. By the middle of the nineteenth century many brooches were now very fine pieces of jewellery, if lacking the naive charm of the older forms, and were being made by established silversmiths in Edinburgh, Glasgow, Inverness, and the North East. The means of fastening them to clothing also changed at this time. Early brooches had very simple pins, similar in function to the pins on ring brooches (the type of pin that was universal in trade-silver brooches, no matter what design). These pins were replaced in the nineteenth century by the sharp steel spring pin and catch that is still used today, possibly because clothing materials were becoming finer and the tight weave could be damaged by the old design. It may also represent a change in the social significance of the brooches. Records and the survival of many early simple heart brooches suggest they were fairly common among the possessions of ordinary people. Their absence in portraits of the period is probably due to the fact that they were owned by people who had neither the means nor the social position to have their portraits painted. By the late nineteenth century, however, the most elaborate versions would have been fairly expensive and could have been afforded only by the better-off. Simpler and less costly brooches did continue to be made and, indeed, are still popular today.

By the second half of the eighteenth century in British North America there was growing use of silver goods for barter within the fur trade, especially by traders operating out of Montreal. Many types of silver ornament were traded with Native Americans, particularly medals, gorgets, ring brooches, and crosses. All helped to "brighten the covenant chain" – or so observers described the strengthening of links between European traders and Native peoples.[4] One type of jewellery found particular favour with Native peoples in the East of the country, namely the heart-shaped brooch. So popular were these small brooches with the Iroquois that the style became something of a national badge.[5]

It is now well accepted that the design of these very distinctive trade-silver brooches originated in Scotland. The first scholar to suggest this and to discuss the significance of the brooches was Ramsay Traquair (1874–1952), the influential professor of architecture at McGill University, whose article "Montreal and the Indian Trade Silver" was published in 1938.[6] Traquair was the Edinburgh-born son of artist Phoebe Traquair and Ramsay Heatly Traquair, the first Keeper of Natural History in the Edinburgh Museum of Science and Art (a forerunner of what is now the National Museums of Scotland). The physical similarities between Scottish brooches and Montreal-made ones are obvious and include the basic heart shape and openwork crowns, as well as complex shapes arrived at by intertwining two hearts. How and why this example of Scottish folk-jewellery became Canadian-made trade silver sought after by Native peoples is a far more complicated matter.

Native American interest in these brooches may have started with seeing Scots settlers – women and children – wearing them. The numbers of Scots settler families in British North America increased after the end of the Seven Years' War, and of course again in the aftermath of the American Revolution. It is quite probable that Scots women wore the brooches as a reminder of emotional ties with the home country. It is also highly significant that Robert Cruickshank, one of the major Montreal-based makers of trade silver, was Scottish. Cruickshank was born on 21 April 1743 and was apprenticed to the London goldsmith Alexander Johnston at the age of sixteen. He became a freeman of the London Company of Goldsmiths on 9 April 1766 and is recorded as a plateworker in Old Jewry from 1766 to 1774.[7] The son of George Cruickshank, a Presbyterian minister in Arbroath,[8] he was possibly related to an earlier Aberdeen goldsmith of the same name. As many Scottish heart brooches were either made or used in the northeast of Scotland, it is certain that Robert Cruickshank would be very familiar with both their design and their cultural significance.

Following in the footsteps of many Scots who migrated first to England before going further afield, Cruickshank came to Montreal around 1773 and soon built up an extensive business making silver and retailing hardware.[9] He was one of the largest suppliers of trade silver to Montreal-based fur traders, many of whom were Scots or of Scots descent. Trade silver was a considerable commercial enterprise, and the fur traders ordered many tens of thousands of silver items. This exchange reached its height during the days of bitter conflict between the Hudson's Bay Company (HBC) and the North West Company (NWC). An order placed with Cruickshank in 1800 by Angus Mackintosh, an agent working for McTavish Frobisher & Co, gives an idea of scale. It included twelve thousand small brooches at 6/6, six thousand small brooches at 8/ and five thousand large brooches at 15/, and was by no means exceptional;[10] other bills and accounts indicate that trade silver was a very large business. At the same time, some idea of the value of the brooches in the fur trade can be derived from the list "Equivalents for barter of goods and skins," dated 1765 which indicated that one silver brooch (although unfortunately the list does not stipulate if it was a heart type) was exchangeable for one raccoon or musquash skin.[11]

Trade-silver double-heart brooch, Iroquois, early nine-teenth century. Gift of David Ross McCord. Courtesy of the McCord Museum of Canadian History (M201)

Group of early-eighteenth-century and late-nineteenth-century Scottish heart brooches. Courtesy of the Trustees of the National Museums of Scotland.

Pocahontas and Her Son Thomas Rolfe, American
School, c. 1800. Photo: D.C. Pitcher. Courtesy of the
Borough Council of King's Lynn and West Norfolk

From the position of a curator of Scottish material culture with no
substantial knowledge of Native American cultures, it would be pre-
sumptuous of me to speculate why this form of brooch, derived from
Scottish folk jewellery, should have become so popular with Native
peoples. The subject merits further investigation by scholars of Native history and material culture. Still, reasons for the widespread exchange of trade silver between Natives and Europeans are hinted at
in a wonderful painting of a Native woman and child that clearly
dates from the early part of the nineteenth century and is erroneously

titled *Pocahontas and Her Son Thomas Rolfe.* The woman's dress is heavily influenced by European style and tailoring and is lavishly decorated with alternating lines of heart and "council square" trade-silver brooches. Her son seems to be wearing a straightforward European shirt, while his sash hints at his Native background. Whoever painted this picture (which is unsigned) was aware of the cultural and ethnic complexity of Native American and European interaction in the context of the fur trade. In Scotland, heart brooches were normally worn only by women or children, and usually one at a time. Native American women seem to have preferred to wear them in large numbers, as did Native American men with other forms of trade silver.[12]

In spite of their widespread use in the fur trade era, trade in silver ornaments decreased dramatically after the amalgamation of the NWC and HBC, since the HBC did not favour the use of trade silver in their business.

SCOTTISH POTTERY

Scottish industrial potteries, from their beginnings in the 1750s, were as interested in export markets as they were in selling at home. It is no coincidence that the first industrial pottery to open in Scotland – the Delftfield Pottery – was established in Glasgow by a company that included Robert Dinwiddie, a Glasgow "tobacco lord" and sometime Lieutenant Governor of Virginia.[13] He was a consummate mercantilist, importing raw materials and through the store system – which the Scots tobacco lords perfected – exporting cheap manufactured goods to the colonists.[14]

The Scottish pottery industry grew throughout the rest of the eighteenth century and into the nineteenth. It was centred on the Firths of Clyde and Forth to take advantage of sea-borne transport, both for importing raw materials and exporting finished goods.[15] The Glasgow-based potteries, in particular, cultivated overseas export markets, but virtually all the Scottish potteries aspired to capture this lucrative trade. By the second half of the nineteenth century potteries in Glasgow, Greenock, Bo'ness, and Kirkcaldy were exporting to the United States, South America, South Africa, and Australia and, most spectacularly, to Southeast Asia.[16] Especially interesting, of course, was the trade with Canada on a very large scale. Direct trade between Scotland and Canada blossomed in the nineteenth century, and the Scottish pottery industry in particular benefited from growing Canadian markets. The trade grew to such an extent that one Scottish company – Robert Cochran & Co., in Glasgow – built a factory specifically to service the North American market.[17]

One of the most ubiquitous types of nineteenth-century pottery found in Canada is sponge-printed and hand-painted ware. This type was so common that it was originally believed to have been manufactured at Portneuf, near Quebec City. In fact, all of it was imported, and much of it was probably made in Scotland, as most Scottish potteries produced this type of ware in huge amounts both for home consumption and for export.[18] Some Scottish potteries went on to produce wares designed exclusively for the Canadian market. One such was John Marshall & Co., which created a very popular transfer-printed pattern called Canadian Sports. Marshall took over the Bo'ness pottery on the Firth of Forth in 1859, and the firm continued in production throughout the rest of the century.[19] In the early 1880s the company devised a series of designs for earthenware dinner and toilet sets based directly on scenes from Christmas cards published by William Bennett & Co. of Montreal. The scenes present a rather idealized vision of a Canadian winter, with children and adults enjoying such pastimes as skating, tobogganing, walking in snowshoes, and clearing snow from the path.[20] These wares seem to have been sold only in Canada – very few examples turn up in Scotland.[21]

This would appear to be a recurring model in the business practices of Scottish potteries. They originally started by exporting wares they were also producing for the home market and then developed specialized lines for export only. The most spectacular example of this model is the astonishing range of patterns produced by the Glasgow firm of J. & M.P. Bell, solely for export to Southeast Asia. This company probably exported millions of these plates, but until the early 1980s this trade was known in Scotland only from a few stray sherds found in the pottery waster dumps. From the Canadian perspective, the best example is Robert Cochran's Britannia factory in the St Rollox area of Glasgow. This was a brand new pottery, built in 1855 "on the most modern lines," with twelve kilns and as fully mechanized as was possible at the time, solely to serve the Canadian

Earthenware bowl, with so-called Portneuf spongeware decoration, but probably Scottish, dating from
the second half of the nineteenth century. Gift of
Mrs J. Geoffrey Notman. Courtesy of the McCord
Museum of Canadian History (M986.136)

Earthenware jug decorated
with *Canadian Sports* transfer-
printed pattern, by J. Marshall
& Co., Bo'ness, Scotland,
c. 1880–1900. Courtesy of the
McCord Museum of Canadian
History (MC988.1.186)

and American market.[22] Robert Cochran – son of a Dumbarton ship-master – already owned an earlier pottery, the Verreville works at Finnieston on the Clyde, but it was somewhat out of date, and by the mid-1850s this astute and innovative businessman saw the potential for increasing his trade with Canada and the United States. In 1856 he sent James Dykes Campbell to Montreal to open a warehouse and build a base for trade with his newly built Britannia Pottery. Two years later Campbell was replaced in Canada by James Fleming, who eventually took over the pottery entirely. Once in Canada, Fleming moved the company's warehouse to Toronto.

The outbreak of the American Civil War badly affected the pottery trade, but Fleming was an astute businessman and turned the problem to his advantage, buying up devalued Union dollars and cashing in when they regained their worth after the war. He used the resulting profit to help enlarge the pottery back in Glasgow, in order to take advantage of the boom in trade at war's end.[23] At that time the Britannia Pottery became one of the biggest and most modern in Scotland. It was geared for mass production – one thousand dozen plates and as many cups and saucers could be turned out each day.[24] Initially the pottery concentrated on producing hardwearing Royal Ironstone China, which, despite its name, was really just hard-fired earthenware decorated with simple relief patterns. It soon moved on to selling transfer-printed wares in the North American market.

Perhaps the ultimate product solely for the Canadian market came in 1880. By this time Robert Cochran's son Alexander, in partnership with James Fleming, ran the Britannia Pottery, and they were commissioned by a Quebec-based china retailer, Francis T. Thomas, to produce a wide-ranging series of dinner, bathroom, and breakfast sets decorated with transfer-printed patterns depicting scenes from Quebec City. Thomas's name appears on the back of many of the pieces, which caused some confusion in the past, as collectors used to think Thomas was the maker. There is no doubt, however, that the pottery was made in Glasgow, since occasionally the marks of both the retailer and the producer appear together on wares. Still, the question remains: Where did the designs originate? Here one must acknowledge the work of the late Canadian pottery historian Elizabeth Collard. She discovered that the transfer prints were based on

Tissue transfer print, *Wolfe's Monument*, from Quebec series of patterns, taken from photographs by L.P. Vallee, produced by R. Cochran's Britannia Pottery, St Rollox, Glasgow, retailed by F.T. Thomas, Quebec, c. 1880s–1890s. Courtesy of the McCord Museum of Canadian History (M965.124.1.9.1)

a series of photographic views of Quebec taken by Louis Prudent Vallée, who had studied photography in New York before returning to Quebec to publish a series of views of the city in conjunction with Charles E. Holiwell, an engraver, printer, and stationer.[25] Albums containing virtually all the scenes that eventually appeared on the pottery were sold specifically to tourists throughout the 1880s and 1890s. We do not know the exact nature of the relationship between Thomas, Holiwell, and Vallée. Thomas may have commissioned Holiwell to produce the engraved plates for the transfers from Vallée's photographs in Canada and then sent them over to Glasgow for production, or he may have simply arranged for Vallée's photographs themselves to be sent directly to Glasgow, where the Britannia Pottery's own engravers could have made up the plates and transfers. The fact that some transfer "pulls," or impressions, still exist in Canada suggests that the transfers may well have been made there. The McCord Museum of Canadian History in Montreal has an excellent collection not only of the pottery itself but also of some transfer pulls and original photographs from which these were taken. This represents a remarkable and inspired bit of collecting and something that very rarely happens with pottery in Scotland.

In all, the Britannia Pottery used almost twenty different views for their Quebec pattern series, including St John's Gate, Breakneck Steps, St Louis Gate, and the Basilica and Seminary. The series had a long life, was especially popular as wedding presents throughout the 1880s and 1890s, and in fact was still being produced in the 1920s. Altogether, many hundreds of thousands of pieces must have been exported to Canada. Again, virtually no examples of this pattern survive in Scotland, and it is known there really only through sherds excavated from the pottery dumps.[26]

CONCLUSION

This chapter offers one small exploration of one of the many remarkably successful commercial contacts between Canada and Scotland. The evidence presented here should not come as any surprise, since potters and silversmiths were businessmen interested first and foremost in making a profit, just like many other Scots traders who had sought their fortunes in North America. They made use of well-established business links and family connections to further their enterprises. They often had interests in several connected businesses. Robert Cochran, for example, had a financial interest in various merchant ships sailing to Canada, and his company produced pottery for some of the shipping lines plying between Glasgow and Canada, including the Allan Line.[27] He was not alone, perhaps just a little more astute than most. What is surprising, however, is that we in Scotland do not know more about the survival of Scottish-produced material culture in Canada.

NOTES

1 N. Jaye Fredrickson and Sandra Gibb, *The Covenant Chain: Indian Cere-monial and Trade Silver* (Ottawa: National Museums of Canada 1980), q.v.
2 *Arma Christi* is Latin for the armorial bearings of Christ, i.e., the instruments of the Passion arranged heraldically on a shield, much used in devotional art in the fifteenth century. *New Catholic Dictionary* (1910).
3 Dr Rosalind Marshall and G. Dalgleish, eds., *The Art of Jewellery in Scot-land* (Edinburgh: Scottish National Portrait Gallery 1991).
4 Fredrickson and Gibb, *Covenant Chain*, 11.
5 Ibid., 52.
6 Ramsay Traquair, "Montreal and the Indian Trade Silver," *Canadian Historical Review* 19, no. 1 (March 1938): 1–8.
7 Arthur Grimwade, *London Goldsmiths 1697–1837*, 2d ed. (London 1982), 481.
8 Hew Scott, ed., *Fasti Ecclesiae Scoticanae* (Edinburgh 1915), vol. 5, 424, 442. I am indebted to René Villeneuve for proving Cruickshank's Scottish roots and for sharing his great knowledge of Cruickshank with me. For more insight into this silversmith, see Villeneuve's chapter in this volume.
9 René Villeneuve, *Quebec Silver* (Ottawa: National Gallery of Canada 1998), 68–70.
10 The source of this order is John E. Langdon, *Canadian Silversmiths, 1700–1900* (Toronto 1966), 18–19; the prices read as six shillings and sixpence, eight shillings, and fifteen shillings, respectively. Before the decimalization of British currency in 1971 there were twelve pence (pennies) in one shilling and twenty shillings, or two hundred and forty pennies, in one pound.
11 Langdon, *Canadian Silversmiths*, 46–7.
12 Fredrickson and Gibb, *Covenant Chain*, 22, 23, 26, 27; coloured plates 6, 7, 8.
13 J. Kinghorn and G. Quail, *Delftfield: A Glasgow Pottery, 1748–1823* (Glasgow: Glasgow Museums and Art Galleries 1986), 11.
14 The "store system" refers to the stockpiling of goods in anticipation of the arrival of trade vessels, to ensure a rapid turnaround and allow sales in bulk. See Thomas Martin Devine, *The Tobacco Lords: A Study of the Tobacco Merchants of Glasgow and Their Trading Activities, c. 1740–90* (Edinburgh: Donald 1975).
15 J.A. Fleming, *Scottish Pottery* (Glasgow 1923).
16 H. Kelly, "The Export Trade of J & M.P. Bell & Co. and Other Scottish-Potteries," *Scottish Pottery Historical Review* 16 (Scottish Pottery Society 1994): 49–58.
17 Fleming, *Scottish Pottery*, 108–16; Henry Kelly, *Scottish Ceramics* (Atglen, PA: Schiffer 1999), 33–51.
18 G. Cruickshank, *Scottish Spongeware* (Edinburgh: Scottish Pottery Studies 1982).
19 Kelly, *Scottish Ceramics*, 23.
20 Elizabeth Collard, *The Potters View of Canada* (Montreal and Kingston: McGill-Queen's University Press 1983), 68–73.
21 Kelly, *Scottish Ceramics*, 24.

22 Fleming, *Scottish Pottery*, 108ff.; Kelly, *Scottish Ceramics*, 33; H. Kelly "The Export Wares of Cochran from the Britannia and Verreville Potteries," in *Scottish Pottery Historical Review* 20 (1990): 33.

23 Fleming, *Scottish Pottery*, 108–10; H. Kelly "The Life of Robert Cochran of Britannia and Verreville Potteries," in *Scottish Industrial History* 18 (1996): 12–14.

24 Fleming, *Scottish Pottery*, 111.

25 Collard, *Potters View of Canada*, 74–80.

26 Kelly, *Scottish Ceramics*, 34.

27 E. Collard, *Canadiana Connection* (Winnipeg: Winnipeg Art Gallery 1998), 63.

EIGHT

A Scottish-born Silversmith in Montreal: Robert Cruikshank

René Villeneuve

When we consider the contribution to the art of silversmithing of Canadian artists of Scottish descent, the name Robert Cruikshank (1743–1809) springs immediately to mind. Although he was one of the first to settle here and the impact of his work was considerable, much remains to be learned about his stylistic influences. Interest in his biography and his activities as a workshop director and merchant has hitherto tended to take precedence.[1] He was born on 21 April 1743, son of the Reverend George Cruikshank, Presbyterian minister of Arbroath (Aberbrothock), in Forfarshire, Scotland, who was himself born around 1705, son of the Aberdeen merchant John C. Cruikshank.[2] Robert Cruikshank served his apprenticeship in London under Alexander Johnston, beginning his training on 4 April 1759 and receiving his freedom on 9 April 1766.[3] His presence in Montreal is documented as of 1773.[4] My aim here is to present a brief survey of his work that illustrates the precise nature of his contribution to the development of silver making in this country.

DOMESTIC WORKS

To begin, it is well worth examining a few of Cruikshank's simple utensils, including a *Soup Spoon with the Monogram of the Duperron-Bâby Family* (National Gallery of Canada [hereafter NGC] 24312). The spoon's Old English style was highly innovative for the period, as was the bright-cut decoration and the use of a thin, light metal. The monogram reveals that Cruikshank had received a commission from the Duperron-Bâby family, a leading family of fur traders.[5] A *Ladle with the Monogram of the Saint-Ours Family* (NGC 24292), similar in terms of style and technique, bears witness to the patronage of the Saint-Ours family, an old and noble French Canadian family, and offers evidence of their new practice of using the family monogram rather than the coat-of-arms to identify their silverware. *Sugar Tongs* (NGC 24289), a *Tea Caddy* spoon (NGC 25709) and a *Skewer* (NGC 24317), while in very much the same spirit as the spoon and the ladle from a stylistic and technical point of view, are all items that had not hitherto been part of the range of table utensils in use in Canada. A *Fish Slice* (NGC 24315) was also something of an innovation, both as a utensil type and in its "fiddle" design. Cruikshank, one of the first artists to introduce this model, decorated the blade with a trellis motif typical of the neoclassicism of the period. Rather different, with its hint of the Rococo, is the more lyrical openwork adorning the blade of another *Fish Slice* (NGC 24321) – proof that Cruikshank was not afraid to break new ground. Finally, the *Salt Spoons* illustrated here are evidently the work of a silversmith who was exploring both new forms and new ornamental approaches, for they display a quite remarkable combination of traditional Scottish motifs and decorative elements drawn from Georgian England.

Cruikshank created hollowware, as well as utensils. Despite its simple style, the *Beaker* (NGC 24076) was a novel piece for the time. This flat-based vessel, shaped like a truncated cone, is undecorated except for the engraved monogram of its owner. It differs in both form and ornamentation from earlier works, which were rounder and squatter and generally adorned with regular mouldings around the rim. A *Mustard Pot* belonging to the Canadian Museum of Civilization is also a unique piece, for it was the first object of its type

Robert Cruickshank (1743–1809), *Pair of Salt Spoons with the Monogram J.P.*, c. 1775–1809, from the collection of the National Gallery of Canada (27845.1-2), gift of the Henry Birks Collection of Canadian Silver, 1979. Courtesy of the National Gallery of Canada

Robert Cruickshank (1743–1809), *Pair of Salt Cellars,*
c. 1790–1800, from the collection of the Metropolitan
Museum of Art (33.120.366,367), bequest of
A.T. Clearwater, 1933. Courtesy of the Metropolitan
Museum of Art

made in Canada. The body of the pot, in the shape of a drum, is decorated with fine engraving around the hinge of the lid. The *Salt Cellars*
illustrated here, now in the collection of the Metropolitan Museum
of Art, were also the first such items to be made in this country. Their
gondola-shaped design, characteristic of the period, had rarely been
employed before in domestically produced silverware. Although
damaged and minus its bottles, a *Cruet Frame* (NGC 27777) is another exceptional piece, since it is the only object of its type ever produced in Canada. Individualized by the rounded corners, the overall
shape of the stand is elegantly refined. The mouldings and elaborate
bright-cut engraving underscore the complex outline of the border.
A *Teapot* (NGC 24094)[6] offers yet a further example of a form that
had not previously been part of the Canadian decorative arts vocabulary. Oval in shape, with pure, quintessentially neoclassical lines, it
boasts the most impeccably polished surfaces. It was in fact created
using industrially produced machine-rolled silver sheet, and thus
marks an early step in the gradual industrialization of the trade.
Similar in general form, the *Teapot with a Monogram Thought to
Be That of Jacques Duperron-Bâby*[7] is a variation on the same
theme, although here the monogram is set against the ground of an
elaborately engraved cartouche. In marked contrast, however, are a

Robert Cruickshank (1743–1809), *Tea Service with the Monogram of the Chartier de Lotbinière Family*, c. 1790–95. Courtesy of the National Gallery of Canada (38441.1-4, purchased in 1997)

matching *Sugar Bowl* and *Milk Jug* (NGC 24133.3–4). The sugar bowl represents another typological innovation, for it is the first such item produced by a Canadian silversmith to employ the gondola shape also used for the salt cellars. The delicate surface engraving that adorns the vessel's edge raises some questions concerning the division of labour within the workshop: an identical decorative frieze can be seen not only on the pendant milk jug but also on the *Teapot* and *Tea Caddy* (NGC 24133.1–2)[8] that complete the set, both of which were the work of Peter Arnoldi. It seems unlikely that Cruikshank would have engraved works made by his partner, and the task was probably entrusted to a craftsman or apprentice employed by the firm. Formally speaking, the ewer shape of the milk jug represents yet another advance.

The *Tea Service with the Monogram of the Chartier de Lotbinière Family* is the oldest silver tea service made in Canada. It confirms the excellence of Cruikshank's reputation, moreover, for its commissioner, Michel Chartier de Lotbinière, was a foremost member of the local nobility.[9] Although many of Cruikshank's creations offer evidence that he was largely responsible for introducing British neoclassicism – specifically the Late Georgian style – into Canadian silver making, this service is one of the very finest examples of the power and quality of his contribution. The double-shouldered teapot, mounted on a foot ring, is the most sophisticated of the five known examples, while its accompanying *Tea Trivet* is the earliest documented. The *Milk Jug* in the shape of a miniature wine jug is another first; although it displays a definite formal similarity to the jug discussed above, the design here is more flowing and assured. The *Tea Service with the Monogram of the Chartier de Lotbinière Family* forms a whole whose value exceeds the sum of its parts. Composed of thick silver, rather than machine-rolled silver sheet, the exquisitely crafted set is unquestionably the finest Canadian tea service produced during the period.

The *Sweetmeat Basket*, published here for the first time, is another exceptional piece, for it is the only pierced-work basket made in Canada before the industrial era. The design follows London prototypes, with beaded, spiral ribs separating different pierced patterns made from the mid-1760s through the 1770s. English baskets with similar features, such as the high foot formed from a pierced band, the narrow gadrooned rim, the base mouldings and the feather-edging, date to the early 1770s. This would indicate that the piece was designed and made shortly after Cruikshank's arrival in Montreal. The piercing has been meticulously executed, without the aid of a die. A masterpiece of elegance and refinement, the basket offers a glimpse of the opulent lifestyle enjoyed by certain of Montreal's citizens during the latter part of the eighteenth century. It is to be hoped that the coat of arms that adorns the inside will eventually be identified, thus establishing who commissioned the piece.[10] This object also provides an important key to understanding the origins of trade silver, in which the art of pierced work played a major role and which represented an important facet of Cruikshank's activity as a silversmith. Several of the motifs seen on the sweetmeat basket confirm that the fashion for pierced work had an influence on this other branch of silver making.

ECCLESIASTICAL WORKS

As well as creating objects for domestic use, Robert Cruikshank made ecclesiastical silver. Although born into a Presbyterian family, he became a member of the Anglican congregation of Montreal's

Robert Cruickshank (1743–1809), *Sweetmeat Basket*, c. 1775–80. Private collection.

Christ Church,[11] for which he made a very simple *Communion Paten* – the only piece destined for the Anglican Church known to be from his workshop.[12] He executed a wide range of commissions for the Catholic Church, however, and was already working for the parish of Vaudreuil in 1775.[13] A *Chalice* (NGC 24354) belonging to the National Gallery is a pivotal work. The decorative impact of the piece resides mainly in its combination of perfect proportions and beautifully polished surfaces. If we compare it to a chalice from around the same period by François Ranvoyzé,[14] who practised a highly ornamental style, the radical simplicity of the new approach becomes evident. The similarly spare *Sanctuary Lamp* from the Varennes church[15] confirms the impression: for this category of object, it was entirely novel. The body of the lamp is elegantly vertical, the entire metal surface is polished to a mirror-like brilliance, and decoration is limited to the graceful hooks around the opening, which were used

Robert Cruickshank (1743–1809), *Monstrance*,
c. 1775–1809, Île-Perrot, Parish of Sainte-Jeanne-de-Chantal.
Image courtesy of the Montreal Museum of Fine Art

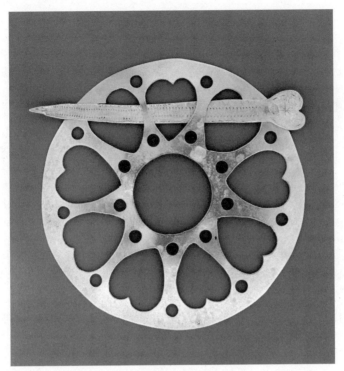

Robert Cruickshank (1743–1809), *Circular Brooch*,
c. 1775–1809, gift of the Henry Birks Collection of
Canadian Silver, 1979. Courtesy of the National
Gallery of Canada (27743.4)

to attach the chains. The overall effect is extremely powerful. For its
part, a *Monstrance* from Île Perrot is fascinatingly hybrid: the shape
echoes that of monstrances made during the French regime, but the
engraved ornamentation is typical of the British neoclassicism of the
period. The result is a synthesis quite unique in the history of Canadian art. The stylized boat shape of the *Incense Boat* (NGC 24355) –
the only known object of its type by Cruikshank – clearly reflects the
influence on a liturgical vessel of a form popular in secular silverware. The engraving that adorns the lid and the edge of the body was
once again inspired by British neoclassicism. Finally, the *Baptismal
Ewer* belonging to the Hôpital général de Québec[16] illustrates the potential offered by this type of object for formal experimentation.
Unique in Cruikshank's work, it echoes the shape of a coffee pot.

TRADE SILVER

The production of silver items for use in the fur trade was a major aspect of the work undertaken in Robert Cruikshank's workshop.[17] An extraordinary number of trade silver pieces were produced there, based on various European prototypes – including the *Scottish Luckenbooth Brooch*[18] – and incorporating elements ranging from Masonic emblems to motifs drawn from Aboriginal cultures. We will look only briefly at a couple of representative pieces, although this corpus warrants its own study. A *Cross of Lorraine* (NGC 27743.3) offers a first splendid example. This age-old Christian symbol is composed here of thin silver sheet, probably machine rolled, whose surface is ornamented with engraving – both common features of Georgian silver. A second, larger *Cross* (NGC 25079), formally and decoratively more elaborate, is an enhanced version of the first. Lastly, a *Circular Brooch* displays the traditional Scottish design of interlinked pierced-work hearts. Exceptionally, this particular example still possesses its original engraved pin.

CONCLUSION

Robert Cruikshank's contribution to the development of silver making in Montreal and in the country as a whole was considerable. In the field of domestic silver he introduced a number of new forms, and several of his secular works are genuine masterpieces. He also furthered the development of Roman Catholic liturgical silver, employing a powerfully concise style to create original, sometimes hybrid pieces inspired by the formal repertoire of domestic silverware. Finally, he must be seen as one of the founders of Canada's trade silver industry. This activity brought him the patronage of Scottish merchants, but his clientele also included members of the middle classes, French Canada's nobility, and the clergy. Although silver objects were imported from the United Kingdom, Cruikshank was undoubtedly largely responsible for the adoption in this country of the British neoclassical style. An in-depth study of his technical innovations and of the division of labour within his workshop is called for if the importance of his role is to be fully recognized. Just as Cruikshank's decorative vocabulary bears witness to his Scottish roots, his approach and his success in the different branches of the market reflect a hardworking, enterprising nature in tune with the popular image of Scots immigrants to Montreal in the late eighteenth century. However, an appreciation of the originality and sophistication of his work and its impact on artistic development subtly alters the picture generally painted of the Scottish contribution by traditional historiography. A full exploration of the impact of his oeuvre is overdue.

NOTES

This chapter was translated from the French by Judith Terry.

1 Robert Derome, "Cruikshank, Robert," *Dictionary of Canadian Biography* 5 (Toronto/Buffalo/London: University of Toronto Press 1983), 217–19.

2 Hew Scott, *Fasti Ecclesiae Scoticanae: The Succession of Ministers in the Parish Churches of Scotland from the Reformation, A.D. 1560, to the Present Time,* vol. 3, part 2, Synods of Aberdeen, and Angus and Mearns (Edinburgh: William Paterson/London: John Russell Smith 1871), 442. I am grateful to Dr James S.S. Armour and George Dalgleish for their help in clarifying this information.

3 Arthur G. Grimwade, *London Goldsmiths, 1697–1837* (London: Faber & Faber 1990), 481.

4 Benjamin Sulte, *A History of Quebec: Its Resources and People* (Montreal and Toronto: The Canadian History Company 1908), 230.

5 The Duperron-Bâby family was remarkably fond of silver tableware during the eighteenth century. See, in particular, the inventory of the communal estate drawn up after the death of Jacques Duperron-Bâby (1731–89) (Archives nationales du Québec in Quebec City, Office of notary Joseph Planté, no. 2508, 8 November 1800). See also René Villeneuve, *Québec Silver from the National Gallery of Canada* (Ottawa: National Gallery of Canada 1998), 36, 37, 57, 65.

6 Reproduced in John E. Langdon, *Canadian Silversmiths, 1700–1900* (Toronto: Stinehour Press 1966), plate 56.

7 Reproduced in Ross A.C. Fox, *Quebec and Related Silver at the Detroit Institute of Arts* (Detroit: Wayne State University Press 1978), 65.

8 The teapot is reproduced in *The Development of Canadian Silver* (Winnipeg: The Winnipeg Art Gallery 1974), no. 177.

9 For information on Chartier de Lotbinière, see F.J. Thorpe, et al., "Chartier de Lotbinière, Michel, marquis de Lotbinière," *Dictionary of Canadian Biography* 4 (Toronto/Buffalo/London: University of Toronto Press 1983), 143–5.

10 Although the owner of these armorial bearings is still unknown, it is interesting to note the presence of boars' heads in the arms of the Gordon family. See John Burke, *Encyclopaedia of Heraldry or General Armory of England, Scotland and Ireland* (London: Henry G. Bohn 1844), n.p.

11 When Cruikshank arrived in Montreal there was no Presbyterian congregation in the city. Presbyterians did not begin gathering to worship until

1791, and although the St Gabriel Street Church opened its doors in 1792, the opening of its registers was not authorized until 1796. Cruikshank married Ann Kay in Christ Church in August 1789, the year of its official establishment by Bishop Inglis. I am grateful to Dr James S.S. Armour for this information.

12 The piece is dated 1786. Reproduced in Colette Godin, ed., *Montréal: La ville aux cents clochers* (Montreal: Fides 2002), 78.

13 René Villeneuve, "Vaudreuil, œuvres d'art de l'église Saint-Michel," *Les chemins de la mémoire III* (Quebec City: Éditeur officiel 1999), 51–2.

14 See, for example, the chalice from the Ange-Gardien church, dating from 1784. Reproduced in Jean Trudel, *Silver in New France* (Ottawa: National Gallery of Canada 1974), 48.

15 Reproduced in Gérard Morisset, *Les églises et le trésor de Varennes* (Quebec City: Médium 1943), plate 28.

16 Reproduced in Gérard Morisset, *Le Cap-Santé, ses églises et son trésor* (Montreal: Montreal Museum of Fine Arts 1980), 346.

17 N. Jaye Fredrickson and Sandra Gibb, *The Covenant Chain: Indian Ceremonial and Trade Silver* (Ottawa: National Museum of Canada 1980), 40–1.

18 Ian Finlay, *Scottish Gold and Silver* (London: Chatto & Windus 1991), 163–5, plate 105.

NINE

"Bonnie Lassies" and a "Coat of Many Colours": Highland-Inspired Clothing at the McCord Museum

Eileen Stack

Though the origins and nature of so-called traditional Highland costume have long been a source of debate among historians and costume enthusiasts, there can be no denying the nineteenth-century popularity of textiles and garments linked to Highland culture.[1] Highland-inspired garments fell into two distinct but often overlapping categories: clothing worn to overtly reference Scottish culture and identity and clothing worn simply to participate in a fashionable trend for Highland dress. Material evidence, pictorial documentation, and textual sources provide insight into the Canadian context of the phenomenon. This paper examines nineteenth-century Canadian clothing inspired by the traditional male dress of Highland Scotland through the costume and photography collection of the McCord Museum.[2]

A key catalyst of this practice was Queen Victoria, who celebrated her distant Scottish ancestry at her reconstructed castle, Balmoral, and dressed her family in kilts and tartans in both public and private.[3] Victoria's enthusiasm for Highland life was matched and inspired by that of her husband, Prince Albert. Costume historian Richard Martin emphasizes the importance of Albert's endorsement of Highland dress to its dissemination into the fashionable mainstream, noting, "Albert's adoption of Highland dress gave sanction and like mind to many other men who would have previously left Highland dress to the festival of the Scots."[4] Likewise, a substantial impact was created by dressing the nine-year-old Prince of Wales in full Highland costume at highly publicized events such as the 1851 opening of the Great Exhibition in London.[5]

Queen Victoria was not acting in isolation, however, but was inspired by a revival of interest in Highland culture and costume initiated in the late eighteenth century and furthered in the nineteenth century.[6] Key events of this revival included the founding of Highland societies in the late 1700s and early 1800s, King George IV's 1822 visit to Edinburgh, and the publication of a series of texts celebrating Scottish Highland heritage.[7] The research into and use of Highland costume were essential elements of this revival, and many cultural societies made Highland dress a key component of their functions.[8] It was through the activities of the revival that a formal definition of Highland costume was established. This definition drew heavily on the standardized uniforms of the Highland regiments and instigated the proliferation of setts, or patterns, to match family and clan.[9]

By the start of the nineteenth century, the core elements of male Highland costume included the short kilt and shoulder plaid made in a clan-linked tartan, a modified military jacket, and accessories such as a sporran and bonnet.[10] Interpretations and fashionable transmutations of this look resulted in a broadened definition of textiles, apparel, and accessories for men as well as for women and children. Notions of tartan fabric were expanded from patterns of woven checks and stripes in heavy-weight wool twills to weaves in lighter-weight wool, as well as silk satins and velvets and even embroidery designs created to emulate the look of tartan setts.[11]

Extant clothing and photographs from the McCord Museum demonstrate that Canadians followed Queen Victoria's lead and

Sergeants of the 78th Fraser Highlanders, Montreal, QC, 1867, William Notman. Courtesy of the Notman Photographic Archives, McCord Museum of Canadian History (I-27497). With their military version of Highland costume, the Highland regiments in Canada would have undoubtedly raised the profile of and piqued interest in what was being viewed internationally as Scotland's national costume.

dressed in clothing inspired by male Highland costume. The majority of these objects date from the second half of the nineteenth century, when Victorian interest in Scottish costume was at its height.[12] Although some artifacts can be interpreted as making an overt reference to a Scottish or Highland identity, others are ambiguous in their intention and may simply reflect a preference for tartan-inspired textiles rather than a deliberate salute to Highland heritage. An examination of these artifacts within the context of their use provides insight into their appeal and significance for nineteenth-century Canadians, as will be seen in the following survey of artifacts and images of men, women, and then children.

Garments and photographs in the McCord collection suggest that men used Highland-inspired costume in various ways over the course of the century and with various intentions. An important facet of masculine Highland costume was brought to Montreal at mid-century, courtesy of the Highland regiments of the British army who were periodically stationed in the city during the nineteenth century.[13] The tartan of the 78th Highlanders, who were stationed in Montreal from 1867 through 1869, was the Mackenzie sett, seen in the illustration here, that was used for kilts, plaid, and trousers.[14] A pair of wool trousers made from Mackenzie tartan in the collection of the McCord Museum bears a striking similarity to the tartan trousers worn by the 78th Highlanders at mid-century, though their broad-fall front construction indicates that they were made about 1830. It is important to note, however, that tartan was being made commercially throughout the nineteenth century, and it is possible that the trousers have no military connection and were worn merely for fashionable reasons.[15]

Indeed, garments made from textiles resembling tartans were a popular choice for men's fashion in the mid-to-late nineteenth century, as an 1868 photograph of Montrealer John Fairie wearing a checked suit attests.[16] Likewise, Montreal mayor Henry Starnes chose to have his photograph taken in 1866 wearing a plaid waistcoat, and a waistcoat done in Berlin woolwork embroidery imitating tartan further supports a trend for this style.[17]

Extant clothing and photographs from the last quarter of the nineteenth century present the most consistent and overt references to

Duncan McIntyre, Montreal, QC, 1892, Wm Notman
and Son. Courtesy of the Notman Photographic
Archives, McCord Museum of Canadian History
(II-96785). There can be little doubt as to the direct
reference intended by the wearing of a complete
Highland costume by Montreal businessman Duncan
McIntyre in the 1890s.

Evening dress in silk tartan inspired by Ogilvie hunting
plaid, worn by Mrs A.W. Ogilvie, née Sarah Leney,
gift of Mrs Hugh Phillipps. Courtesy of the McCord
Museum of Canadian History (M974.15.1-3)

Highland costume and identity, and it is interesting to speculate as to
the evolution of the garments and the context of their use. In 1870,
A. Ramsay wore a complete Highland costume as fancy dress to a
skating carnival held at Montreal's Victoria Rink in honour of Prince
Arthur.[18] In 1873, Montreal architect John James Brown had his
photograph taken wearing a Balmoral bonnet trimmed with a dis-
creet cap badge adorned with a thistle.[19] William MacLennan, a celebrated Highland dancer who visited and performed in Montreal,
had his photograph taken in 1890 at the Notman studio in full
Highland costume.[20] Finally, in 1892 Montreal businessman Duncan
McIntyre, a founder of the Caledonian Society in 1855 and twice
president of the Saint Andrew's Society, was photographed in com-

*Joseph Family Members, Fancy Dress Costumes, QC,
about 1880*, gift of Miss Annette R. Wolff. Courtesy of
the Notman Photographic Archives, McCord Museum
of Canadian History (MP-1983.63.4-13). This page
from a scrapbook features members and friends of
the Abraham Joseph family in fancy dress, including
Maud Joseph dressed as a variation of a Highland
Lassie, wearing a tartan skirt, shoulder plaid and sporran.

plete Highland costume. This survey of photographic evidence demonstrates a variety of uses of Highland fashion motifs, from re-
strained accessory to complete Highland costume. The employment
of Highland fashion also ranges from the exceptional occasion of
fancy dress to the working attire of a professional dancer and the representation of the Scottish heritage of a Montreal business baron.

Material evidence at the McCord Museum suggests that women's
nineteenth-century use of Highland-inspired costume ranged from
the adoption of tartan as a fashion fabric in conventional women's
clothing and the use of this fabric to make a fashionable reference
to Scottish heritage to the appropriation and feminization of male
Highland costume for fancy dress and theatrics.[21] For example,

Young Boys in Highland costume, Montreal, QC, about 1855, gift of Mr M.S. Reford. Courtesy of the Notman Photographic Archives, McCord Museum of Canadian History (MP-1975.67.25).

photographs in the Notman archives from the 1860s show women wearing dresses made of tartan-inspired textiles that might have been worn to acknowledge their Scottish ancestry or perhaps simply to participate in a trend for a popular fabric design.[22] In contrast, a silk evening dress made in Ogilvie hunting tartan said to have been worn by Mrs A.W. Ogilvie for a reception for the Prince of Wales in 1860 was likely chosen by its wearer for its ability to communicate the Ogilvies' cultural lineage.[23] Ogilvie's husband, Alexander Walker Ogilvie, would become president of the Saint Andrew's Society of Montreal in 1870.[24]

Photographs from the last quarter of the nineteenth century and into the early twentieth show women appropriating the traditionally male garb of Highland costume. This costume was worn for fancy dress or theatrical outings as women adopted the guise of a new kind of female character, the Highland Lassie, dressed in shoulder plaid, kilt-like skirt, and sometimes a sporran. This personality can be seen in a scrapbook of photographs featuring members and friends of the Abraham Joseph family of Quebec City, dating from about 1880. At an 1870 skating carnival in Montreal at least six women were dressed as Highland Lassies.[25] Prescriptive references of the period, such as Ardern Holt's *Fancy Dresses Described, or What to Wear at Fancy Balls*, listed variations of the Highland Lassie, including "Flora MacDonald" and "Flora McIvor," though the characters shared similar dress.[26] The popularity and evolution of this character can be seen in a photograph of 1909 featuring a theatrical group entitled the *Bonnie Lassies*, and it is visible in the persona of the Highland Lassie used to promote cigarette tobacco in the twentieth century.[27]

In keeping with Queen Victoria's children, who were dressed and documented in Highland-inspired costume in the late 1840s and the 1850s, Canadian children wore and had their photographs taken in diminutive versions of the Scottish ensembles. Rare insight into a child's experience of this style of clothing can be found in the diary of Fanny Joseph, a daughter of Abraham Joseph. Living in Quebec City, Fanny's nine-year-old brother Montefiore Joseph was sent to school in 1860 dressed in a "scotch kilt dress" that had been acquired in Edinburgh. Fanny describes the garment and the reception her brother received at school: "it was a brilliant tartan & the boys plagued him by calling 'Joseph the coat of many colors' & he was

Master Hugh Allan, Montreal, QC, 1866, painted
photograph, William Notman and John Arthur Fraser,
gift of Mrs Gertrude H. Bourne. Courtesy of the
Notman Photographic Archives, McCord Museum
(N-1981.16.1)

Waistcoat, about 1840, gift of the estate of Mrs Emily Ross Crawford. Courtesy of the McCord Museum of Canadian History (M9532). This waistcoat, dating from the 1840s and embroidered with thistles, roses, and shamrocks, can be interpreted as suggestive of Scottish heritage.

very unhappy about it till he was given dark tweed suits. I remember how our chums Charlie & John Stewart helped us to persuade Mother to give him real boy's clothes."[28] As a Canadian Jew of Portuguese-Spanish descent, it is unlikely that Montefiore Joseph was wearing the kilted garment to reference a Scottish heritage, but, rather, he was likely wearing it because the style was part of a clothing trend favoured by nineteenth-century mothers – though at times clearly less popular with their children.

In contrast to this use, a painted photograph of Master Hugh Allan, son of leading nineteenth-century Montreal businessman Hugh Allan, presents an obvious tribute to Highland heritage. Allan's son is dressed in Highland costume and assuming the pose of a young laird fishing in the playground of a painted Highland backdrop. Much deliberate effort went into the creation of this contrived image, and the wearing of Highland costume plays a key role in the performance of identity captured here. Much like the photograph of Montreal businessman Duncan MacIntyre dressed in full Highland ensemble, this image is telling of the significance that Highland costume held for many Scots living in Canada during the nineteenth century, even for someone like Hugh Allan Sr, who was born in Lowland Scotland.

Material evidence from the McCord Museum indicates that Canadians of different backgrounds actively participated in the fashionable trend for clothing inspired by male Highland costume with a variety of intentions and adaptations. In the case of artifacts such as a plaid dress or embroidered waistcoat, it can be difficult to determine whether this usage was intended overtly to reference Scottish identity. In other instances, however, it is readily apparent that a deliberate allusion was being made to Highland culture. Since use of this tradition was not restricted exclusively to those of Scottish origin, the phenomenon also illustrates how Highland culture had become part of the emerging nineteenth-century Canadian identity.

NOTES

1 For an examination of the history and debate surrounding tartan and Highland costume, see Hugh Cheape, *Tartan: The Highland Habit* (Edinburgh: National Museums of Scotland 1995); Hugh Cheape, "Researching Tartan," *Costume* 27 (1993): 35–46; Malcolm Chapman, "'Freezing the Frame': Dress and Ethnicity in Brittany and Gaelic Scotland," in *Dress and Ethnicity: Change across Space and Time*, ed., Joanne B. Eicher (Oxford: Berg Publishers 1995), 7–28; Richard Martin, "Transmutations of the Tartan: Attributed Meanings to Tartan Design," *Textiles as Primary Sources: Proceedings of the First Symposium of the Textile Society of America, Minneapolis Institute of Art, September 16–18, 1988* (1988): 51–62; W.A. Thorburn, "Military Origins of Scottish National Dress," *Costume* 10 (1976): 29–40; Hugh Trevor-Roper, "The Invention of Tradition: The Highland Tradition of Scotland," in *The Invention of Tradition*, ed., Eric Hobsbawm (Cambridge: University of Cambridge 1983): 15–42.

2 Founded in 1921, the McCord Museum of Canadian History collects, among other things, costume and textiles made, used, or worn in Canada. Its collection of costume and textiles numbers approximately sixteen thousand objects. Among the Museum's other noteworthy collections is the Notman Photographic Archives, which contains over one million images. Many of the artifacts and photographs referred to in this article can be viewed on the museum's website, www.mccord-museum.qc.ca.

3 Cheape, *Tartan*, 61–3; Kay Staniland, *In Royal Fashion: The Clothes of Princess Charlotte and Queen Victoria* (London: Museum of London 1997), 138–42; Frances Dimond, "Queen Victoria and Fashions for the Young," *Costume* 21 (1987): 7.

4 Martin, "Transmutations," 57.

5 Staniland, *In Royal Fashion*, 142.

6 This revival was in part born of the Romantic movement and the cult of the noble savage that emerged in Europe at the end of the eighteenth century and took as its subject the character of the indomitable Highlander (Trevor-Roper, "Invention of Tradition," 25; Chapman, "'Freezing the Frame,'" 20).

7 David Stewart, *Sketches of the Character, Manners, and Present State of the Highlanders of Scotland* (Edinburgh: A. Constable 1822); James Logan, *The Scottish Gael, or Celtic Manners as Preserved among the Highlanders* (London: Smith Elder 1831); James Logan, *The Clans of the Scottish Highlands* (London: Ackermann 1845); John Sobieski Stuart, *Vestiarium Scoticum* (Edinburgh: William Tait 1842); and John Sobieski Stolberg Stuart and Edward Charles Stuart, *The Costume of the Clans* (Edinburgh: William Tait, 1845); Martin, "Transmutations," 54–6.

8 For example, a primary goal of the Highland Society of London, established in 1778, was the repeal of the Act of Proscription of 1747 that forbade civilian use of Highland dress. The society also initiated research into and preservation of clan-specific tartans in the early 1800s (Cheape, *Tartan*, 48–9).

9 Highland regiments were exempt from the Act of Proscription of 1747, and their controlled use of Highland costume established dress traditions that became intrinsically linked to nineteenth-century notions of Highland costume. These practices included tartan differentiation according to group affiliation and a systematic manner of costume display (Trevor-Roper, "Invention of Tradition," 25; Thorburn, "Military Origins," 31).

10 Thorburn, "Military Origins," 33.

11 Cheape, *Tartan*, 52; Martin, "Transmutations," 56–9. The term "tartan" is commonly believed to have come from the French word *tiretaine*, a half-wool, half-linen cloth, though recent scholarship suggests a Scottish-Gaelic origin for the name. The term "tartan" was first associated with Scottish costume in the sixteenth century. It was used during this period in a nonspecific way to describe checked or coloured cloth (Cheape, *Tartan*, 3, 13). It was not until the early 1800s that the term "tartan" began to be used to describe specific checked patterns signifying clan identity (Trevor-Roper, "Invention of Tradition," 29).

12 By the mid-nineteenth century, popular perception had appropriated, expanded, and made Highland culture, costume, and identity largely interchangeable with that of the whole of Scotland. See J.M. Bumsted, "Scottishness

and Britishness in Canada, 1790–1914," in *Myth, Migration and the Making of Memory: Scotia and Nova Scotia, c. 1700–1990*, eds. Marjory Harper and Michael E. Vance (Halifax, NS: Fernwood 1999), 93–4; Martin, "Transmutations," 54.

13 Cameron Pulsifer, "A Highland Regiment in Halifax: The 78th Highland Regiment of Foot and the Scottish National/Cultural Factor in Nova Scotia's Capital, 1869–71," in *Myth, Migration and the Making of Memory: Scotia and Nova Scotia, c. 1700–1990*, eds. Marjory Harper and Michael E. Vance (Halifax, NS: Fernwood 1999), 144–6; Thorburn, "Military Origins," 39.

14 The Mackenzie sett is a variation of the government or Black Watch sett, with white and red overcheck added (Pulsifer, "A Highland Regiment," 144). Tartan trousers would have been an obvious nod to Highland trews, "a form of tight trousers," references to which first appear in the seventeenth century (Cheape, *Tartan*, 18–19).

15 This conclusion was reached courtesy of correspondence with André Gousse of Parks Canada, Allan Carswell of the National War Museum of Scotland, and Wayne Moug of Canadian Heritage.

16 *John Fairie, Montreal, QC, 1868*, William Notman, Notman Photographic Archives, McCord Museum, I-30864.1. A similar checked suit was found in a fashion plate from the *Gentleman's Magazine of Fashion*, February 1875–78, owned by J.B.P. Beauregard, a Montreal tailor.

17 *Mayor Starnes, Montreal, QC, 1866*, William Notman, Notman Photographic Archives, McCord Museum, I-20690.1. Berlin woolwork, a type of counted-thread embroidery, was widely popular as a form of domestic needlework in the mid-nineteenth century.

18 *A. Ramsay, Montreal, QC, 1870*, William Notman, Notman Photographic Archives, McCord Museum, I-43735.1.

19 *John James Brown, architect, Montreal, QC, 1873*, William Notman, Notman Photographic Archives, McCord Museum, I-85652.

20 *William MacLennan, Montreal, QC, 1890*, Wm Notman and Son, Notman Photographic Archives, McCord Museum, II-91677.

21 In an examination of the "feminization" of heavyweight woollen fabrics traditionally designated for menswear to lighter-weight textiles for womenswear in the 1865–85 period, Lou Taylor notes the production of "lighter-weight tartan wool cloth" as an example of the new textiles being produced for this use. She also notes the appearance of "Ladies Scotch Plaids" being shown at the Great Exhibition of 1851. See Lou Taylor, "Wool Cloth and Gender: The Use of Woollen Cloth in Women's Dress in Britain, 1865–85," in *Defining Dress: Dress as Object, Meaning and Identity*, eds. Amy de la Haye and Elizabeth Wilson (Manchester: Manchester University Press 1999), 38.

22 Examples include *Mrs Ashworth, Montreal, QC, 1861*, William Notman, Notman Photographic Archives, McCord Museum, I-479; and *Miss Esther Matthews, Montreal, QC, 1861*, William Notman, Notman Photographic Archives, McCord Museum, I-2390.

23 "Hunting" and "dress" tartans were created as variations of existing clan setts during the mid-nineteenth century (Cheape, *Tartan*, 61).

24 Alexander Walker Ogilvie was the founder of Ogilvie Flour Mills.

25 *Montreal Gazette*, 2 March 1870.

26 Ardern Holt, *Fancy Dresses Described, or What to Wear at Fancy Balls*, 6th ed. (London: Debenham and Freebody 1896), 100, 232–3.

27 *"Bonnie Lassies" Group, Montreal, QC, 1909*, Wm Notman and Son, Notman Photographic Archives, McCord Museum, II-172610. The use of women dressed in Highland-inspired costume to promote tobacco use is visible in an advertisement in the collection of the McCord Museum dating from 1904–17 that invited consumers to "Smoke Highland Lassie" (M999.70.6.20). This character was modified and further disseminated in the advertising campaigns of Canadian tobacco company Macdonald Stewart, which developed the trademark image of a woman wearing a Macdonald of Sleat tartan kilt and plaid for their line of Export A cigarettes in 1935. "Macdonald Stewart of Canada," NATCD *Star* 102, no. 105 (September 1973): 5–6; RJR-Macdonald Inc., "La Compagnie Macdonald," *RJR-Macdonald Inc.* 6 (1979): 4–5.

28 Anne Joseph, *Heritage of a Patriarch: A Fresh Look at Nine of Canada's Earliest Jewish Families* (Quebec City: Editions du Septentrion 1995), 302.

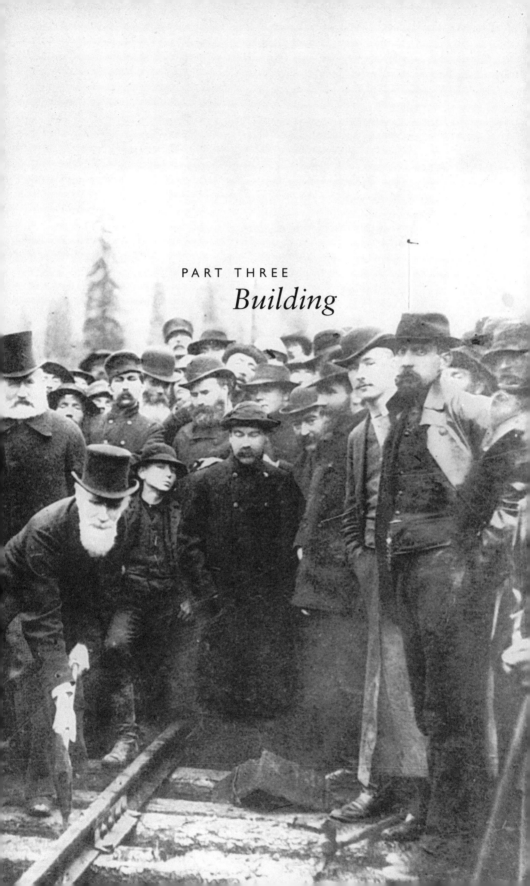

PART THREE
Building

Sir William Logan and Sir J.W. Dawson: Victorian Geology as Scottish Science in a New World Environment

Suzanne Zeller

The catchy title of a popular book by Arthur Herman, *How the Scots Invented the Modern World* (cannily subtitled *The True Story of How Western Europe's Poorest Nation Created Our World and Everything in It*), offers a fair indication of the appreciation for Scottish culture that has enjoyed a resurgence over the past generation or so. Not only have the great intellects of the Scottish Enlightenment earned renewed scholarly admiration for Scotland as an eighteenth-century "hotbed of genius";[1] cultural historians of nineteenth-century "invented traditions" have also highlighted the more remarkable – if that is possible – complex social networks that so effectively supported and transported Scottish culture abroad, across oceans as well as across the social spectrum.[2] In offering only a superficial account of Scottish influences in Canada, with but little specific mention of Montreal, Herman's work challenges Canadian specialists to construct a more nuanced picture upon foundations already laid by Canadian students of the Scottish cultural heritage.[3]

My own contribution to this collective effort involves a close examination of Canada's two leading scientists of the nineteenth century: Sir William Edmond Logan (1797–1875), a native Montrealer
born into the city's influential Scottish business community and
founding director of one of Canada's first permanent scientific institutions, the Geological Survey of Canada (GSC, 1842), which head-
quartered in Montreal until 1881; and Sir John William Dawson
(1820–99), the Nova Scotian son of a Scottish bookseller, stationer,
and printer, adopted Montrealer, and founding principal of a revitalized McGill College (1855).[4] The common factor of Montreal in
this scenario was no mere coincidence; nor were the Scottish background, the natural history training at the University of Edinburgh,
and the specific focus on geology that Logan and Dawson had in
common. Inheriting and transposing important aspects of Scottish
scientific culture to Montreal, they joined a well-rehearsed dialogue
between Old and New Worlds, participating in a process that transformed both their New World surroundings and their own community's Old World cultural heritage.

SCOTTISH CULTURE INHERITED

Herman recounts multiple dimensions of the Scottish Enlightenment
outlook that lent such force to Scottish culture from the late eighteenth
century. He enumerates classic assumptions that, as members of
Montreal's Scottish community, Logan and Dawson accepted and actively fostered. In particular, their worldview exalted industry, knowledge, and humanity, interpreting Christian doctrine as "the very
heart of what it meant to be modern."[5] This intellectual foundation
prized a growing commerce sustained by worldwide trade and communication lines; widespread literacy in society and with it public education, lending libraries, and the book trade; innovative fields and
forms of knowledge that ranged beyond traditional classical curricula; historical approaches to the study of nature, including human
nature; and practical and theoretical knowledge as two sides of the
same coin, with science seen as key to both.[6]

The science of geology as Logan and Dawson practised it during
the Victorian age offered a powerful means to realize these Scottish
Enlightenment values, not only in Montreal but farther afield – by

16533

Sir William Edmond Logan, Geologist, Montreal, QC,
1865, William Notman. Courtesy of the Notman
Photographic Archives, McCord Museum of Canadian
History (I-16533.1)

Sir William Dawson, Montreal, QC, 1895, Wm Notman
and Son. Courtesy of the Notman Photographic
Archives, McCord Museum of Canadian History
(II-109802)

applying them to the vast British North American hinterland that lay beyond the city. As arguably the quintessential Victorian science, linking the theoretical inextricably to practical results, geology was widely perceived as closely linked to Scotland's industrial take-off, apparent proof of the revitalized Baconian adage that "knowledge is power."[7]

Scottish contributions to modern geology by the 1830s included, on the one hand, the theoretical approaches of James Hutton (1726–97) and Sir Charles Lyell (1797–1875) to a "uniformitarian" understanding of the earth as the historical product of similar forces acting over time and, on the other hand, practical field training to pinpoint coal and other valuable mineral deposits in the complex Scottish terrain. Perhaps nowhere were geological discussions livelier than at the University of Edinburgh during the early nineteenth century, and perhaps no one thirsted more for geological information about all the earth – or was better positioned to obtain it – than Robert Jameson, Edinburgh's influential natural history professor and founder of the Royal Museum of Scotland, a major repository for worldwide collections of specimens and other scientific information during the fifty years before his death in 1854.[8]

Both Logan and Dawson had imbibed Scottish scientific and educational priorities well before they attended the University of Edinburgh during its heyday as a centre for natural history: Logan at Alexander Skakel's grammar school in Montreal and Dawson at the Reverend Thomas McCulloch's Pictou Academy in Nova Scotia. In their turn these teachers had been educated during the height of the Scottish Enlightenment, Skakel (1776–1846) at the University of Aberdeen and McCulloch (1776–1843) at the University of Glasgow. Both immigrated to British North America as active promoters of Scotland's widely extolled three-way partnership between science, education, and industrialization.[9]

The Edinburgh education, which reinforced the values imparted by Skakel and McCulloch, was already behind both Logan and Dawson when they encountered Charles Lyell on his first North American geological tour at Pictou in 1841. While Dawson served as Lyell's geological guide through Nova Scotia's great coalfields, Logan embarked on his own regional tour to garner more evidence for his recently published theory of coal's *in situ* formation. Having lost his long-term position as manager of the Forest Copper Works in Swansea, South Wales, Logan was visiting family in Montreal at the time. Lyell became Dawson's lifelong mentor, encouraging both scientists to channel colonial data into the imperial geological discourse in which his was a leading voice.[10]

Logan and Dawson practised to the full their neo-Baconian belief in the combined power of education, science, and industrialization to improve the quality of life in their colonial societies. An experienced cartographer whose model cross-sectional maps had been adopted by the Geological Survey of Great Britain, Logan understood the colony's need for a school for field geologists, a function he introduced and went to personal expense to preserve under the aegis of the GSC, before the province of Ontario finally secured a School of Mines at Queen's University, Kingston, in 1893. In the same educational vein he funded McGill College's Logan Chair and Logan Medal to encourage the study of geology in Canada. He also supplied Canadian public schools with geological specimens and maps as educational resources.[11]

For its part, Dawson's scientific educational mission proved even broader . An advocate of science curricula while serving as Nova Scotia's Superintendent of Education in 1850, Dawson took charge at McGill College in 1855 just when Scottish universities were setting important educational precedents. That same year, the University of Edinburgh appointed George Wilson to its inaugural Regius Professorship of Technology. Wilson was the brother of Daniel Wilson (1816–92), the Scottish archaeologist who became professor of English and history at University College, Toronto, in 1853, and later Dawson's friend and counterpart as president of the University of Toronto. Also in 1855, the University of Glasgow appointed the physicist W.J.M. Rankine professor of engineering. While Rankine began scientizing the conceptual foundations of British engineering over the next few years, Dawson set about founding McGill's innovative chairs in practical scientific fields, including botany, meteorology, and applied mineralogy, along with popular public lecture series on scientific topics and themes. His preferred educational dream, the establishment of a department of applied science at McGill, took more time to accomplish. When Dawson finally succeeded in 1870, inaugurating what soon became McGill's Faculty of Engineering, he

confessed that in exchange for this achievement he would willingly
have foregone his illustrious geological career.[12]

SCOTTISH CULTURE TRANSPOSED

It was, above all, in building and deploying effective lines of communication that the Montreal Scottish community excelled in dis-
persing its culture, at least where its geological applications were
concerned. Several waves of immigration in the late eighteenth and
early nineteenth centuries included scientifically trained British military officers who had served in Canada during the War of 1812 and
were reappointed to colonial administrative positions after the peace
of 1815. They rounded out a growing network of geological patrons,
protagonists, and practitioners whose influence extended, already by
the 1820s and 1830s, across British North America to the Pacific and
Arctic Oceans.

In addition to the Scottish-born, Edinburgh-educated Earl of Dalhousie (himself a powerful early influence in shaping colonial scientific and literary culture, first as lieutenant governor of Nova Scotia
from 1816 and then as governor-in-chief of British North America
from 1820, founding the pioneering Literary and Historical Society
of Quebec in 1824), the patrons also included members of the
McGill, Redpath, and other families with Scottish connections who
constituted a vital sector of the influential Montreal business community, to which the Logan family belonged. The level of this community's impressive philanthropic generosity reached its height during
the 1890s, when the tobacco magnate Sir William C. Macdonald
endowed McGill College with three fully-equipped, state-of-the-art
science buildings, complete with professorships.[13]

In turn, these wealthy Scottish patrons found public expression for
their common outlook through Montreal's Scottish contingent of
protagonists: newspaper owners, editors, and booksellers, including
David Chisholme (1796–1842), editor of the Montreal *Gazette*, the
Montreal *Herald*, and the *Canadian Magazine and Literary Repository* and founder of the *Canadian Review and Literary and Historical Journal*, to accompany Dalhousie's Literary and Historical
Society of Quebec, in 1824. By the 1830s, Robert Armour (1781–
1857) had revitalized the *Gazette*, with his son Robert Jr (1806–45)

as editor. These Scottish literati joined educators and other middle-class professionals, many of them fellow Scots, including Alexander Skakel, to follow Dalhousie's example by forming the Natural History Society of Montreal in 1827.[14]

David Chisholme, in particular, spoke for a growing cohort in British North America who shared Dalhousie's conviction that colonists were entitled to the full rights and privileges of British subjects, with the state acting to investigate and develop the land and its resources. They advocated a geological or mineralogical survey to ascertain British North America's agricultural and industrial potential. Chisholme is credited with publishing the work of Edinburgh-educated John Jeremiah Bigsby (1792–1881), a medical officer who served with the International Boundary Commission along the Great Lakes in 1819–20. Bigsby's work was one of the first scholarly treatises on geology written in British North America.[15] Chisholme also publicized the mineralogical assessments of the Glasgow-educated William "Tiger" Dunlop (1792–1848), who was the Canada Land Company's warden of the woods and forests in the Huron Tract, over a million unsettled acres extending from the eastern shore of Lake Huron deep into what is now Southern Ontario. In other words, decades before Logan returned to Montreal in 1841 and Dawson arrived in 1855, the social structures of Montreal's Scottish community were solidly in place, enabling it to lobby not only for a state-supported geological survey of the commercial hinterland of the metropolis, but also for such a survey to be entrusted not to an imperial officer but, rather, to one of its own. William Logan, self-styled "practical coalminer of education," attained the position notwithstanding important gaps in his geological expertise, including his lack of a thorough knowledge of palaeontology.[16]

Logan dreaded from the outset the unspeakable possibility that the province of Canada was bereft of coal, that invaluable industrial fuel, after recognizing in the geological strata around Montreal "a coal field, with the coal left out." Crucial to his success, and to the long-term survival of the GSC, was Logan's decision to draw upon support from valuable sources on the scene who would otherwise have remained silent and anonymous. He consulted a preexisting community of geological practitioners who were, once again, mainly Scottish immigrants and who had accumulated a wealth of local information, especially along canal routes in the Ottawa-Rideau valleys. They included the Reverend Andrew Bell (1803–56) of L'Orignal, Upper Canada, whose son Robert (1841–1917) joined the GSC as an apprentice when he was only fifteen, before capping off his formal science education at the University of Edinburgh and eventually directing the GSC himself. Like the elder Bell, the less well-known James Wilson, an Edinburgh-trained surgeon at Perth, Upper Canada, had assembled an extensive local reference collection of minerals and fossils. Thomas Roy (?–1842), a New Brunswick–born son of Scottish settlers, moved to Toronto as an engineer during the 1830s and constructed a pioneering geological map of eastern North America, a helpful basis for Logan's cartographical enterprise. Finally, Logan's indefatigable first assistants, Alexander Murray (1810–84) and James Richardson (1810–83), also Scottish immigrants, readily grasped Logan's vision of the GSC's mandate as a sacred mission with the very future of the country riding on its success.[17]

A still wider circle of links in the Scottish social-scientific network included that master of communication lines, the civil engineer Sir Sandford Fleming (1827–1915). Fleming founded the Canadian Institute at Toronto in 1849, drawing lustre during the 1850s from Logan's scientific reputation by naming him its first president. Moreover, Logan had attended the Edinburgh High School with George Barnston (1800–83), a Hudson's Bay Company fur trader with a lifelong interest in natural history. Barnston extended the Scottish pursuit of the geographical distribution patterns of plants, birds, and minerals northwestward into the Arctic Circle – with related speculations about the global reach of God's intentions for the British Empire.[18]

Barnston in turn sent his son James (1831–58) to the University of Edinburgh. James found confirmation of his father's wide-ranging geographical perspective on natural history through the botanical teachings of J.H. Balfour, who emphasized the earth's vast unexplored territories, including British North America, as untapped repositories of scientific knowledge. Encouraged by Logan and Dawson to lobby for McGill's new chair of botany, James Barnston returned to Montreal, duly attaining the post in 1856. But his untimely death months later shifted the focus of this Scottish-style exploratory botany (for the promotion of which Barnston had organized the

Botanical Society of Montreal) to a newly immigrated fellow Scot and student of Balfour, George Lawson (1827–95). As professor of chemistry and natural history at Queen's University, Lawson founded the Botanical Society of Canada in 1860, defining yet another circle of like-minded Scots, to whom Logan entrusted the GSC's enormous plant collections.[19]

SCOTTISH CULTURE TRANSFORMED

This barest outline of a community's richly textured, broadly focused cultural window on the world perhaps offers sufficient evidence that, for all their outstanding scientific and administrative achievements, Logan and Dawson hardly acted alone. They represented the visible tenth of an extraordinarily expansive cultural community whose vision, predicated more on natural than on political boundaries, sharpened over time into a powerful ideological tool of ambition for no less than a transcontinental reconfiguration of British North America. As early as 1845, Logan had envisioned his GSC as a mere dress rehearsal for a future survey of British North America's entire unexplored northwestern territory. A decade later, Dawson articulated a theme that has resonated in Canadian history ever since, declaring more pointedly: "As naturalists, we hold [British North America's] natural features as fixing its future destiny, and indicating its present interests, and regard its local subdivisions as arbitrary and artificial." Logan pushed his GSC outward from its political limits in the province of Canada as far as Newfoundland, even after that colony rejected Confederation, with Dawson, too, supporting an integrated geological survey over the "bad hands" of rival local geologists in the maritime colonies. Extending inquisitive scientific tentacles ever outward well before it was politically warranted (or even justified), Logan and Dawson's geology, like the arctic natural history of their contemporary, George Barnston, helped to normalize public perceptions of a transcontinental Canada as a "natural" development.[20]

The road to this point had not been at all straightforward, nor was it inevitable. Logan had originally envisaged the GSC and its British counterpart as "mutually serviceable" institutions, with Canada, ever the linchpin in a North Atlantic triangle, offering "the measure of a correct geological comparison" between Europe and America. Indeed, he and Dawson determined early on to entice both the American and the British Associations for the Advancement of Science to hold unprecedented annual meetings in Montreal. They succeeded in 1857 and 1884, respectively, and hoped to carve a place for Canadian science in both wider forums.[21]

But Logan also found himself "mortified" at discovering cartons of Canadian fossils that he had sent in good faith stowed away unopened and ignored in the British Geological Survey's basements. Dawson, too, suffered bitter rejections as a "mere colonist," passed over twice for appointments to the University of Edinburgh by the British Geological Survey's general director, Sir Roderick Murchison (himself a Scot, no less) – despite Charles Lyell's vigorous support of his applications. When Logan felt compelled to consult New York reference collections for territorially contiguous geological strata and their fossils – and therefore to translate between British and American nomenclatures and to some extent to adopt the American version when parsing Canadian formations – he nevertheless vowed to let scientific evidence alone challenge British imperial stratigraphic declensions. Yet he too found his achievements repeatedly undermined by Murchison's systematic imperial campaign to modify Canadian geological analyses to suit his own iterations, including Logan's famous *in situ* theory of coal.[22]

Logan in fact won a significant victory in retaining the Canadian name "Laurentian" for the Precambrian Shield over Murchison's preferred Scottish term "Lewisian." He also adopted the British Geological Survey's conventional colour codes for GSC maps, harmonizing contiguous American strata with British representations as far as possible. But it comes as no surprise that he eventually spearheaded efforts to synchronize international geological nomenclature and mapping schemes, in order to eliminate the difficulties that resulted from this constant lack of coordination.[23]

Even though the Scottish scientific gaze was territorially expansive in so many ways, it nevertheless manifested crucial blind spots in the culturally contested site of Montreal. As a further characteristic of the Scottish outlook, Arthur Herman highlights its means of dealing with problems of identity: "How to deal with a dominant culture that one admired but that threatened to overwhelm one's heritage, and oneself with it ... [when no] amount of political wishful thinking could close the cultural gap."[24] This relentless Scottish question of identity, Herman explains, had been framed in Great Britain during the eighteenth century vis-à-vis the dominant English culture. There, the Scottish answer had been a determination, with some success, to modify British culture to suit Scottish interests. But this self-confident tradition played itself out in relation to French Canadian culture, at least in Dawson's case, in a self-defeating narrow-mindedness at feeling "under siege." Dawson's dichotomized perception of Canadian society, with Montreal as its microcosm, committed him to a "double-fisted fight" between Anglo-Celtic Protestant modernity, on the one hand, and Franco-Catholic ultramontane "popery" on the other hand, leading him to overlook important potential allies, especially at Laval University, in his own anti-Darwinian battle.[25]

Among the ironies that punctuated Logan's and Dawson's scientific careers, perhaps none is as telling as the issue of succession in both cases. Logan, so much of whose own successful career derived from his status as a Canadian-born member of the Montreal business community, purposefully selected as his 1869 successor in the GSC directorship the English-born A.R.C. Selwyn (1824–1902). Selwyn had trained with the Geological Survey of Great Britain and had then directed the geological survey of Victoria, Australia. In passing over Canadian-born aspirants, including Robert Bell, Logan left Selwyn to deal with a work environment so poisoned by bitterness that a public inquiry was launched to investigate the GSC's situation in 1884. For his part, Dawson took pride in arranging the admission of his son, George Mercer Dawson (1849–1901), to the Royal School of Mines in London, only to see him succeed as the prize-winning student of T.H. Huxley, "Darwin's bulldog," and join the next generation of Canada's leading scientists, all trained in modern evolutionary science, in rejecting the older Baconian natural history tradition preferred by the elder Dawson.[26]

More intriguing is evidence that if this generational transition represented a decline, it was a decline not of Scottish influence in science per se but rather of the Edinburgh mode of practising it. My own research has turned in recent years from natural history to the history of physical sciences, leading straight back to McGill and Montreal. A recent awarding-winning study, *The Science of Energy*, by Crosbie Smith, brilliantly illuminates the powerful impact of yet another cluster of remarkable Scots, this time of physicists and engineers at Glasgow. With William Thomson, Lord Kelvin (1824–1907), in the lead they transformed classical Newtonian mechanics into the modern sciences of thermodynamics and energy physics, supported once again by a wealthy and practical-minded Scottish business community.[27]

How, one wonders, might this new approach have played itself out in Canada, where the outstanding student of energy physics was Ernest Rutherford (1871–1937), a New Zealander who acceded to the Macdonald Chair of Physics at McGill in 1898? Rutherford's Nobel Prize in chemistry in 1908 honoured research that he began at McGill on the transmutability of chemical elements and the atomic structure of matter itself. His remarkable "genius for astonishment" can be traced only with dissatisfaction to the unconventional cosmological theories of A.W. Bickerton, his expatriate English science professor at the University of Canterbury, New Zealand. By inquiring still farther back to Rutherford's earlier life, however, one finds him the son of a versatile, innovative, and mechanically inventive Scottish-born father and a schoolteacher mother whose children are said to have completed their daily homework at her behest by reciting aloud, "All knowledge is power."[28] There must be something to this Scottish cultural heritage in Canada after all, at least as far as science is concerned, and I for one am persuaded.

NOTES

1 David Daiches, Jean Jones, and Peter Jones, eds., *A Hotbed of Genius: The Scottish Enlightenment, 1730–1790* (Edinburgh: Edinburgh University Press 1986).

2 See for example Hugh Trevor-Roper, "The Invention of Tradition: The Highland Tradition in Scotland," in Eric J. Hobsbawm and Terence O. Ranger, eds., *The Invention of Tradition* (Cambridge: Cambridge University Press 1983), 15–42.

3 Arthur Herman, *How the Scots Invented the Modern World* (New York: Crown Publishers 2001), chaps. 13–14; see also W. Stanford Reid, ed., *The Scottish Tradition in Canada – A History of Canada's Peoples* (Toronto: McClelland and Stewart, in association with the Multiculturalism Program, Department of the Secretary of State and the Publishing Centre, Supply and Services Canada 1976).

4 C. Gordon Winder, "Logan, Sir William Edmond," in *Dictionary of Canadian Biography* [DCB], vol. 10, Francess G. Halpenny, gen. ed. (Toronto and Quebec: University of Toronto Press and Laval University Press 1972), 444–9, and Peter R. Eakins and Jean Sinnamon Eakins, "Dawson, Sir John William," in DCB, vol. 12 (1990), 230–7. See also Morris Zaslow, *Reading the Rocks: The Story of the Geological Survey of Canada, 1842–1972* (Ottawa: Macmillan and Department of Energy, Mines, and Resources 1975).

5 Herman, *Scots*, 165.

6 Ibid., *Scots*, 15–22, 51–4, 81–5, 159–61, 172, 207.

7 Roy Porter, *The Making of Geology: Earth Sciences in Britain 1660–1815* (Cambridge: Cambridge University Press 1977), 152, 171–3; and Roy Porter, "The Industrial Revolution and the Rise of the Science of Geology," in Mikulas Teich and Robert Young, eds., *Changing Perspectives in the History of Science* (London: Heinemann Educational 1973), 320–43. On Baconianism see Suzanne Zeller, *Inventing Canada: Early Victorian Science and the Idea of a Transcontinental Nation* (Toronto: University of Toronto Press 1987), 14–15, and Suzanne Zeller, "'Merchants of Light': The Culture of Victorian Science in Sir Daniel Wilson's Ontario, 1853–92," in Marinell Ash and colleagues, *Thinking with Both Hands: Sir Daniel Wilson in the Old World and the New*, Elizabeth Hulse, ed. (Toronto: University of Toronto Press 1999), 116.

8 Stephen Jay Gould, *Time's Arrow, Time's Cycle: Myth and Metaphor in the Discovery of Geological Time* (Cambridge, MA: Harvard University Press 1987); Zeller, "Nature's Gullivers and Crusoes: The Scientific Exploration of British North America, 1800–1870," in *North American Exploration*, John L. Allen, ed., vol. 3, *A Continent Comprehended* (Lincoln: University of Nebraska Press 1997), 194–5, 200–3; see also Zeller, "The Colonial World as Geological Metaphor: Strata(gems) of Empire in Victorian Canada," in *Nature and Empire: Science and the Colonial Enterprise*, Roy MacLeod, ed., *Osiris* 15 (2001): 85–93.

9 Winder, "Logan," 444; Eakins and Eakins, "Dawson," 230; Stanley B. Frost, "Skakel, Alexander," and Susan Buggey and Gwendolyn Davies, "McCulloch, Thomas," in DCB, vol. 7 (1988), 809, 529; See also B. Anne Wood, *God, Science and Schooling: John William Dawson's Pictou Years, 1820-1855* (Truro: Nova Scotia Teachers College 1991).

10 Zeller, *Inventing Canada*, ch. 2.

11 Ibid., ch. 3.

12 These points are elaborated in Zeller, "'Merchants of Light'," 115–16; Zeller, "Darwin Meets the Engineers: Early Timber Researches at McGill University, 1894–1910," *Environmental History* 6, no. 3 (July 2001): especially 429–35; Zeller, "Roads Not Taken: Victorian Science, Technical Education, and Canadian Schools, 1844–1913," *Historical Studies in Education* 12, nos. 1–2 (spring and fall 2001): especially 8–12.

13 Here again the DCB offers a wealth of background information on the Scottish roots and professional careers of George Ramsay, Earl of Dalhousie (1770–1838), James McGill (1744–1813), Peter McGill (1789–1860), John Redpath (1796–1869), and Sir William C. Macdonald (1831–1917). On the latter, see also Zeller, "Darwin Meets the Engineers," 429–32.

14 Carl Ballstadt, "Chisholme, David," in DCB, vol. 7 (1988), 179–80; George L. Parker, "Armour, Robert," in DCB, vol. 8 (1985), 21–2; Zeller, *Inventing Canada*, ch. 2.

15 John Jeremiah Bigsby, "On the Utility and Design of the Science of Geology," no. 2 (1988), *Canadian Review and Literary and Historical Journal Canada*, 2, (December 1824).

16 Anthony W. Rasporich, "Bigsby, John Jeremiah," in DCB, vol. 11 (1982), 72–3; Gary Draper and Roger Hall, "Dunlop, William," in DCB, vol. 7 (1988), 260–3; see also Zeller, *Inventing Canada*, ch. 1–2; Zeller, "Colonial World," 90–3.

17 Zeller, "Colonial World," 96; H.J. Bridgman, "Bell, Andrew," in DCB, vol. 8 (1985), 72–3; W.A. Waiser, "Bell, Robert," in DCB, vol. 14 (1998), 55–6; Robert F. Leggett, "Roy, Thomas," in DCB, vol. 7 (1988), 760–1; Richard David Hughes, "Murray, Alexander" in DCB, vol. 11 (1982), 630–2; David R. Richeson, "Richardson, James," in DCB, vol. 11 (1982), 731–2; Zeller, *Inventing Canada*, ch. 1–3.

18 Fleming is best known for engineering the Intercolonial and Canadian Pacific Railways, proposing the worldwide adoption of standard time, and promoting a worldwide British imperial telegraph line; see Clark Blaise, *Time Lord: The Remarkable Canadian Who Missed His Train and Changed the World* (Toronto: Vintage Canada 2001); Mario Creet, "Fleming, Sir Sanford," in DCB, vol. 14 (1998), 359–62; Zeller, "'Merchants of Light,'" 118–19, 130–1; Jennifer S.H. Brown and Sylvia M. Van Kirk, "Barnston, George," in DCB, vol. 11 (1982) 52–3; Zeller, "The Spirit of Bacon: Science and Self-Perception in the Hudson's Bay Company, 1830–1870," *Scientia Canadensis* 8, no. 2 (fall/winter 1989): 79–101.

19 Suzanne Zeller and John H. Noble, "Barnston, James," in DCB, vol. 8 (1985), 61–2; Zeller, "Lawson, George," in DCB, vol. 12 (1990), 539–43; Zeller, *Inventing Canada*, ch. 12.

20 Zeller, *Inventing Canada*, ch. 5; Zeller, "Spirit of Bacon"; Zeller, *Land of Promise, Promised Land: The Culture of Victorian Science in Canada/La nouvelle Terre promise: La culture de la science victorienne au Canada*, Canadian Historical Association Historical Booklet no. 56 (Ottawa: Canadian Historical Association 1996).

21 Zeller, "Colonial World," 95–6.

22 Ibid., 96–8; Susan Sheets-Pyenson, *John William Dawson: Faith, Hope, and Science* (Montreal and Kingston: McGill-Queen's University Press 1996), ch. 4, 6.

23 Zeller, "Colonial World," 98–102.

24 Herman, *Scots*, 99. See also Alan Gordon, *Making Public Pasts: The Contested Terrain of Montreal's Public Memories, 1891–1930* (Montreal: McGill-Queen's University Press 2001).

25 Zeller, "Environment, Culture, and the Reception of Darwin in Canada, 1859–1909," in Ronald L. Numbers and John Stenhouse, eds., *Disseminating Darwinism: The Role of Place, Race, Class, and Gender* (Cambridge: Cambridge University Press 1999), 94; Luc Chartrand, Yves Gingras, and Raymond Duchesne, *Histoire des Sciences au Québec* (Montreal: Boréal 1987), 167–79.

26 Suzanne Zeller and David Branagan, "Australian-Canadian Links in a Geo-logical Chain: Sir William Logan, Dr. Alfred Selwyn and Henry Y.L. Brown," in *Dominions Apart: Reflections on the Culture of Science and Technology in Canada and Australia, 1850–1945*, Roy MacLeod and Richard Jarrell, eds., *Scientia Canadensis*, 17, nos. 1–2 (1994): 71–102; Suzanne Zeller and Gale Avrith-Wakeam, "Dawson, George Mercer," in *DCB*, vol. 13 (1994), 257–61; Zeller, "Environment, Culture, and the Reception of Darwin," 95–6, 103–5; Carl Berger, *Science, God, and Nature in Victorian Canada*, The Joanne Goodman Lectures (Toronto: University of Toronto Press 1983); Sheets-Pyenson, *Faith, Hope, and Science.*

27 Smith, *Science of Energy.*

28 *http://www.nzedge.com/heroes/rutherford.html* [accessed 5 September 2002].

ELEVEN

The Seed, the Soil, and the Climate: The Scottish Influence on Canadian Medical Education and Practice, 1775–1875

Jock Murray and Janet Murray

During its formative period from 1775 to 1875, Canadian medical practice and education was deeply influenced by the history and concepts of Scottish medicine and medical training. Many historical factors converged in this period to make this influence a profound one. Scots were then immigrating to Canada, Australia, the United States, and other new lands of opportunity, and Scottish educators, physicians, and marine engineers could be found in positions of social prominence in colonies around the world. At this time medical schools and medical organizations were being founded in the colonies, and Scotland had an established reputation as world leader in the field. This reputation persisted well into the nineteenth century, even when, in practice, Scottish medical training had been eclipsed by developments in France, Germany, and, later, the United States. Those individuals with medical degrees from the foremost Scottish schools thus commanded deference, and in Canada, as elsewhere, they designed schools, hospitals, and medical organizations after the Scottish institutions where they had trained.

THE DEVELOPMENT OF ORGANIZED MEDICAL EDUCATION IN SCOTLAND

Before the sixteenth century, European medicine was open to anyone who wished to offer medical advice, medicines, and herbals, or even surgical procedures. Many who did so had useful skills to practise, but quacks and charlatans also used every manner of deception to take money from people who were gullible, frightened, and sick. Initial attempts at regulating the profession created only two classes – qualified physicians and everyone else – but did not stop the unqualified from plying their trade, sometimes even to good effect. The standards thus varied greatly, and as some have suggested, the person who fell into a physician's hands was the object more of pity than of hope.[1] It was in this context that Scottish universities and the Royal Colleges of Physicians and Surgeons of Scotland slowly but progressively developed standards of education and qualification that put them ahead of the rest.

There were early attempts at universities in St Andrews, Edinburgh, Aberdeen, and Glasgow to teach medicine or a medical science such as anatomy. They did not, however, organize these classes as formal medical training or the beginning of an actual medical school but, rather, as a series of lectures on physic given in the same vein as lectures on the other philosophies and sciences. Aberdeen University was the first to establish regular medical teaching when, in 1494, a "mediciner" was appointed for the annual salary of £12 and the right to fish salmon on the Don River.[2] At St Andrews, Scotland's oldest university (formed in 1411), an occasional physician delivered lectures as part of an arts program rather than as a medical course; this tradition continued for 150 years. John Knox said in his Book of Discipline in 1560 that St Andrews should be Scotland's medical school, and the university was given the right to grant medical degrees, but still it did not teach a medical curriculum. Rather, medical degrees were granted to those who applied if they had received some medical training or completed an apprenticeship elsewhere. A medical degree was received after payment of a fee, and "mail-order degrees" were not uncommon. In fact, for some two centuries one could essentially buy a medical degree from St Andrews – Edward Jenner and Jean-Paul Marat provide two prominent examples, but not all were as distinguished. It was not until 1897 that a formal medical school was established there. Glasgow University is nearly as old as St Andrews, dating from 1451, but regular medical teaching did not begin there until William Cullen was appointed in 1744, and he stayed only a year before moving to Edinburgh. Finally, although the Royal College of Physicians and Surgeons was in Glasgow as early as 1599, its role was simply to examine the fitness of candidates to practice; it did not provide medical education or grant medical degrees.

Medical teaching in Scotland reached its apex in this period in Edinburgh. During the reign of James IV (1473–1513), a patron of medicine, the town council of Edinburgh gave a charter to the Barber Surgeons. The Incorporation of the Royal College of Barbers and Surgeons (1505) and the Royal College of Physicians of Edinburgh (1681) allowed the founders to solidify recognition of the profession and control the qualifications of practitioners within the city.[3] Medical lectures were part of the curriculum from the beginning at the University of Edinburgh (1583), but the formation of a medical school occurred only later. In 1726 four Scottish physicians who had trained at Leiden University in the Netherlands petitioned the Edinburgh town council to establish a medical school. Their names were John Rutherford, Andrew St Clair, Andrew Plummer, and John Innis, and they would be the school's founding doctors. The high rate of poverty and illness in the city at that time and the primitive state of medical practice, despite the earlier formation of the two colleges, augured poorly for what would become an outstanding medical school.[4] Nevertheless, fellows of the College of Physicians were central to the medical school's formation. George Drummond, then the provost of the College, wanted a truly international medical school to counteract Edinburgh's recent decline in stature – the city had lost its parliament, mint, and many members of its aristocracy.[5] From its outset the medical school of Edinburgh welcomed international students. The birth of this school was followed in three years by the hospital that would become the Royal Infirmary.

The teaching methods used at Leiden, particularly the bedside instruction of Hermann Boerhaave, greatly influenced the founders of
the Edinburgh school, just as Scottish methodologies would one day
influence those who trained in Edinburgh and then went off to the
colonies to form new schools and teach new physicians. By 1780 Edinburgh had a growing international reputation as a centre of medical excellence – the city now had a medical school and two royal
colleges, as well as many private lecturers, hospitals, and dispen-
saries.[6] In Britain most well-trained physicians of the day were Edinburgh-trained, as were one-third of the physicians in the army,
navy, and East India Company.

THE STATE OF MEDICINE IN SCOTLAND

From the beginning it was recognized that the medical school at Edinburgh must address the needs of the poor. Two physicians at the
fledgling school took it upon themselves to treat the poor three af-
ternoons a week, and the necessary medicines were provided with the
support of an endowment of the Royal College of Physicians. Much
of the medicine was botanical, and the four founding doctors themselves had a physic garden. Referring to the Faculty of Medicine at
Edinburgh as a living organism, and not just a series of buildings,
W.R.O. Goslings stated:

For the subject I am dealing with here, I would like to identify the seed
with the teaching, its content and quality; the soil with the total student
body, its motivation and its avidness to learn, but also its critical attitude to what is taught; and the climate with the organization and management of the university, both of which are closely related to the
socio-politico-economical characteristics of the society or community
from which the university originates. It is only rarely, and mostly only
for a limited time, that the interaction of these three factors, the seed,
the soil and the climate, work synergistically to reach a pinnacle.[7]

Certain unique approaches at Edinburgh explain how it came to
be regarded as the leading medical school in the world by the end of
the eighteenth century. At a time when many physicians acquired
their training through apprenticeship or a few brief courses of lec-

tures or visits to a teaching centre, Edinburgh had a three- and, later, four-year course, leading to a degree by examination and thesis. Teaching was done not only in the lecture halls but at the bedside. The Edinburgh Faculty of Medicine incorporated excellence in the teaching of anatomy and the medical sciences and focused on care of the poor and prevention of the epidemics that ravaged the tenements of the city; it was nonsectarian, thus attracting students who could not attend Oxford or Cambridge (which admitted only Anglicans). Most importantly, the Edinburgh school took a multidisciplinary approach to medicine; faculty were known for their expertise in anatomy, ethics, social medicine, pharmacology, therapeutics, obstetrics, and surgery.

Between 1790 and 1826, 2,309 medical graduates and 2,722 diplomas were granted by the Royal College of Surgeons. Many more studied at Edinburgh but did not graduate, perhaps finishing their studies and graduating elsewhere. It was not uncommon for students to take the medical course but not take the exams, which many found expensive. As in the past, the lack of a degree did not prevent self-proclaimed doctors from practising, nor did it prevent them from tacking "MD" to the end of their shingle. Others added months or a few years at Edinburgh to cap off their training, as the description "trained at Edinburgh" enhanced one's reputation.

Edinburgh's own renown was the result of the fact that it promised a rigorous, if somewhat repetitious, education delivered by faculty who were regarded as leaders in their profession. Great teachers of the emerging sciences at Edinburgh attracted students from all over the world, as did leading figures in the social and public health movements that transformed nineteenth-century medical practice.[8] The physician-instructors at Edinburgh recognized the importance of public health, observing as they did epidemics in the crowded and unsanitary streets and back alleys of Old Reekie. Their students would soon carry this message to the colonies.

MEDICINE IN CANADA: THE EARLY SCOTTISH PHYSICIANS

The first Scottish physicians arrived in this country with the early waves of immigrants in the late eighteenth and early nineteenth century or as military physicians and surgeons. Many of these would settle and practise in Canada. There were also the many Canadians who travelled to Scotland, particularly Edinburgh, to pursue a medical education. When these Canadians and expatriate Scots established their practices in the new world, they attracted other physicians as their apprentices, providing them in turn with a medical education based on the Edinburgh approach. When these Scottish-trained and influenced physicians formed early Canadian medical institutions they did so on the basis of the principles they had observed and acquired in places like Edinburgh University and the Edinburgh Royal Infirmary.

In his book, *The Scotsman in Canada*, Wilfred Campbell lists pages of Scottish physicians practising in Upper and Lower Canada in this period.[9] Almost all growing populations in British North America were likely to have had Scottish-trained physicians, whose education afforded them prominent positions in both their chosen profession and their communities. In a number of places, especially garrison towns, there were so many Scottish physicians that some were forced to take administrative and sinecure positions to make ends meet, practising medicine on a part time basis. Three examples are of interest:

Dr Adam Mabane (1734–92) practised in Quebec. An Edinburgh graduate, he came to Canada on General Amherst's ship as a surgeon's mate in 1759, and from 1767 to his death was physician to the Hôpital Général de Quebec and its Réligieuses. Known as a man of "great erudition and broad culture,"[10] he was selected by General Murray for the newly formed council and made a judge of common pleas for the district of Quebec and Montreal. Although he was a respected physician, his time was increasingly spent on judicial and administrative matters, and during attacks by American rebels he was involved in raising and organizing the Canadian Militia. He continued as the surgeon to the Garrison until 1783 and maintained his legal and administrative duties until his death. In discussing early physicians of foreign origin in Quebec, Maude Abbott lists Mabane first, as the earliest and the most prominent.[11] He also perfectly illustrates the common phenomenon of the physician/colonial administrator whose education and social prominence resulted in a career branching into many fields.

Dr James Douglas was an Edinburgh graduate who led an adventurous life as a ship's surgeon to the Arctic Circle, the Mosquito Coast, and India. Escaping charges of body snatching for dissection in Utica, New York, he came to Canada in midwinter 1825–26 and soon settled in Quebec City. Some years later he was asked to share the headship of the Marine and Emigrant Hospital, which was then deteriorating in the hands of an alcoholic surgeon. He converted it into an excellent school of practical surgery, applying his experience with Robert Liston and James Syme in Edinburgh. With no anesthesia, Douglas used hypnosis on his surgical cases. He predicted the arrival of cholera and, later, typhus in Quebec and was sought out for his experience, having encountered these diseases on his travels. Subsequently asked to examine the care of the mentally ill, Douglas reported that they were kept in deplorable conditions, in filthy cells, often handcuffed for many years. He leased a large house in Beauport and brought the patients there, gave them bright, clean rooms and good food and saw an almost immediate improvement. He would continue in this line of work for the rest of his career, and his efforts came to be regarded as a model for care of the mentally ill.

Dr James Barry was yet another Edinburgh graduate who travelled the world as a military surgeon and exercised influence in Canada; this remarkable physician was later revealed to be a woman. James Miranda Stuart Barry graduated in 1812, at the tender age of twelve or thirteen, at a time when women were not knowingly admitted to the study of medicine at Edinburgh. After years of contrived resistance to the idea, women were finally admitted in 1869, but regulations still did not allow them to graduate. They were merely granted a certificate of proficiency, until an 1876 act of Parliament enabled universities to grant degrees to women. Dr Barry became inspector general of all military hospitals in Canada in 1857 and head of the entire military medical services in December 1858. In a twist of historic irony, Elizabeth Garrett Anderson became Britain's first officially recognized woman physician in 1865, the same year that Dr Barry died after a long military career. Although rumors had previously circulated, Barry's true gender was not revealed until the postmortem examination.[12]

Campbell provides an accurate picture of the Scots' influence on the development of Canada, including their disproportionate influence in politics, public administration, education, business and finance, journalism, literature, art, and the law. He continues:

There is another class of men in every community who are a class too often ignored, but who deserve more honor and respect than any other – namely, the members of the medical profession.

    This important profession in Canada has, and has had, in its ranks a large percentage of Scotsmen; many of whom are, and were, among its ablest representatives. One has only to read the list of medical professors on any university board to note the great number of Scotsmen, or men of Scottish extraction, who stand high in the ranks of medicine in Canada.[13]

Campbell lists the Scottish physicians who came with the Loyalist regiments, and those who practised in the communities and often took on local administrative duties. He notes that later in the nineteenth century some of these doctors made their mark in other fields, namely Tait McKenzie as a sculptor, Andrew McPhail as a writer and editor, and W.H. Drummond as a poet.

MEDICAL EDUCATION IN CANADA

In the early nineteenth century a young man who wished to become a physician could apprentice to a respected physician, take courses at a medical school, or travel to Edinburgh, Philadelphia, or another urban centre to enter a course towards a medical degree. Abbott lists the early licentiates of Quebec for the period 1792–1841, including many who were born locally and trained in Edinburgh. One such physician was Thomas Fargues, to whom she refers as the most important English-Canadian in early-nineteenth-century Quebec. Fargues studied at both Edinburgh and London, and in 1823 would become a professor of medicine at McGill. There were, however, no stringent regulations at this time governing qualifications for the practice of medicine, and many would-be practitioners acquired their skills under the tutorship of respected local physicians. Before long the apprentices of Scottish-born and Scottish-trained physicians

pervaded the lists of those granted licenses to practise in various ju-
risdictions in Canada. If one could not afford Scottish medical training, one could at least apprentice to a Scottish graduate.

The first medical school in Canada was established at McGill University, where it was developed by Edinburgh-trained physicians and
designed on the pattern of the Edinburgh Faculty and Royal Infirmary. Its founders were responding not only to the need for medical
training at home but also to the mounting number of charlatans and
quacks plying their trade in the cities and towns of the New World.
Two of the founders of the McGill Medical School were already
teaching – for example, Dr John Stephenson gave classes in anatomy, physiology, surgery, and practical anatomy at the Montreal General Hospital in August 1822, and Dr A.F. Holmes gave a course in
chemistry. Together, they drew up a statement indicating the need for
formal education in medicine. The fifth consideration reads: "They
are further encouraged to attempt the formation of a medical seminary, when they reflect that the medical school of Edinburgh, the
basis of which they would adopt for the present institution, now justly considered the first in Europe, is of comparatively recent formation, it being little more than 100 years since medical lectures were
first delivered in that city. The early history of the Edinburgh Infirmary is not dissimilar to that of the General Hospital."[14]

Stephenson and Holmes, along with William Caldwell, William
Robertson, and a new member, Henry P. Loedel, presented the memorandum to Governor General Lord Dalhousie. Dalhousie, whose
Scottish home was just a few miles from Edinburgh, was known for
his enlightened attitudes towards education, and towards Edinburgh education in particular. He accepted the application and the
suggestion that they constitute a reformed board of medical examiners. This step, however, was not taken without some opposition.
There was concern in the medical community of Montreal about the
Britishness of the new board – every member had a Scottish medical
degree, and only two were Canadian-born. A stipulation in the
statement from Lord Dalhousie that the board should be remodelled
and that henceforth only British medical qualifications would be
accepted was greatly resented by the physicians who had qualified
elsewhere. Further criticism that the medical institution was not
associated with any "Seminary of Learning" led to an association

with the fledgling Burnside University of McGill College, which as yet existed more in theory than in practice.[15]

Later clamour from the medical community resulted in a new act and a new board of examiners, who insisted that William Logie, the first graduate of McGill in 1833, submit to an examination from the board. He refused. Following a year of wrangling about this issue in the medical organizations, the legislature, the press, and eventually the courts, the question was settled in Logie's favour, but he had long since moved to New Orleans. He would spend his entire career in the United States, thus beginning an all too familiar pattern in the history of Canadian medicine.[16] Other early McGill students nevertheless went on to build successful careers closer to home. As just one example, Archibald Hall (1812–68) was born in Montreal, apprenticed under William Robertson, and began his medical studies at McGill. He then went on to Edinburgh, graduating in 1834. Hall returned to Canada, set up practice in Montreal, and was appointed a member of the McGill faculty, teaching *materia medica*,[17] chemistry, and midwifery. He also became a pioneer in Canadian medical publishing, editing three early Canadian medical journals, including the *British American Journal of Medical and Physical Sciences* (1845–50).

The careers of the four Scottish-trained "founders" of the McGill Medical School deserve some mention:

John Stephenson (1796–1842) was born in Montreal and was apprenticed in 1815 to William Robertson. He enrolled at Edinburgh, where he received his degree in 1820. Subsequently he returned to Montreal to begin a large surgical practice. Stephenson initiated the idea of establishing a medical institution, and he became the first professor of anatomy at McGill.

William Caldwell (1782–1833) was born in Ayrshire, Scotland, and studied at Edinburgh but received his degree from Aberdeen. He became a British army surgeon and was posted to Canada during the War of 1812. He retired from the army in 1815, stayed in Canada, practised in Montreal, and joined the staff of the Montreal General Hospital, as well as the Montreal Medical Institution, which later became the McGill Medical Faculty. Caldwell was professor of principles and practice of medicine and, unfortunately, died of typhus, which he contracted in the hospital.

William Robertson (1784–1844) was born in Perthshire, Scotland, studied at Edinburgh, and became a ship's surgeon and then surgeon to a regiment stationed in Cape Breton. He retired from the army in 1815 and started a medical practice in Montreal. Robertson joined the staff of the Montreal General when it opened, and performed the first recorded surgery there, the amputation of a limb. He then became head of the newly formed Montreal Medical Institution, where he taught midwifery and diseases of women and theory and practice of medicine.

Andrew Fernando Holmes (1797–1860) was born in Cadiz, in the south of Spain, and arrived in Canada in 1801. He started as an apprentice in Montreal and then moved to Edinburgh, where he obtained an MD in 1819. After further study in Paris he returned to practise in Montreal, where he taught chemistry, botany, *materia medica*, and principles and practices of medicine. He was the first to hold the title of dean when the McGill Medical Faculty was reorganized in 1854. Abbott refers to him as the singular "founder" of the McGill Medical School.

As members of the first medical board of the new Montreal General Hospital – an institution established to bring healing to the distressed poor – the four founders of McGill insisted that the hospital become the basis of the medical school. As early as 1819 Dr Charles Perrault indicated to the House of Assembly that a hospital would benefit the community twofold: by healing the sick and by teaching the healing arts. Three months after the new hospital building was opened, Dr Stephenson advertised lectures on anatomy and physiology in the *Montreal Gazette*; the same ad indicated that soon surgery and all other branches of the profession would be taught. Thus was formed the Montreal Medical Institution. A clear statement in the draft of its founding memorandum indicated that the Edinburgh model would be followed.

LAVAL UNIVERSITY

The Scottish influence extended to other parts of British North America, including, to a lesser extent, to the simultaneously developing French school in Quebec City. In the 1820s a medical licence was

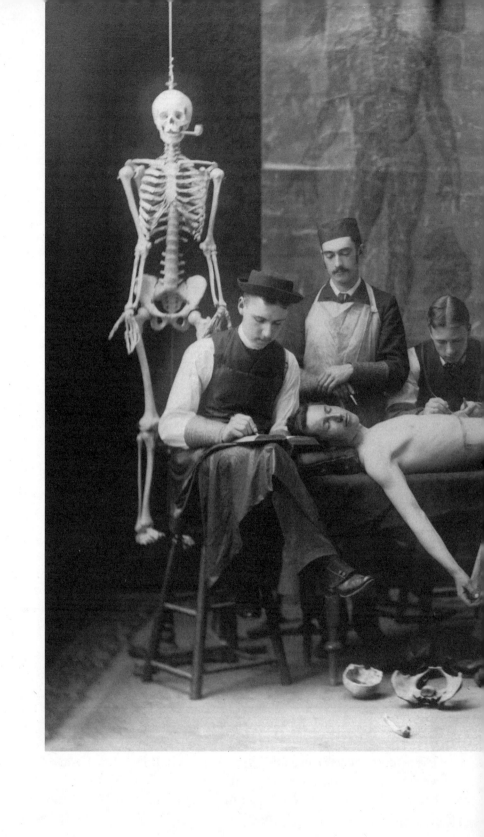

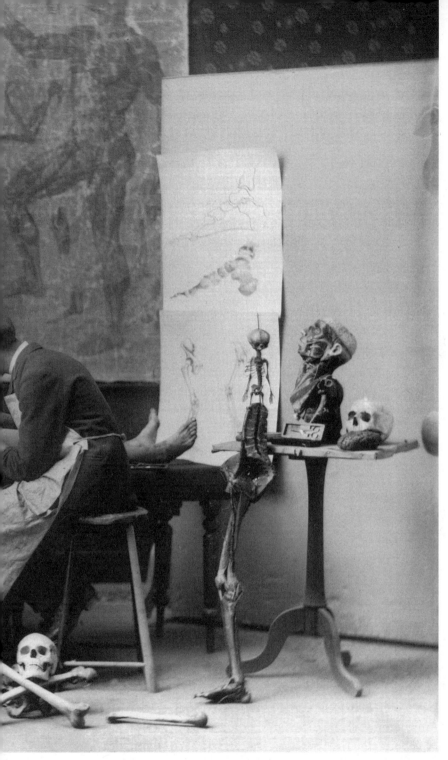

Anatomy Study, McGill Medical Students, Montreal, QC, 1884, Wm Notman & Son. Courtesy of the Notman Photographic Archives, McCord Museum of Canadian History (II-73328).

granted to another graduate of Edinburgh, Pierre Beaubien, who would become dean of the Laval Medical School.[18] The origins of the medical school at Laval were with the 1848 École de médicine incorporée de la Cité de Québec. Although some short-lived medical schools had existed in Quebec before this time, Laval was the only one to survive into modern times.[19] The president was Joseph Morrin, a Scot raised in Quebec who, after an apprenticeship, studied in Edinburgh and London. Edinburgh graduates could also be found among the founders of the Medical Faculty of the Université de Montréal.

QUEEN'S UNIVERSITY

Although Scots physicians had less influence in Toronto and Upper Canada, 71 of the 260 medical men who practised in Upper Canada between 1783 and 1850 had been educated in Scotland (43 trained in England, 40 in the United States and 28 in Ireland). It is hardly surprising that Scots were instrumental in initiating medical education soon after the formation of Queen's University, in Kingston. The goal in establishing this Upper Canadian institution was to create a new Edinburgh University, and this project would not be complete without a medical school. Queen's was in fact born of a desire of the Synod of the Presbyterian Church in Canada, in connection with the Church of Scotland, to have ministry training in Canada similar to that of the Scottish National Universities. Classes opened in 1842, and a medical faculty was formed in 1854.

DALHOUSIE UNIVERSITY

As mentioned earlier, Lord Dalhousie was favourably disposed to creating new Canadian institutions of higher learning based on the Edinburgh model. As lieutenant governor of Nova Scotia he established Dalhousie College in 1818, using the Castine fund,[20] which was under his direction, and with the stated desire that the new college would be based on the Edinburgh example. Charles Tupper, an Amherst physician pushed into politics by his community who soon became premier of Nova Scotia, argued there should be a nonsectarian college at Dalhousie, and some years later he also argued there should be a medical school in the Maritimes associated with Dalhousie. He was able to pass legislation to allow the Anatomy Act,[21] and along with Joseph Howe he persuaded the Dalhousie board to create a medical school. At a first meeting on the subject the local physicians, virtually all Edinburgh graduates, were initially reluctant, since they did not believe enough qualified teachers could be found. A second meeting was more positive, and the Dalhousie Board reluctantly agreed.[22] Many of the first staff of the teaching hospital, the Provincial and City Hospital (later the Victoria General Hospital), were graduates of Edinburgh and Glasgow, and they provided cutting-edge clinical teaching for the first class of twelve students. One, William Almon, a leader in the medical community and a graduate of Glasgow, had first used chloroform, prepared by the Pictou pharmacist J.B. Fraser, in an operation performed within months of the anesthetic's discovery by J.Y. Simpson of Edinburgh.

THE CANADIAN MEDICAL ASSOCIATION

In addition to taking leadership roles in medical training, physicians trained in Scotland took the lead in organizing Canadian medical societies. The most important of these was the Canadian Medical Association (CMA), born in the year of Confederation, 1867. The driving force behind the CMA was Dr William Marsden of Quebec, who had just returned from a meeting of the American Medical Society. On 18 June the Quebec Medical Society sent a notice to every medical practitioner in Canada proposing a meeting for the second Wednesday in October – one hundred days after Confederation – to discuss the formation of a national association. The meeting was chaired by James Sewell, president of the Quebec Society, and held at Laval University, with 164 physicians attending from all over the new Dominion. They unanimously elected Charles Tupper their first president. In his acceptance speech, Tupper said, "our leading objects are to protect the health and lives of the people of this Dominion from the unskilled treatment of incompetent men, and to provide in the most effective manner for the due qualification of the members of a profession as important as our own."[23]

The first slate of officers of the CMA included James DeWolf of Nova Scotia, a friend of Tupper from their days at Edinburgh, and Duncan MacCallum of Quebec, who had studied at Edinburgh and

Dublin after graduating from McGill. Tupper served three terms as president of the CMA and was followed in the presidency by Daniel MacNeil Parker, his life-long friend and roommate from Edinburgh.

CONCLUSION

In the early nineteenth century a Scottish medical education was re-garded as the best in the world, and the concepts and principles de-veloped in the Scottish universities were influential across the British Empire, and beyond. Graduates of ground-breaking Scottish institu-tions, particularly the University of Edinburgh, developed colonial medical schools and hospitals based on the plan they saw as the best – that of their alma mater. They became leaders in Canadian medi-cine during the period 1775–1875, and a Scottish degree garnered re-spect and status that also often translated into social prominence and positions of colonial administrative authority. Canadian medical ed-ucation was undoubtedly created in the image of its Scottish prede-cessor, and thus the pattern of medical education at McGill, Queen's, Dalhousie, and other nineteenth-century medical schools in Canada owes its approach and plan to the Scottish graduates who were the founders and early professors.

NOTES

1 Douglas Guthrie, *The Medical School of Edinburgh* (Edinburgh: Oliver and Boyd 1964), n.p.
2 See ibid.
3 C.G. Drummond, "Introduction," in *The Early Years of Edinburgh Medical School*, R.G.W. Anderson and A.D.C. Simpson, eds. (Edinburgh: Edinburgh University 1976), n.p.
4 See Anderson and Simpson, *Edinburgh Medical School.*
5 See Anand C. Chitnis, *The Scottish Enlightenment and Early Victorian Eng-lish Society* (Dover, NH: Croom Helm 1986), 8.
6 See Chitnis, *Early Victorian*, 9–13, and Chitnis, *The Scottish Enlightenment: A Social History* (Totowa, NJ: Rowman & Littlefield 1976), 129–30, 136–8.
7 W.R.O. Goslings, quoted in Drummond, "Introduction."
8 R.D. Lobban, *Cambridge Introduction to the History of Mankind*, Trevor Cairns, ed. (Cambridge, MA: University of Cambridge Press 1980).
9 Wilfred Campbell, *The Scotsman in Canada*, vol. 1 (Toronto: Musson n.d.), 392–4.

10 M.E. Abbott, *History of Medicine in the Province of Quebec* (Montreal: McGill University 1931), 38.

11 Ibid.

12 Charles Roland, in his contribution on Dr James Barry in the *Dictionary of Canadian Biography*, vol. 9, suggests that Dr Barry may have been a hermaphrodite.

13 Campbell, *Scotsman in Canada*, 391–2.

14 Abbott, *History of Medicine*, 59.

15 Ibid., 60.

16 B. Tunis, "Medical Licensing in Lower Canada: The Dispute over Canada's First Medical Degree," *Canadian Historical Review* 55 (1974): 489–504.

17 The study of remedial substances used in medical practice.

18 Abbott, *History of Medicine*, 54–5.

19 N. Tait McPhedran, *Canadian Medical Schools: Two Centuries of Medical History, 1822–1992* (Montreal: Harvest House 1993), 89.

20 Dalhousie University's initial funding came from customs duties collected at Castine, Maine, during the British occupation in 1814–15.

21 The Anatomy Act was introduced by Charles Tupper in Nova Scotia. Among other things, it permitted the use of human cadavers for the purpose of teaching anatomy. The act was an essential step towards the creation of Dalhousie Medical School, since before the act, obtaining corpses for this purpose was illegal.

22 The board's reluctance stemmed from the belief that the school would be a great expense to the University, a prediction that would hold true for the next 135 years.

23 Hugh Ernest MacDermot, *History of the Canadian Medical Association, 1867–1956* (Toronto: Murray 1935), 34.

FURTHER READING

Bensley, E.H. *McGill Medical Luminaries*. Montreal: Osler Library, McGill University 1990.

Benvie, R.M. "West River Medical Doctors," *Nova Scotia Medical Bulletin* 26 (1947): 81–5.

Birkett, Herbert S. "A Short Account of the History of Medicine in Lower Canada." *Annals of Medical History* 3, no. 1 (1939): 315–24.

Bordley, J., and A.M. Harvey. *Two Centuries of American Medicine: 1776–1976*. Philadelphia: WB Saunders 1976.

Cleveland, D.E.H. "Canadian Medicine and Its Debt to Scotland." *Canadian Medical Association Journal* 52 (1945): 90–5.

– "The Edinburgh Tradition in Canadian Medical Education," *Bulletin of the Vancouver Medical Association* 28 (1952): 216–20.

Gibson, A.D. "Some Medical Highlights of Early Saint John (New Brunswick)." *Canadian Medical Association Journal* 76 (1957): 896–99.

Gosse, Margaret E. "Medical Journalism in the Maritimes." *N.S. Medical Bulletin* 32 (1953): 253–7.

Heagerty J.J. *The Romance of Medicine in Canada*. Toronto: Ryerson Press 1941.

– "The Romance of Medicine in Canada," *Canadian Public Health Journal* 32 (1941): 130–1.

Howell, William Boyman. *Medicine in Canada*. CLIO MEDICO series. New York: Paul B. Hoeber 1923.

MacKenzie, K.A. "A Century of Medicine in Nova Scotia." *Nova Scotia Medical Bulletin* 32 (1953): 290–5.

– "The First Physicians in Nova Scotia." *Canadian Medical Association Journal* 68 (1953): 610–12.

– "Founders of the Medical Society of Nova Scotia." *Nova Scotia Medical Bulletin* 32 (1953): 240–5.

MacLeod, J.R. "Of Interest to Dalhousians Old and New," *Nova Scotia Medical Bulletin* 25 (1946): 185–91.

Miller, Genevieve. *Bibliography of the History of Medicine of the United States and Canada (1939–1960)*. Genevieve Miller, ed. Baltimore: The Johns Hopkins Press 1964.

Nichols, Roberta Bond. "Early Women Doctors of Nova Scotia." *Nova Scotia Medical Bulletin* 29 (1950): 14–21.

Reid, J.W. "Presidential Address to the Medical Society of Nova Scotia." *Canadian Medical Association Journal* 70 (1954): 335–7.

Rendall, J. "The Influence of the Edinburgh Medical School on America in the Eighteenth Century." *The Early Years of the Edinburgh Medical School*. R.G.W. Anderson and A.D.C. Simpson, eds. Edinburgh: Royal Scottish Museum 1976, 96–124.

Stewart, C.B. "A Few Thoughts on Medical Education." *Dalhousie Medical Journal* 8 (1960): 7–11.

TWELVE

A Scout of the Past: Ramsay Traquair and the Legacy of the National Art Survey of Scotland in Quebec

Irena Murray

A Scottish influence on Canadian architectural education and the development of a national consciousness of architectural heritage in Canada is clearly demonstrated in some dozen architectural *fonds* that form the core of the John Bland Canadian Architecture Collection (CAC) of McGill University.[1] Originally a modest teaching archive, the CAC has its roots in the work and influence of two of the three Scottish-born directors of the McGill School of Architecture – Percy Erskine Nobbs and Ramsay Traquair – who, much like their colleagues in medicine, helped shape professional norms and practice in Quebec.[2] Housed in Percy Erskine Nobbs's 1921 extension to the Redpath Library (the original building was designed by another Scottish native, Andrew Thomas Taylor) and furnished with examples of Nobbs's furniture and decorative objects, the Scottish *fonds* in the CAC provide important clues to understanding the transmission of ideas of design, as well as those of architectural representation, along the Edinburgh-Montreal axis.

Another place from which Scottish architects came to Montreal was Inverness. Two examples are Robert Findlay (1859–1951) – architect of the Westmount Public Library and Westmount City Hall and of such prominent residential projects as the Mortimer B. Davis House and the Halward House, both of which are now part of the McGill campus – and James Rhind, who designed details and supervised the construction of the Royal Victoria Hospital.

In 1924, on the occasion of the British Empire Exhibition, Percy E. Nobbs, in his capacity as president of the Province of Quebec Association of Architects, offered a somewhat caustic description of the Canadian architectural profession in a lecture later published by the Royal Institute of British Architects.[3] Having listed two groups – "born Canadians who have studied abroad" and "American immigrants trained in the United States" – he added a third: "British immigrants, the majority hailing from Scottish offices, often immature, and picking up their experience in Canada before becoming practitioners."[4] He certainly would not have considered his friend Ramsay Traquair immature, and besides, Traquair followed a trajectory opposite from his own. When Traquair succeeded Nobbs as director of the McGill School of Architecture, it was largely because of Nobbs's wish to divide his time between teaching and practice, a wish the university had some trouble agreeing to. In 1912, when Traquair applied to be appointed to the Macdonald Chair in Architecture at McGill, a chair that Nobbs had held since 1903, he was quick to state, in a letter to the principal, Sir William Peterson, that "in the event of my application being successful I should like to regard teaching as my life work with only so much practice as to keep in touch with realities."[5] This commitment not only helped secure his appointment but allowed Traquair to redesign the school's curriculum. It also gave him the opportunity to become involved with a variety of pursuits within the university and the museum community,[6] and within an impassioned group of ethnologists and historians who shared his many interests.[7]

The legacy of his parents, Dr Ramsay Heatley Traquair, a distinguished specialist in fossil fish and a keeper of natural history at the Royal Scottish Museum in Edinburgh, and Phoebe Anna (Moss) Traquair, an illustrator of Dante and one of the foremost artists of the arts and crafts movement in Scotland,[8] shaped Traquair's far-ranging humanistic approach and, at the same time, instilled in him the need to record, classify, and analyze his findings, as collector, historian, and bibliophile. Nowhere is this more visible than in his pioneering study of historic Quebec architecture, documented by some twelve hundred measured drawings of ecclesiastical and civic buildings. These drawings, which he and his McGill students produced after 1920, became the primary material on which detailed reports were published in the *Journal of the Royal Architectural Institute of Canada*. Subsequent reprints of these reports in the McGill Publications Series 13 (Arts and Architecture) would also be based upon them.[9]

If character and circumstance colluded to make Traquair a distinct force in documenting the historic architecture of Quebec, it was primarily due to his earlier experience as a bursar of the National Arts Survey of Scotland, a brainchild of the noted Scottish architect Sir Rowand Anderson (1834–1921).[10] As Ian Gow points out, "the idea of an archive illustrating our [Scottish] national architecture" was central to Anderson's vision of improving architectural practice through better education and was innovative in two important ways: it replaced the more common perspective sketches with "accurate measured surveys rendered in plan, elevation and section," and it provided, by virtue of a collection of these surveys, a true foundation "for the idea of a Monuments Record."[11] Recording historic architecture of Scotland was also a way of stimulating national pride and of gaining a new awareness of the importance of built heritage. The present-day Royal Commission on the Ancient and Historic Monuments of Scotland, which carries out a program of field surveys of the built national heritage, continues the work begun by Anderson on a much greater and more systematic scale.

In 1896, while a senior student at the Edinburgh School of Applied Art, of which Anderson was honorary director, Ramsay Traquair became one of the early appointees at the survey staff, thanks to a bursary arranged for by Anderson. His meticulous work, exemplified by measured drawings of the Argyll Lodging in Stirling,[12] was so valued that it garnered a special prize at the 1899 Owen Jones competition for measured drawings.[13] The subsequent publication, sold by subscription, of a selection from some fifteen hundred pencil-and-wash

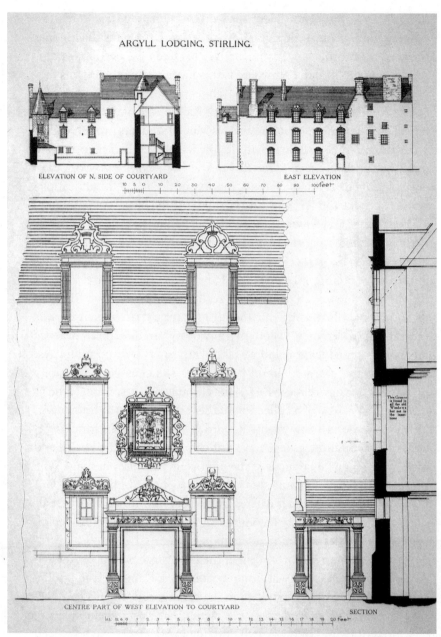

ARGYLL LODGING, STIRLING.

ELEVATION OF N. SIDE OF COURTYARD

EAST ELEVATION

CENTRE PART OF WEST ELEVATION TO COURTYARD

SECTION

Argyll Lodging, Stirling (elevation and details of
fenestration), measured drawing by Ramsay Traquair,
1896, National Art Survey of Scotland (STD 139/4).
Courtesy of the Royal Commission on the Ancient
and Historical Monuments of Scotland

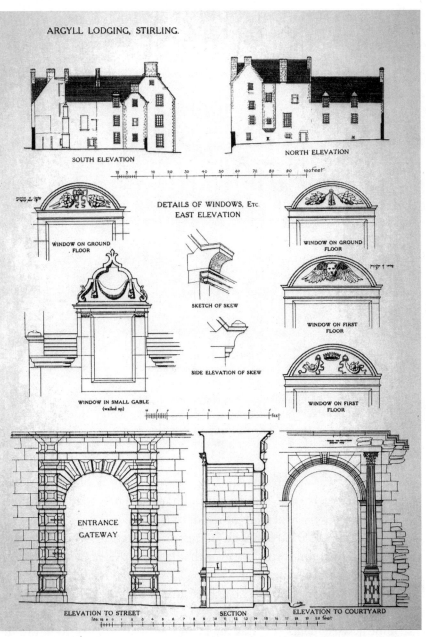

ARGYLL LODGING, STIRLING.

SOUTH ELEVATION

NORTH ELEVATION

DETAILS OF WINDOWS, ETC.
EAST ELEVATION

WINDOW ON GROUND
FLOOR

WINDOW ON GROUND
FLOOR

SKETCH OF SKEW

WINDOW ON FIRST
FLOOR

SIDE ELEVATION OF SKEW

WINDOW IN SMALL GABLE
(walled up)

WINDOW ON FIRST
FLOOR

ENTRANCE
GATEWAY

ELEVATION TO STREET

SECTION

ELEVATION TO COURTYARD

Argyll Lodging, Stirling [elevations], measured drawing
by Ramsay Traquair, 1896, National Art Survey of
Scotland (STD 139/5). Courtesy of the Royal
Commission on the Ancient and Historical
Monuments of Scotland

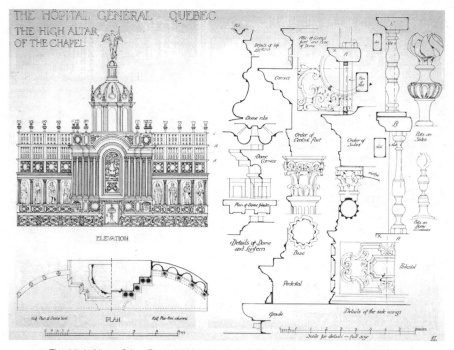

The High Altar of the Chapel, Hôpital général, Québec,
measured drawing by Ramsay Traquair, Fonds Ramsay
Traquair, (6.0). Courtesy of the John Bland Canadian
Architecture Collection, Rare Books and Special
Collections Division, McGill University Libraries

drawings was anticlimactic, in the sense that it took place only much
later, between 1921 and 1933, and had been preceded by disputes
concerning the ownership of the drawings.[14]

What is remarkable about Traquair's adaptation of his experience
with the National Arts Survey is that he took the model used by Anderson and his students, made it part of the McGill curriculum, and
improved upon it by increasing the amount of measured interior details and of photographic evidence. Furthermore, he added important new elements, such as the inclusion of silverwork found in the
religious and civic buildings he had surveyed and which he viewed as
a singular manifestation of a culture in which "French renaissance
art [was] flourishing long after that art disappeared in its native

Hôpital général, Québec (exterior), Fonds Ramsay Traquair
(105789). Courtesy of the John Bland Canadian Architecture
Collection, Rare Books and Special Collections Division,
McGill University Libraries

Hôpital général, Québec (exterior view from garden), Fonds Ramsay Traquair (105790). Courtesy of the John Bland Canadian Architecture Collection, Rare Books and Special Collections Division, McGill University Libraries

Photographs of the old silver of Quebec, Fonds Ramsay Traquair (102914-102917). Courtesy of the John Bland Canadian Architecture Collection, Rare Books and Special Collections Division, McGill University Libraries

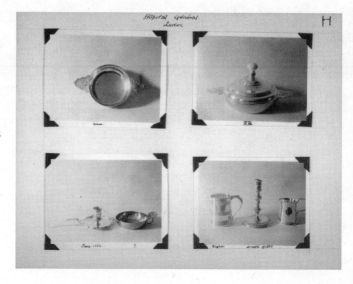

land."[15] The way he developed the Scottish experience as viable model of surveying the built heritage of Québec not only attracted scholarly and public attention to a "forgotten artistic legacy"[16] but also gave birth to the book that remains Traquair's most enduring legacy: *The Old Architecture of Quebec.*[17]

NOTES

1 The John Bland Canadian Architecture Collection (http://cac.mcgill.ca; hereafter CAC) was established in 1974 by the late Professor John Bland (1911–2002), director of the McGill School of Architecture from 1941 to 1972, to document the work of architects associated with the school and the university. The collection now numbers some two hundred thousand drawings, photographs, architectural models, and textual records dating back to the nineteenth century. The records of Scottish architects represented in the CAC include those of Andrew Thomas Taylor (1850–1937), Hugh Allen Inglis Valentine (1904–78), James R. Rhind, John Smith Archibald (1872–1934), Ramsay Traquair (1874–1952), Percy Erskine Nobbs (1875–1964), and Robert Findlay (1859–1951), among others.

2 Rebecca M. Bailey, *Scottish Architectural Papers* (Edinburgh: Rutland Press 1996). McGill principal Sir William Peterson, who came from University College Dundee, appointed S.H. Capper (1896), Nobbs (1903), and Traquair (1912) on the advice of his friend Gerald Baldwin Brown (1849–1932), who was until 1930 the Watson-Gordon professor of fine art at the University of Edinburgh.

3 Percy Erskine Nobbs, *Architecture in Canada* (London: The Royal Institute of British Architects 1924).

4 Ibid, 13.

5 Quoted in John Bland, "Ramsay Traquair: Biography," in *Ramsay Traquair and His Successors: A Guide to the Archive*, vol. 1 (Montreal: Canadian Architecture Collection 1987), 10. In Edinburgh, where Traquair had been associated with Capper and others, his own practice was brief. His most notable buildings are the First Church of Christ Scientist on Inverleith Terrace (1911) and the Skirling House for Lord Carmichael in Peeblesshire (1908).

6 Traquair's role in shaping the Blackader Library of Architecture was particularly prominent. He edited the first two editions of the library's catalogue in 1920 and, again, in 1922; he sought out books to be added to the library's collection and donated some of the most precious volumes held by the university library at large, most particularly G.B. Piranesi's *Opere varie* (1750).

7 For examples of Traquair's contribution as architect, historian, pedagogue, and collector see http://cac.mcgill.ca/cac/traquair. Traquair's professional and personal papers are held both by the McGill University Archives and the John Bland Canadian Architecture Collection, and include lecture notes,

manuscripts, correspondence and sketches, scrapbooks, notes on the history of different localities in Quebec, measured drawings, and publications.

8 Phoebe Anna Traquair's contribution to such diverse areas as mural painting, the book arts, and furniture decoration was recognized in a major exhibition of her work. A catalogue by Elizabeth Cumming, *Phoebe Anna Traquair* (Edinburgh: Scottish National Portrait Gallery 1993), details her achievement in these varied fields.

9 Bland, "Biography," 18.

10 An authoritative history of the project has been given by Scottish architectural historian Ian Gow in his article "Sir Rowand Anderson's National Art Survey of Scotland," *Architectural History* 27, (1984): 543–4.

11 Ibid., 544.

12 *Examples of Scottish Architecture from the Twelfth to the Seventeenth Century: A Series of Reproductions from the National Art Survey Drawings*, vol. 1 (Edinburgh: G. Waterston and Sons 1921–33).

13 Ibid., 546.

14 Ibid., 547. The drawings were transferred out of the school to the National Portrait Gallery, an act bitterly resented by Anderson, who lived to see the first volume appear.

15 Ramsay Traquair, *The Old Silver of Quebec* (Toronto: Macmillan 1940), and Robert Derome "Ramsay Traquair, l'histoire de l'orfèvrerie ancienne au Québec et les archives de l'Université McGill," in *Ramsay Traquair and His Successors*, 48–77.

16 "M.R. Traquair nous révèle un patrimoine artistique oublié," *Le Canada* 6 (31 January 1934): 12.

17 Ramsay Traquair, *The Old Architecture of Quebec: A Study of the Buildings Erected in New France from the Earliest Explorers to the Middle of the Nineteenth Century* (Toronto: Macmillan 1947).

THIRTEEN

Scottish Identity and British Loyalty in Early-Nineteenth-Century Montreal

Gillian I. Leitch

Founded in 1835 under the pressure of political and social unrest, the Saint Andrew's Society of Montreal was an important community institution that played a vital role in the development and interrelationship of Montreal's "national" societies. It provided the city's Scottish community with a stage on which to celebrate its identity and its elite members with a platform from which to promote this celebration within a wider British identity and in pursuit of political goals and ideals. Through its activities, both alone and in conjunction with the Saint Patrick's, Saint George's and German Societies, the Saint Andrew's Society asserted itself and its beliefs to the wider Montreal public.

This chapter analyzes the public acts of the Saint Andrew's Society between 1835 and 1850, focusing on parades and dinners that were principally connected to the celebration of Saint Andrew's Day and demonstrating how the distinct identity of the Scot was integrated into the more general one of a loyal Briton. In so doing, it explains the persistence of this Scottish-British identity beyond the Rebellion years and its general acceptance by the community.

Newspapers provide a rich source of information on Montreal's early British community. They demonstrate clearly the public image that the Saint Andrew's Society members wished to display and the reaction of readers to it, both positive and negative. Hugh Allan's *Narrative of the Proceedings of the Saint Andrew's Society of Montreal*, published in 1855, provides a further glimpse into the motivations and private actions of the society. The *Narrative* is edited, however, and so the picture it provides is incomplete, but because the archives of the society are at present closed to researchers, these are the few sources available for assessing the role it played in Montreal and its Scottish community.

HISTORICAL INTRODUCTION

There was a great deal of political conflict in the years preceding the Rebellions of 1837–38; it manifested itself most notably during elections. The elections in Montreal West in 1832 were particularly violent and resulted in the deaths of three men. They were important politically because the ruling British Party lost to the Patriotes (formerly the Parti canadien), and the events of the election, from polling irregularities to riots, appeared often in postelection rhetoric. A great deal of the tension, though political in origin, manifested itself in ethnic divisions, primarily between the British and French Canadians but also between specific British groups.

One reaction to the turmoil was the tendency to split along ethnic lines and organize into "national" societies.[1] The societies were not explicitly political in nature; rather they were aimed at charitable action. Nevertheless, they were linked closely to political action, most significantly in the case of the Constitutional Association,[2] which was founded in December 1834.[3] The different societies may have been divided by ethnic heritage, but they were united with the same political vision.

Of all the ethnic groups in Montreal, the Scots played by far the most significant role in Montreal society. As Gerald Tulchinsky notes, Scots dominated the city's political and economic life disproportionately in relation to their numbers.[4] Many of the same men who held power in business and government also held high office in the Saint Andrew's Society. As a result, the society reflected not only their identity as Scots but their aspirations to power in Lower Canada.

SOCIETAL FORMATION

It was in the beginning of 1834 that societies began to form along ethnic lines. Following the celebration of Saint Patrick's Day by a group of Reformers, prominent and conservative-minded Irishmen met to form the Saint Patrick's Society, which was the first of several national societies to form in Montreal within a little over a year.[5] It was followed by "Aide-toi, le ciel t'aidera," which became the Saint-Jean Baptiste Society,[6] the only "national" society to form in this period that did not have conservative leanings.[7] In January 1835 the Saint George's Society met for the first time. It welcomed all sons of England, Wales, and Scotland but expressed a hope, in the newspaper account, that "the sons of St Andrew will not be slow in following the example set them by their English and Irish brethren,"[8] advice that they heeded within a few months. The German Society then formed in April.[9]

The process of formation was not a smooth one, nor was it instantaneous. All societies required a measure of momentum, willingness on the part of a number of men to join, and agreement on the type of structure to be used. The Scots had formed themselves previously into special-interest societies such as the Montreal Curling Club in 1807 and the Waverly Institute (honouring Sir Walter Scott) in 1833. These societies were oriented towards Scottish culture but had limited appeal. As a national society, the Saint Andrew's Society was a first for the Scottish community.

It cannot be said that the formation of national societies, specifically those aligned to the British Party, received universal approval. They were severely lambasted by the English-language reform newspaper, the *Vindicator*:

THE CONSTITUTIONALISTS of this city carried out their "National origin" principles, in the course of last spring, by cutting up their followers into squads, and separating them into political parties or "societies," according to the country, they, or their forbearers came from. The Scotch Tories were parceled out into a "Saint Andrew's Society," the English Tories into a "Saint George's Society ... All this was done in order to be able through these Subdivisions, to move the whole Tory phalanx, with ease, whenever required.[10]

The Société Saint-Jean Baptiste was more inclusive of other ethnicities at this time, welcoming political allies into the fold, such as the Scot John McDonnell[11] and Irishman John Turney.[12] The Hibernian Benevolent Society (founded in 1823) was another avenue, for Irishmen at least, to pursue their identity without aligning themselves with the conservative cause. From 1835 to 1837 the *Vindicator* chose to cover the Hibernian celebration over that of the Saint Patrick's Society, seeing it as a more legitimate and reform-minded celebration.[13] It is clear that those who did not support the British Party did not join the Saint Andrew's, Saint George's, Saint Patrick's, or German Societies but chose instead to be members of the Société Saint-Jean Baptiste or the Hibernian Benevolent Society.

THE SAINT ANDREW'S SOCIETY

Saint Andrew's Day, 30 November, had been commemorated in Montreal to some extent for several years. It was first celebrated in 1816,[14] and occasionally from then on, with dinners organized by interested Scots. But there had been a lapse of eight years between celebrations when the Scots of Montreal met once again in 1834.[15]

The celebration of Saint Andrew in November of that year was an exceptional circumstance, since it reunited Montreal's elite – Scottish and otherwise – in an environment of political and social solidarity. For participants, it was a celebration of loyalty. The event was extensively covered in the *Montreal Gazette*, and the impetus of the get-together was described in the following manner:

A Public Dinner, of an extensive nature, to celebrate the return of a day dear to every true CALEDONIAN, had not taken place in Montreal in the last eleven years [as stated above, it had in fact been eight years], but the recent proceedings at the West Ward election had brought together so many fellow-countrymen, united in one common cause, the party to which they were opposed had so diligently and virulently attacked their principles, their country and all that is dear to SCOTCHMEN that it was deemed advisable to form a union of all who professed and acknowledged the same attachments."[16]

This positive and cohesive portrayal of Scottish identity marks the first celebration of Saint Andrew's Day brought forward to a larger public through newspaper coverage. It demonstrates that Scottish identity was not incompatible with a larger British identity, one that was political and conservative and encompassed all manner of groups in Montreal, as evidenced by the convivial presence of the representatives of the other ethnic groups at the dinner.

This celebration of Saint Andrew's Day was considered a success, and the momentum it created enabled the Scottish community to take the next step in March of 1835 and organize the Saint Andrew's Society of Montreal.[17]

POLITICS

In founding the Saint Andrew's Society, its elite members were attempting to create a popular opinion in their favour. As Hugh Allan explained years later, "It had long been felt that there was a want of concentration and unanimity, amongst the Anglo-Saxon community, for although its members on all leading points were sufficiently unanimous, yet the machinery did not exist whereby the views and opinions of the more prominent of 'the British Party' as it was called, could be diffused and impressed on the community at large."[18] The society was considered a mechanism for social and political action, appealing to the "patriotic feeling which societies strictly national would have."[19]

If the political aims of the society were never openly displayed during the turbulent 1830s, neither were they hidden. The reform press often allied the British and German Societies with the Constitutional Association. This connection was easily made, since many of the more prominent members of the society, such as Peter McGill, founding president of the Saint Andrew's Society, were also active members of the Constitutional Association and, as shown above, the national societies had the same political aims as the Constitutional Association. However, the majority of the members of the Constitutional Association were not members of any of the national societies.[20]

There was no formal connection between the Constitutional Association and the national societies; their operations were entirely separate. However, an alliance was formed between the Saint Andrew's, St George's, St Patrick's, and German Societies. Through formal agreement each of the four societies participated actively in the ceremonial occasions of the others.[21] The four societies were significantly connected until 1839; their connection was the most prominent indication of their politicization, since it demonstrated their solidarity and their will.

The societies used their activities not only as social occasions but also as a means of promoting – through social interaction, planned activities, and ritual – a clear political ideal. Scottish identity was closely aligned through these activities with a loyal and conservative political identity. Symbols visualized in the form of banners, transparencies, flags, and regalia highlighted both their unique heritage and their British allegiance.

According to Hugh Allan, in 1836 the Saint Andrew's Society purchased from Scotland transparencies of the Scottish heroes Sir William Wallace, John Knox, Sir Walter Scott, and Robert Burns and of a Highland chief in full costume; the flags of the Royal Arms of Scotland and the Royal Standard of Scotland; and banners with representations of "Caledonia" and of an "ancient Caledonian" (no other description of them is provided).[22] Additionally, the wives and daughters of the Saint Andrew's Society also created a society banner, which they formally presented before the march to church on Saint Andrew's Day, 1835.[23] It consisted of blue silk trimmed in silver lace, with Saint Andrew surrounded by thistles, the Scottish national motto (*nemo me impune lacesset* [no one attacks me with impunity]), and on the back, Scottish dress and weapons. Two male members representing the ladies "resident in Montreal, Scotch by birth, and others descended from and connected with Scotchmen" presented this banner to the society.[24] Their speeches were printed verbatim in the *Gazette* afterwards as part of the extensive coverage of Saint Andrew's Day that year.

Society members dressed suitably for processions and other functions in "collars of green velvet, embroidered with silver thistles,"[25] thus elaborately demonstrating their belonging. Each member also had a certificate that was designed locally but printed in New York.[26] The society decided early on to purchase symbols of membership, and they were expensive: the banners alone cost the society £115.[27] These symbolic decorations were meant to impress upon both members and the audiences at more public occasions the honour of belonging and the power of the group. They found good use in ceremonial activities of both the society itself and its sister societies.

The four connected societies chose to honour their respective "nationalities" with a special day, the British groups choosing the day of their patron saint, the Germans choosing the date of the Hanoverian succession.[28] The societies' anniversaries, as the annual celebrations were called, used three separate forms, or rituals. They began in the morning with a church service, the Scots celebrating their patron saint at various Presbyterian churches (alternating between St Gabriel Street, St Paul's and St Andrew's Churches), the Germans and the English celebrating at the Anglican Christ Church, and the Irish at Notre-Dame Catholic Church. All groups attended the services of the other societies, regardless of denomination.

A procession by the societies typically preceded church services. The societies marched through the major streets of the city with their banners and military bands, in an order devised through agreement and based on the dates of their respective celebration days.[29] At the end of the service the procession assembled again and marched back through the streets to the hotel rooms where they had begun.

The evening saw the societies gather together for an elaborate dinner at a prestigious hotel, in rooms festooned with banners, flags, and transparencies. The dinner would be followed by a long series of toasts that demonstrated to the assembled members and to the general public (through the detailed reports of the event printed in the newspapers) the loyalty of Montreal Scots to the Crown and its institutions, as well as their specific national pride.

These toasts promoted a connection to Scotland and to the larger British whole. They were all remarkably similar in content and procedure to those made by the other societies on their celebration days, doing honour to national heroes and British institutions; the British Crown and its representatives in particular figured prominently. For example, in 1836, the Saint Andrew's Society toasted, in this order, the day, the king, the queen and the royal family, Princess Victoria, the "land o' cakes" (Scotland), the navy and the army, the sister colonies, the United States, the garrison of Montreal, the "land we live in," the earl of Dalhousie, Wallace and Bruce, the parish schools of Scotland, the rose, thistle, and shamrock, the ladies, and Sir Francis Bond Head.[30] Altogether, these tributes reflected the dual identity of society members as Scots and Britons.

CHARITY

Aside from the celebration of Saint Andrew's Day, arguably the most important day in the society's calendar, the Saint Andrew's Society held other activities for its members. One of its most visible components was its charitable committee, whose members were elected in the same manner as the other officers in the society. In presenting their banner in 1835, the ladies had remarked that the Saint Andrew's Society's primary purpose would be "administering relief to such of the natives of Scotland and others claiming kindred therewith, as may have fallen into poverty and distress."[31] Aid subsequently dispensed by the committee was mostly for the cost of transportation for new arrivals. For example, in 1836 the society aided 187 people, many of whom had arrived from the Highlands in the latter half of the season and in poor condition. It was a point of pride for the society that many of them came to Montreal "much in need of the Society's bounty, without which, indeed many of them must out of necessity have recourse to the alternative of obtaining charity from the public."[32] The bulk of the money spent by the charitable committee over the years went to immediate relief and transportation out of Montreal, either to Upper Canada and the United States or back to Scotland. Thus, in effect, they sent the problem away.[33]

In essence, the charitable committee served two functions. First, it satisfied the charitable impulse of Scots wanting to help their fellow Scots in distress: the Scottish community was helping itself. According to Hugh Allan,

Saint Andrew, patron saint of Scotland, surrounded by
thistles and holding his characteristic X-shaped cross
(on which he is said to have been martyred). From a
late-nineteenth-century album of prints and drawings
by John Henry Walker. Courtesy of the McCord
Museum of Canadian History (M930.50.1.670)

the grand cause to which they owe their origin, was the fact that it had
long been a matter of complaint and regret that no institution existed in
Montreal, for the encouragement and assistance of emigrants from the
British Isles. To a person far removed from the land of his nativity, and
at a distance from his friends to whom he could apply for relief when in
the hour of misfortune and distress, the friendly assistance of those who
own a common home, and boast a common origin is always cheering to
the heart and acts as a balm to the wounded spirit.[34]

On the other hand, the charitable activities of the society can also be viewed as a means of controlling the newer members of the community and of controlling the image that the community presented to the wider Montreal society. The society took great pride in the fact that it took care of its own, rather than letting Scots rely on public charity. Furthermore, by sending many of the poorer arrivals on to other places, rather than having them all settle in Montreal, it helped ensure that the Scots were not viewed by the greater public as a burden. This same activity also reflected positively on the image of the society and its members. Every annual report printed in the newspapers focused on the charitable endeavours undertaken during the year. The society placed itself in the realm of other respectable Montreal charitable organizations, such as the Ladies Benevolent Society, and in this way lent itself nobility and prestige.

SOCIAL INTERACTION

Because of its political origins, the Saint Andrew's Society can easily be seen as a political and class-oriented organization that in its various functions controlled and organized the idea of Scottish identity in Montreal to its own ends. However, had this been the sum of its worth the society would have had a very limited appeal and probably would not have persisted beyond the time of the Rebellions to the present day. Open only to Scots and those of Scottish descent and limited additionally through election to its ranks, membership in the Saint Andrew's Society provided a place where Scots of similar backgrounds and beliefs could meet and interact. It offered its members, in a word, sociability.

Saint Andrew's dinners were a shining example of this sociability. These lavish events were highly symbolic, using decorations, ritual, and toasts to reinforce the image of what constituted a proper Scot and a proper British subject. They were also parties on a very large scale, and they appear to have been a great deal of fun for the participants, who were a select group. The all-male atmosphere allowed for behaviour not normally acceptable in mixed company;[35] the guest list was also limited to members and special guests and to those who could afford the price of admission. Guests to the dinner numbered between 100 and 150 men. This did not reflect the number of mem-

*Saint Andrew's Society Ball, Windsor Hotel, Montreal,
QC, 1878*, composite photograph, Notman & Sand-
ham, 1879. Courtesy of the Notman Photographic
Archives, McCord Museum of Canadian History
(II-51688).

bers of the society, which in this early period ranged from 384 in
1835, to 226 in 1840.[36]

The dinners typically involved a fair amount of drinking. Toasts
were chosen with care and consideration and laced with much symbolic and patriotic feeling. They were also frequent: fifteen to twenty official toasts were often followed by several voluntary toasts. In
each case, it was considered polite and an honour to the subject of
the toast that alcohol be in the glass and that a portion of it be
drunk.[37] Over the course of the evening, then, in addition to the wine
served with the meal, a participant could expect to drink several
more glasses of wine and other liquors, particularly Scotch. John
Greenshields, who proposed the toast to the ladies in 1845, described
the atmosphere: "it was the last toast of the night, and some people
were pretty far gone and there was such a noise that I could hardly
myself hear the sound of my own voice. I also sang a song, 'My Highland Home.' The dinner went off very well."[38]

The day-to-day interaction of members through other events such as regular or special committee meetings was as important as the annual dinner. Because of its exclusivity, the Saint Andrew's Society gave its members a place where they could encounter others of the same heritage, make business contacts, and work towards common goals. This creation of a social network among Montreal Scots was an important aspect of all of its functions.

The Saint Andrew's Society provided an opportunity for many of its members to solidify their social prestige by holding office as president or treasurer or as a committee member. J.I. Cooper points out that "the societies served ... a useful social purpose in keeping together the well-to-do, who monopolized the executive posts, and the very miscellaneous persons comprising the 'ordinary' membership."[39] In short, these offices reinforced the moral authority of the elite. The society was also able to funnel the ambitions of many Scots through its auspices and provide them with valuable political experience. Presidents of the society, such as Peter McGill and James Ferrier, served as mayors of Montreal.

BEYOND THE CRISIS YEARS

Many societies that were formed in Montreal in a time of political crisis simply folded once the crisis was over. Such was the case with the Constitutional Association, which formed at the same time and for the same reasons as the national societies but which had no reason to continue once the Rebellions were over. Because the Saint Andrew's Society was based not only on political goals but on charitable goals as well and because it gave members a venue for sociability by providing a social network based on ethnic ties and common interests, it was able to carry on past the initial turmoil and serve the broader needs of Montreal's Scottish community. The Scottish identity the society represented resonated with Montreal's Scottish population.

Still, politics were an important part of the Saint Andrew's Society, and while it was not overtly political and did not play an official role in government, it was strongly allied through its membership with the conservative cause in Canada. The society made one of the few overtly political gestures in 1849, following the passing of the

Rebellion Losses Bill, which provided payments to persons in Canada East for losses suffered in the Rebellion of 1837. Its terms were so generous that Tories regarded it as equivalent to compensating disloyalty, and they urged Lord Elgin, the governor general, to withhold his signature. After royal assent was nevertheless given to the bill, the society's members held a special meeting and in a grand gesture kicked Lord Elgin out of the society.[40] Their resolutions were published in the *Montreal Gazette*:

Resolved 1st. That the Earl of Elgin has so conducted himself in his Government as to insult and outrage the feelings of every British Subject in Canada, and to disgrace the Scottish name, the society, with the deepest regret, consider him unworthy to continue as its Patron, and that he is henceforth removed from that office.

Resolved 2d. That the name of the Earl of Elgin be erased from the list of Honorary Members of the Saint Andrew's Society ... It was felt humiliating to the pride of Scotchmen and to the glory that one of her noblemen had been found so destitute of proper ideas of his duty, as to put his name to an act which, for infamy, is unparalleled in history.[41]

Members of the society considered the actions of the governor general to be contrary to all they believed in as Scots and Britons. Their gesture was particularly cruel considering that Lord Elgin had been a very supportive member who had donated much money to their charitable fund and, unlike other governors general, had actually attended their Saint Andrew's Day celebrations. He was also a descendant of Robert the Bruce, whom they toasted at their dinners without fail. The expulsion of Lord Elgin was a political act. It is clear that the majority of the society's members were conservative men and that their ideology provided an important aspect of their identity. For them, being Scottish and British also meant being a Tory.

The participation of the societies in each other's celebrations, which marked the early years of the Saint Andrew's Society, ceased in the period following the upheaval caused by the Rebellions. Nevertheless, saints' days were still celebrated, albeit without the intense cooperation of the past. The identities of Scot and loyal Briton remained strong components in the celebrations, and the Saint Andrew's Society continued to celebrate Saint Andrew's Day in the same manner as it had before the Rebellions, with a church service, a parade, and an elaborate dinner. It used the same toasts, to the same people, in much the same order, since by now these events had become traditional.

CONCLUSION

The Saint Andrew's Society was founded in an atmosphere of political turmoil as an expression of both Scottish identity and British loyalty. It was the action of a group of conservative, or Tory, men who resorted to unifying along common lines of ethnic heritage. The Saint Andrew's Society, unlike the Constitutional Association, offered its members an opportunity to contribute to the welfare of fellow Scots with charitable aid, to celebrate their customs and traditions, host an annual dinner, and to offer fellowship and prestige to its membership. It remained strongly linked to British political institutions with its support of the British Party during the Rebellions. Some members, chiefly office holders, also believed the society served a greater purpose: that of building a cohesive population under the auspices of the British Party and directing energies towards loyal activities. The Saint Andrew's Society aligned the Scottish identity of its members under the umbrella of loyalty.

It may not have counted all Scots in Montreal as members – it was composed mainly of the business and social elite – but the Saint Andrew's Society, acted, rightly or wrongly, in the belief that its interests were common to all Scots. Dissent in the Scottish community against the Saint Andrew's Society and its role simply took the form of not joining. Consequently, the Society's very public displays of identity were not openly contested in this period.

It would appear that in Montreal, being Scottish meant not only identifying with the heroes of the land, its poets, and its culture and celebrating Saint Andrew's Day but also identifying with the British institutions in British North America, the Crown, and the government.

NOTES

1 Jean-Claude Robert, *Atlas Historique de Montréal* (Montreal: Art Global /Libre Expression 1994), 93.

2 Elinor Kyte Senior, *Redcoats and Patriotes: The Rebellions in Lower Canada, 1837–38* (Ottawa: Canadian War Museum, Historical Publications no. 20, 1985), 12. The Constitutional Association was founded by opponents of the Parti Patriot, including former Papineau associate John Neilson, and had as its objective defence of the constitution and reform through peaceful means.

3 *Montreal Gazette*, 16 December 1834.

4 See Gerald Tulchinsky, "The Montreal Business Community, 1837–1853," in *Canadian Business History, Selected Stories, 1497–1971*, David Macmillan, ed. (Toronto: McClelland and Stewart 1972), 134, and *The River Barons: Montreal Businessmen and the Growth of Industry and Transportation, 1837–1853* (Toronto: University of Toronto Press 1977), 19.

5 John Loye, "St Patrick's Day in Montreal, 1835," *Montreal Gazette*, 16 March 1935; Kevin James, "The Saint Patrick's Society of Montreal: Ethnoreligious Realignments in a Nineteenth-Century National Society," Master's thesis, McGill University, 1997, 3.

6 Robert Rumilly, *Histoire de la Société Saint-Jean-Baptiste de Montréal: Des Patriotes au Fleuridisté, 1834/1948* (Montreal: Société Saint-Jean-Baptiste 1975), 16.

7 *Vindicator*, 27 June 1834.

8 *Montreal Gazette*, 15 January 1835.

9 *Montreal Gazette*, 14 April 1835.

10 *Vindicator*, 9 October 1835.

11 Criticisms of McDonnell's lack of attachment to his Scotch heritage appear in the *Montreal Courier*, 24 April 1840.

12 *Montreal Courier*, 27 June 1834.

13 For example, see the *Vindicator,* 20 March 1835.

14 *Montreal Herald*, 7 December 1816. The Saint Andrew's Society of Montreal places the first celebration of Saint Andrew's Day in 1804; however, this cannot be verified. Mary Johnston Cox, *The Saint Andrew's Society of Montreal Handbook* (Montreal: Saint Andrew's Society 2000), 5.

15 The last recorded celebration of Saint Andrew's Day before 1834 was covered in the *Canadian Courant*, 6 December 1826.

16 *Montreal Gazette*, 4 December 1834.

17 Hugh Allan, *Narrative of the proceedings of the Saint Andrew's Society of Montreal from its formation on the 9th March 1835, until 1st January 1844, to which is now appended lists of the officers, members, and constitution of the society* (Montreal: JC Becket 1855), 6.

18 Ibid., 3.

19 Ibid.

20 A comparison was made between the membership lists of the Constitutional Association published between 1834 and 1837 in the *Montreal Gazette* and the lists of the ethnic societies published in the *Gazette, Herald, Transcript, Courier*, and *Pilot* between 1834 and 1850. Of a total of

337 Constitutional Association members, only 46 were also members of the Saint Andrew's Society, 27 of the Saint Patrick's Society, 31 of the Saint George's Society; and 14 of the German Society.

21 Allan, *Narrative*, 8.

22 Ibid., 7.

23 *Montreal Gazette*, 1 December 1835.

24 Ibid.

25 Edgar Andrew Collard, "The Traditions of the St Andrew's Society," in *Montreal Yesterdays* (Toronto: Longmans Canada 1962), 206.

26 *Montreal Gazette*, 14 November 1835.

27 Allan, *Narrative*, 16.

28 *Montreal Gazette*, 2 April 1835.

29 Allan, *Narrative*, 8–9.

30 *Montreal Gazette*, 1 December 1836.

31 Ibid., 1 December 1835.

32 Ibid., 12 November 1836.

33 The charitable actions of the Saint Andrew's Society as a society were controlled by a narrow definition of what kind of aid they could provide and to whom they could provide it. When the society was asked to help some destitute Highlanders in the townships in 1842, it had to decline, but individual members banded together to provide for the settlers (*Montreal Gazette*, 17 August 1842). Over time the rules for aid were expanded, and more requests for assistance could be accommodated, such as the help to the victims of the *Montreal Steamer* in 1857, who were lodged in the recently opened Saint Andrew's Home (*Canadian News*, 22 July 1857, 471).

34 Allan, *Narrative*, 4.

35 In 1848 the tradition of a dinner was dropped in favour of a ball, which naturally included women, but the following year the society reverted back to the all-male dinner. Women were not included until 1871.

36 Allan, *Narrative*, 8–9, 14.

37 To go against this convention could be a deliberate insult. For example, in 1835 some guests toasted the governor-in-chief with cold water, and others in silence with glasses reversed – a fact that raised the ire of the *Vindicator* (2 December 1835).

38 John Greenshields to Eliza Black, 9 December 1845, Greenshields Family Fonds, McCord Museum of Canadian History Archives, PO11, 421.

39 J.I. Cooper, "The Social Structure of Montreal in the 1850s," *Canadian Historical Association Report* (1956): 69–70.

40 The society rectified this insult in 1972, when it invited the present Earl of Elgin to be an honorary member of the society. Cox, *The St Andrew's Society*, 12.

41 *Montreal Gazette*, 30 April 1849.

FOURTEEN

"In the Hallowed Name of Religion": Scots and Public Education in Nineteenth-Century Montreal

Roderick MacLeod

Anyone familiar with the religious history of Scotland or with Scots as an ethnic group may not find irony in the juxtaposition of the terms "religion" and "public education," but for those used to the notion of a public school system such as it is generally understood in North America, this juxtaposition rings out as something of a paradox: if it is "public," how could it do anything in the name of religion? Even in the province of Quebec, where education was eventually divided along confessional lines, the drive for public schooling in the first half of the nineteenth century was articulated in nonconfessional, or at any rate nondenominational, terms. As in most parts of North America, opponents of public schooling promoted separate religious institutions. In Montreal this tension was addressed by creating Catholic and Protestant public school boards in 1846, but for many years the Protestant board seemed dead in the water, rejected by some as too secular and by others as too much in the hands of the state. It was the Scots who found the balance and forged a school system that did credit to the city and inspired the rest of the province.

Scottish tradition had worked out a happy marriage between the religious and the public. Protestants in general placed a great deal of importance on literacy – not just being able to read the Bible, but to study it, understand the issues, and appreciate the power of the Word. Scots were by no means the only people to promote school as both a venue for Bible study and a vehicle for literacy, but they were a good deal less afraid of public money than many Protestant groups, especially American Nonconformists, who tended to be deeply suspicious of official institutions.[1] Scotland had a long tradition of governments obliging property owners to make regular financial contributions towards the maintenance of a local school that all children (in theory) could attend. This tradition was very much in contrast to the Anglican attitude, which held that education had much more to do with social reproduction than with personal salvation; if social reproduction had no meaning for you, then you did not really need to be educated. For Scots (again, in theory) this made no sense: education for all should be the business of all.

Culture and institutions are, of course, never transferred neatly from one part of the world to another, and the immigrant and colonial experience changes all the rules. Nevertheless, Scottish families do appear to have come to British North America with the expectation that their children would go to school. Like their Nonconformist counterparts who came to Lower Canada from the United States towards the end of the eighteenth century, Scottish settlers were quick to set up schools and hire teachers – long before they were able to build churches. We see this pattern in early centres of Scottish settlement such as Terrebonne or the Argenteuil, where Scots opened schools within the first decade of the nineteenth century, as well as in the communities established by Scots in the 1820s and 1830s at Inverness in the Megantic, at Lochaber in the Ottawa Valley, and at New Glasgow in the Laurentians.[2]

Early Scottish settlers seem to have been more willing than the Nonconformists of the Eastern Townships to turn to the Royal Institution for the Advancement of Learning for help in establishing schools. These settlers were generally predisposed to put their faith in a system of government funding. But in time they, too, clashed with the Royal Institution, which had been formed in 1801 to provide public schooling in all Lower Canada communities but which in practice, especially by the 1820s, was operated by the Anglican establishment and seemed bent on imposing Anglican rules and regulations on its schools. In 1829 the Assembly of Lower Canada began to fund schools, and the Royal Institution gradually withdrew from the business of administering elementary education; the trustees opted to concentrate their efforts on their most prestigious property, Burnside, on which they hoped to build McGill College. The next generation of Scottish settlers was only too happy to turn to this new source of government funding: the community of New Glasgow, for example, received money from the Assembly in 1829 that met half the costs of building a schoolhouse.[3] The most famous student at the New Glasgow school was Sir Wilfrid Laurier, who attended in the early 1850s, his liberal parents believing his education would benefit from a dose of English grammar – and Scottish discipline.[4]

Most Scottish immigrants to Lower Canada settled in the cities, however, and there they rubbed shoulders with Roman Catholics, Anglicans, Methodists, Congregationalists, Baptists, and American Presbyterians. Protestant denominations quickly grew sensitive to their differences and particular as to how they stood apart from each other: one's congregation was like a club or a clan, and one's church an important cultural landmark. In Quebec, St Andrew's Presbyterian Church vied for civic prominence with the Anglican parish church and the Catholic cathedral, each an expression of a separate ethnicity and its place within urban society. Matters were more complex in Montreal, where divisions within Presbyterianism led to the establishment of new congregations and the building of even more churches: the original Scottish church on St Gabriel Street was soon joined by St Andrew's in 1805, the American Presbyterian Church in 1825, St Paul's and Erskine in 1834, and the Free Presbyterian Church in 1844. Montreal also boasted several Methodist chapels, a Congregational church, and a Baptist church by the end of the 1830s. This diversity within Protestantism made it seem unlikely that enough common ground could be found upon which to build an educational system – to say nothing of having to accommodate French-speaking Catholics within such a system. Nevertheless, such was the goal of the educational reformers of the 1830s and, later, of those who shaped the new Province of Canada.[5] This goal was expressed in a series of Education Acts, beginning with one passed in late 1841, within months of the Union of Upper and Lower Canada.

What sort of schooling was available to urban Scottish families before the Union? The Royal Institution continued to operate a grammar school in each of the two cities, and these were the schools of choice for the Protestant elites of Quebec and Montreal. The Royal Grammar Schools offered an advanced curriculum that would prepare students for higher studies – not that there was any institution capable of providing higher studies at this time, other than McGill's Medical Faculty. It is difficult to say if the students at these schools were mostly Anglican, but the schools themselves were Anglican in character: the Royal Institution that ran them was overwhelmingly Anglican, the visitors were Anglican, and in Quebec the teacher was Anglican. The Scots of Quebec did have an alternative as of 1829 in the form of St Andrew's School, which was located just beside St Andrew's Church and was obviously affiliated with it, yet received funding from the Assembly.[6] It outlasted Quebec's Royal Grammar School, which closed in 1836 when the Royal Institution decided to cut its losses at the same time that political tensions resulted in the Assembly suspending all funding to schools. The two National Schools, once run by the Royal Institution, were now operated by the Anglican Society for the Promotion of Christian Knowledge and were essentially charity schools for the children of poorer families.[7]

Montreal's Scots were fortunate in having as teacher of its Royal Grammar School Alexander Skakel, a Scottish educator whose local career had begun at the turn of the century at the Classical and Mathematical School, which he himself had founded. He brought to the grammar school curriculum the Scottish tradition of classical rigour and a spirit of scientific inquiry, reputedly devoting half of class time to the study of the classics and dividing the other half between English, scripture, and mathematics.[8] Although a popular teacher with both pupils and the public at large – to whom he gave evening classes on practical science – Skakel began to complain by the later 1820s that a Presbyterian institution was drawing students away from his school; he must have been referring to the Montreal Academical Institution, a school taught by Henry Esson, minister of the St Gabriel Street Church. Esson had opened his school in 1822 and would soon boast of having 78 students.⁹ As he was known for his liberal theology and rational approach to matters spiritual, it is reasonable to suppose that the Montreal Academical Institution was not exclusively Presbyterian. Even more liberal was the expressly nondenominational British and Canadian School, which had an enrollment of 275 in the late 1830s, 63 of whom were Presbyterian.¹⁰

Montreal had no counterpart to St Andrew's School in Quebec, which was church-affiliated yet received public money. The nearest example was a school adjacent to St Paul's Presbyterian Church that was built in the early 1830s by private subscription and was taught by the Reverend Edward Black.¹¹ Notwithstanding the source of its financing, the St Paul's school probably differed little in curriculum from St Andrew's in Quebec, unless it was more evangelical in its leanings. Black began as an assistant to Henry Esson at the St Gabriel Street Church, but a faction within the congregation came to prefer his passionate "fire and brimstone" style of preaching to Esson's plodding rationalism, and in 1831 this group broke away to found St Paul's. The school may well have been intended for the children of those Scots who found both Esson's Academical Institution and Skakel's Grammar School too weak on Presbyterian theology. That this school did not seek financial assistance from the Assembly had nothing to do with its curriculum and everything to do with the wealthy members of the congregation wishing to retain control over it. Nevertheless, the idea that such schools should form part of a system was gaining ground: in 1834 the minister of St Andrew's Church in Montreal, Alexander Mathieson, called upon the newly established Synod of the Presbyterian Church of Canada to arrange to fund a school for every Presbyterian congregation in Upper and Lower Canada – though it is not clear whether Mathieson had in mind the publicly funded school in Quebec or the privately funded St Paul's School in Montreal as an example.¹² At any rate, public funds dried up after 1836, and the Synod became bogged down in its struggle with the Church of England over Presbyterian rights to the income generated from the Clergy Reserves.

Some Montreal Scots stepped out of their box at this time and joined forces with members of other denominations, even with francophone Catholics, to form the Society for the Promotion of Public Education. These Scots included Henry Esson, the Reverend William

Taylor of Erskine Church, and John Dougall, editor of the *Canada Temperance Advocate* and future editor of the *Montreal Witness*, each in turn the mouthpiece of the temperance movement. The object of the society was to promote "moral and religious education" through a system of publicly funded schools; the result of such a system, they argued, would be that "crime [would] be diminished and vice essentially repressed."[13] The society advocated a vision of moral and religious education that would still haunt the framers of curricula over 160 years later: "The slight differences arising from opinions on the forms of Church government, or the more philosophical distinctions inculcated by various denominations, may be safely entrusted to the Ministers of each faith, while the teacher of the common school, who has a more varied and more extensive duty to perform, establishes the general foundation upon which those distinctions are subsequently erected."[14] Such views, which were consistent with the 1830s educational reform movement elsewhere, would typify modern liberal schooling as it evolved over the course of the century – and, arguably, would characterize Protestant education as it emerged in Quebec.[15]

One set of rebellions later, the Durham Report came to very similar conclusions and also shared the society's view that school was more about producing good moral citizens than about inculcating doctrine. Accordingly, the framers of the 1841 Education Act provided the mechanism with which Montreal residents could establish a network of common schools. They would be nondenominational – which is not to say they would eschew religion in the manner of the American educational system. Legislators took their cue from the Scottish tradition of using the Bible as a study tool in the teaching of such diverse subjects as reading and writing, history, and moral instruction. Many Catholics and Anglicans were unhappy with what they saw as a watering down of their own religious agendas, but Scottish Presbyterians, even the evangelical factions, seem to have required nothing more than this creative use of scripture for their acceptance of the common-school idea – though they were adamant that they would accept nothing less.[16]

Across Quebec, communities took up the challenge of establishing common-school commissions, except in Montreal and Quebec, where religious turf was jealously guarded. Anglicans and Catholics clung to their own institutions; Catholics had even added some new ones, in the form of the Christian Brothers and the Congrégation Notre-Dame, whose deep sense of vocation challenged anything that Protestants had to offer. For their part, Protestants looked hopefully to an imposing building that neared completion on the slopes of Mount Royal: the long-awaited McGill College. Many were growing concerned, however, over the distinctly Anglican character of the college, personified by the principal himself, John Bethune. Bethune was a Scot – son of Quebec's first Presbyterian minister – but had taken Anglican orders and was now the rector of Montreal's Christ Church. With McGill's opening imminent, Bethune was attempting to make it college policy that professors attend religious services at the Anglican Church and not teach principles that were deemed contrary to those of the Church of England.[17] Anticipating an unfavourable religious climate, Reverend Black of St Paul's School declined an offer of a McGill professorship to teach history, geography, logic, and rhetoric (an offer, incidentally, that speaks to an appreciation for Black's teaching skills.) To Scots and those of other denominations, McGill College promised to be no less in the Anglican pocket than the Royal Institution's schools had been, and with Alexander Skakel nearing seventy and ripe for retirement, there was every possibility that an Anglican Royal Grammar School would become the only path to higher education at McGill. The need for a network of elementary schools took second place to the need to counter the Anglican monopoly at the higher level. This monopoly, of course, had little meaning for the majority of Protestant families who simply wanted their children to receive a basic education, but it had enormous importance for the community as a whole, at least as represented by several leading citizens. Access to McGill, and access to the means of access to McGill, was crucial to social advancement, professional certification, and power.

Accordingly, the city's Protestant elite closed ranks and gathered in April 1842 to establish the High School of Montreal. Several Scots were involved in this project, chief among whom was James Ferrier, a prominent merchant whose political career had already taken him to the city council, would soon see him mayor of Montreal, and would later take him to the Legislative Council and the Canadian Senate. A convert to Methodism, Ferrier was a deeply religious man who was nevertheless convinced that education must be practical. The proposed high school curriculum was to emphasize the study of the classics, but also mathematics and science – a deliberate adaptation of the Scottish education tradition; it was also to be liberal in outlook and nondenominational. Ferrier and the others on the steering committee made it clear in their plan that if McGill failed to provide the kind of pragmatic, nondenominational education that the Protestant community required, then the high school could be expanded as an alternative university.[18] The High School of Montreal opened in a private house, but within two years its subscribers had purchased a lot on Belmont Street in the Square Mile and put up a building that was completed in 1846.[19] That date coincided with the death of Alexander Skakel and with the consequent absorption of the Royal Grammar School by the new high school. An even more significant coup was the government-imposed reform of the Royal Institution into a governing body for McGill College, with its clerical leadership replaced by heads of business, chief among them James Ferrier. It was not long before John Bethune was forced out of office and McGill was launched on a more practical course – a process that would be largely carried out under the long principalship of another Scot, John William Dawson.

No effort had been made, however, to create a public school system, despite much lip service to the obvious moral benefits of having an educated population. Sensing that the city's Protestants were finding common ground but that no cooperation seemed likely with its Catholic leadership, the legislature passed another Education Act in 1846 requiring that a school board be established. The act called for twelve commissioners to be separated into two "corporations," one Catholic and one Protestant, of six members each.[20] Essentially this resulted in two boards, and they were retooled as such at the time of Confederation (and abolished only in 1998). Members were to be appointed by the government, and by custom three were chosen from the clergy and three from the lay population.[21] (This custom was very much by way of contrast to the rural parts of Quebec, where board members were elected by property owners.)

Presumably, some effort was taken to select appropriate board members with experience, or at least an interest, in education. If so, the first choice was not particularly inspired, at least on the Protestant side, suggesting that membership was not seen as a privilege. The three clergy appointed were certainly not the city's leading Protestant figures: Charles Bancroft, an Anglican priest without portfolio (as it were) who would leave the city a little over a year later; Caleb Strong, the minister of the American Presbyterian Church who would die within two months of the board's first meeting; and John Mockett Cramp, the president of the Baptist College in Montreal.[22] Scottish Presbyterians were conspicuous by their absence: Edward Black of St Paul's had died the year before, and his successor, Robert McGill, was overlooked, perhaps because he had a long career fighting for educational rights for Presbyterians – which in the eyes of the government may have made him an undesirable candidate. The only Scot on the first board was John Dougall, the temperance advocate, whose campaign for social reform and whose business career in general did not leave much time for building schools. Indeed, as one later commissioner put it, the early members were generally apathetic, "too listless or too much engaged in transacting their own business, to attend the meetings."[23]

The board, in fact, began life "without a school house, without a competent available teacher, and, for the most part, without sympathy from the public."[24] There seems to have been little confidence that an appointed body of men from wealthy families whose time was already committed to the operation of McGill, the high school, and many charitable institutions, would be able to implement an effective public school system. The board was also seriously impeded by having almost no funds: whereas rural school boards raised school taxes (not always easily) from property owners, the Montreal commissioners were obliged to rely on annual grants transferred from the municipal and provincial governments. For many years these grants were delivered only sporadically and never amounted to very much – the board could do no more than pass small amounts on to various private schools in the city.[25]

It was only towards the end of 1848 that, due to the chair's sudden death, Robert McGill was brought onto the board and moved more aggressively to establish two public schools in rented accommodation. McGill died early in 1856 and was replaced on the board by his successor as minister of St Paul's Church, William Snodgrass. He did not serve as chair, however, until after another commissioner, an Anglican archdeacon, had filled that office for an uneventful five years. The number of schools under the board's control remained at two until 1866, when the directors of the old British and Canadian School, which enjoyed an excellent reputation, decided to transfer its administration to them.[26]

This decision was made mostly through the efforts of the school board's (English) secretary, William Lunn, who also served as a director of the British and Canadian School. It also reflected a renewed confidence in the Protestant board as a key player in establishing educational rights for Protestants at the time of Confederation. Not coincidently, 1865 brought to the board three outstanding Scottish personalities and a fourth member, John Jenkins, who, though Welsh by birth and a Methodist by upbringing, had succeeded Snodgrass as minister of St Paul's Presbyterian Church. His term as chair would make it thirty almost uninterrupted years that the minister of St Paul's would serve at the head of the board – a testament to the rigorous intellectual life at that church. The Scots now on the board were James Ferrier, Hector Munro, and Donald Harvey MacVicar. Munro was a building contractor turned architect who proved very useful; he was put in charge of all school building and repairs, and even after the end of his term he continued to serve as the board's architectural consultant.[27] MacVicar was minister of the Free Presbyterian church and in 1868 became a teacher at the new Presbyterian College; a conservative in religious matters – which put him in the intellectual company of Edward Black, Robert McGill, John Dougall, James Ferrier, and William Dawson – MacVicar presided over the board, with some interruptions, from Jenkins' retirement to his own death in 1902.

The board now dedicated itself to the preservation of a Protestant form of education beyond Confederation – an event widely seen as a vehicle for asserting Catholic hegemony over public institutions in Lower Canada. For Scots, it threatened a return to the days of the Royal Institution, when their only recourse was to create islands of independence by means of separate, religion-based schools. Of course, moral and religious education had a crucial place in modern society, as did the Bible, but for it to be effectively implemented in the Calvinist tradition, it would have to form part of civic life, and not remain the preserve of competing religious constituencies. Thirty years earlier many Protestants and Catholics were able to agree on the need for a kind of civic religion that could be taught in schools, but now their differences had been institutionalized, and it was impossible for them to agree on the form this aspect of the curriculum would take. The British North America Act did allow for the effective creation of separate school systems, but within the Protestant camp it was the Scottish notion of an education system that was public, without being secular, that triumphed.

The key to maintaining a Protestant school system was for the board to gain control over funding. This was technically impossible, because it was the municipal government that collected taxes from the city ratepayers and redistributed the revenue to the boards according to the relative size of the two populations. Although circumstances had improved considerably since the 1840s, the Protestant share of this revenue was still inadequate to meet the commissioners' ambitious needs. The Protestant board argued that, as it was not allowed to collect taxes in the manner of other school boards in the province, it should at least receive a share of the revenues relative to the amount paid by Protestant ratepayers, an arrangement that would have given Protestant children a distinct advantage per capita over their Catholic counterparts.[28] This is a difficult argument to understand today, and an even harder one to condone, but it should at least be seen as a reflection of the importance of property, that is, of the old Scottish idea that public education relied on property owners making an obligatory payment for the upkeep of the local school. While this was a reasonable approach to take in a rural or village context, it made considerably less sense in an industrial city where a great many people – a great many Catholics especially – lived in rented accommodations and a disproportionate number of property owners were Protestant. Nevertheless, a distribution of revenue according to how much property tax each community paid was widely accepted, even by many Catholics.[29] To amend this aspect of the Education Act required presenting a bill in the legislature, which was a comparatively simple matter for the commissioners given that one of their members, James Ferrier, was a senator. The bill was duly passed, and the board's disposable income increased dramatically by the end of 1869. With this windfall the commissioners set to work building elementary schools across the city; by the 1890s they had established a network that seemed to serve adequately the rank and file of the Protestant community.

With a larger operating budget and, more importantly, a greater degree of prestige within the community, the school board rather quickly ceased to be an also-ran institution lurking in the shadows of the high school and McGill College. A nondenominational McGill had taken over the administration of the high school in 1852, making it, in effect, the college's preparatory school; McGill's principal, J.W. Dawson, was also the principal of the high school and taught several courses there. By early 1870 the Royal Institution had decided to transfer the high school, building and grounds (now located on University Street), to the school commissioners, who were only too happy to run it as the city's main Protestant secondary institution.[30] Along with the school came Dawson himself, who was symbolically appointed a member of the school board in 1872. In theory this transfer meant that the high school was no longer private, and by setting up an array of scholarships, the commissioners felt they had successfully breached the class gap. There was now, they said, "no Protestant boy of ability, no matter how humble in life, or however straitened in their circumstances his parents may be, who may not obtain free, and yet with honour to himself, an education equal in all respects ... to that which is given to the sons of the wealthy."[31] The interests of Protestant girls were addressed five years later when the board bought land on Metcalfe Street and built a grand new high school with separate floors for boys and girls.[32] Like its predecessor, this institution was by definition a school for the city's elite, and it was soon served by its own preparatory school, which the board built specifically as an elementary school for those students who were clearly high school material.

The new high school also contained the board's office and meeting room, which was very convenient for its members, who did not have to travel far to attend meetings. By this time not only were the homes of the city's Protestant elite nearly all located in the Square Mile area, but so were almost all the churches: Saintt Andrew's, St Paul's (which later merged), Erskine and the American Presbyterian Church (which later merged). Slightly later, the Free Presbyterian Church and even St Gabriel's all moved uptown to where the members of their congregation lived.[33] There is, of course, nothing specifically wrong with

all the members of a school board coming from one well-to-do sub-
urban community, but with so much focus on the high school and
McGill it must have been a constant temptation to ignore what went
on below the hill. No fear of that, however, as the commissioners'
time was increasingly taken up with the needs of elementary schools
across the city, and with the needs of an expanding immigrant community whose presence strained the definition of Protestant.

The boards' vision remained consistent, however – and this vision
was arguably a Scottish one at heart. Just as the wealthiest Montreal
Scots were reshaping Canada as a modern industrial nation, so was
the school board in which they held such a prominent place reshaping education. Through its network of elementary schools, through
the province's leading public secondary school, and through its links
to McGill University, the Normal School (of which Dawson was also
the principal), and the Protestant Committee of the Department of
Public Instruction, Montreal's Protestant school board led the way
in the establishment of modern schooling. The commissioners best
expressed this vision in the early 1870s when they made the following appeal to the city and its citizens:

This wealthy and populous city will deserve to be a reproach and a by-
word in the land, if through the selfish views of tax-payers, it be allowed
to fall behind its sister cities ... Parks may be laid out in the environs of
the city, contributing to its beauty and to the health and recreation of its
inhabitants; lines of Railway may be projected and constructed so as to
augment its commercial prosperity; but there rests upon Montreal [no]
higher duty than the provision ... of a scheme of Common and Superi-
or Schools equal to the wants of the whole population. For the inaugu-
ration of such a scheme the Protestant School Commissioners again and
earnestly plead in the name of true Progress and Civilization, and not
less in the hallowed name of Religion.[34]

A reference to progress and civilization juxtaposed with a reference to religion clearly did not strike the commissioners as any sort
of paradox. This fact speaks to the influence of a Scottish attitude to
education. It was this vision that would shape the Protestant education system in Quebec for almost another century.

NOTES

This paper forms part of a larger study of Protestant schooling in Quebec, undertaken at McGill University's Quebec Protestant Education Research Project and made possible thanks to generous funding by the Foundation for the Advancement of Protestant Education in Canada. There are useful articles in the Dictionary of Canadian Biography on many of the individuals discussed throughout, including Alexander Skakel, Henry Esson, Edward Black, Alexander Mathieson, John Dougall, John Bethune, James Ferrier, John William Dawson, Robert McGill, William Snodgrass, William Lunn, John Jenkins, Hector Munro, and Donald H. MacVicar.

1 For a discussion of the tensions between the Anglican-led Royal Institution for the Advancement of Learning and the mostly American settlers of Quebec's Eastern Townships in the early nineteenth century, see Réal Boulianne, "The Correspondence of the Royal Institution, 1801–1829," PhD diss., McGill University, 1970, and Stanley Brice Frost, *McGill University for the Advancement of Learning* (Montreal: McGill-Queen's University Press 1980), chap. 2.

2 Boulianne, "Correspondence," 271, 322, 369, 671; Gwen Rawlings Barry, *A History of Megantic County: Downhomers of Quebec's Eastern Townships* (Lower Sackville, NS: Evan's Books 1999), 230.

3 Archives nationales du Québec à Québec [hereafter ANQ-Q]: E-13, no. 413: 13 November 1843.

4 Joseph Schull, *Laurier: The First Canadian* (Toronto: Macmillan 1965), 19.

5 For more on the educational reform movement and its impact on education legislation during the 1840s, see Bruce Curtis, "The State of Tutelage in Lower Canada, 1835–1851," *History of Education Quarterly* 37, no. 1 (1997): 25–43, and Jean-Pierre Charland, "Le réseau d'enseignement public bas-canadien, 1841–1867: Une institution de l'état libéral," *Revue d'histoire de l'Amérique française* 40, no. 4 (1987): 505–35.

6 Robert Stewart, *St Andrew's Church, Presbyterian, Quebec: An Historical Sketch of the Church and Its Ministers* (Quebec: Chronicle-Telegraph, 1928), 14–15. See also Statutes of Lower Canada [hereafter SLC] 9 George IV, Cap. XLVI.

7 Newton Bosworth, *Hochelaga Depicta* (Montreal 1839), 136.

8 Elson Rexford et al., *The History of the High School of Montreal* (Montreal: Old Boys' Association of the High School of Montreal 1950), 65.

9 Boulianne, "Correspondence," 412.

10 Bosworth, *Hochelaga Depicta*, 149.

11 Ibid., 120; Elizabeth Ann McDougall, *The Presbyterian Church in Western Lower Canada, 1815–1842*, PhD diss., McGill University, 1969, 213–14; J.S.S. Armour, *Saints, Sinners and Scots: A History of the Church of St Andrew and St Paul, Montreal, 1803–2003* (Montreal: The Church of St Andrew and St Paul 2003), 42.

12 John S. Moir, *Enduring Witness: A History of the Presbyterian Church in Canada* (Don Mills, ON: Presbyterian Church of Canada 1987), 100.

13 *Montreal Gazette*, 22 September 1836.

14 Ibid., 22 September 1836.

15 For more on the evolution of Protestant schooling, see Roderick MacLeod and Mary Anne Poutanen, *A Meeting of the People: School Boards and Protestant Communities in Quebec, 1801–1998.* (Montreal: McGill-Queen's University Press 2004).

16 Moir, *Enduring Witness*, 100.

17 Frost, *McGill University*, 85–7.

18 Rexford et al., *High School of Montreal*, 5, 12.

19 McGill University Archives [hereafter MUA]: RG.4 (Royal Institution for the Advancement of Learning) – c.187/13/1: deed of sale, 7 June 1845.

20 SLC 9 Victoria, Cap. XXVII.

21 *Reports of the Protestant Board of School Commissioners for the City of Montreal, 1847–1871* [hereafter *Reports PBSC*], 5, 15.

22 Bancroft would return to Montreal in the 1860s and serve once again on the school board, with somewhat greater distinction.

23 *Reports PBSC*, 12.

24 Ibid.

25 Ibid., 6.

26 English Montreal School Board Archives [hereafter EBSBA], Minutes, 22 October 1866.

27 EBSBA, Minutes, 28 September 1869.

28 *Reports PBSC*, 16.

29 Ibid.

30 EBSBA, Minutes, 11 January 1870.

31 *Reports PBSC*, 36.

32 EBSBA, Minutes, 2 May 1874. Rexford et al, *High School of Montreal*, 65.

33 Rosalyn Trigger, "God's Mobile Mansions: Protestant Church Relocations and Extension in Montreal, 1850–1914," PhD diss., McGill University, 2004.

34 *Reports PBSC*, 73.

FIFTEEN

Butcher, Baker, Cabinetmaker?
A View of Montreal's Scottish
Immigrant Community from
1835 to 1865

Heather McNabb

Scottish immigrants and Canadians of Scottish descent played an important role in the development of Canada throughout the nineteenth century. Many writers and historians would agree with Pierre Berton, in *The National Dream: The Great Railway 1871–1881*, when he explains of the Scots that the "Irish outnumbered them, as they did the English, but the Scots ran the country. Though they formed only one-fifteenth of the population they controlled the fur trade, the great banking and financial houses, the major educational institutions, and, to a considerable degree, the government."[1]

During the nineteenth century, Montreal became the undisputed economic centre of Canada. The city developed exponentially, it seems, from a small but important hub for the fur trade into the commercial powerhouse of Canada. Many Scots and Canadians of Scottish descent were leaders in Montreal's business community and as such were certainly among the most powerful and influential men in the colony and in the country throughout most of the nineteenth century. Familiar are the life stories of many of these newcomers to Montreal who participated in the city's development through their financial or commercial endeavours; many of them predate Confederation. Peter McGill, John Redpath, and John Young, as well as Hugh Allan, George Stephen, and Donald Smith (better known as Lord Strathcona), appear most often in the history books. Most of the available literature reinforces the popular perception of the Scots in Montreal as a prosperous and prominent group of merchants and businessmen.

Without a doubt, the Scottish community developed an influence disproportionate to their numbers in Montreal. The census of 1861 recorded only 3,235 natives of Scotland, compared with 4,394 natives of England, and 14,469 natives of Ireland living in the city of Montreal.[2] Apart from the successful individuals, however, very little is known about members of the Scottish community in nineteenth-century Montreal.[3] The original research behind this chapter was undertaken in an attempt address this problem and was inspired by photographs held in the Notman Photographic Archives of the McCord Museum of Canadian History.

The collection of the archives numbers over one million images, including about 450,000 from the work of the Notman Studio in Montreal, spanning 137 years from 1856 to 1993. Pictured within are some of Canada's most successful Scots, as well as their homes, businesses, recreations, and charitable efforts.[4] Despite the enormous number of photographs available, it is actually quite difficult to identify an unremarkable, average Scottish immigrant or person of Scottish descent within these files. Among the very few images of tradesmen in costume that the Notman Studio produced is one portrait of a grocer in his shop apron: his name is Alexander McGibbon, and he is of Scottish descent. Further research, however, shows that in 1866, when the photograph was taken, Mr McGibbon was far from being an average, unremarkable Montrealer. He was at that time a member of the Montreal City Council and could also be termed an active participant in the cultural affairs of Montreal's Scottish community, as he would later become president of both the Saint Andrew's Society and the Caledonian Society. During the North-West Rebellion, he was the quartermaster general and chief transport officer for the military forces. He was appointed government inspector in the Department of Indian Affairs in 1886.[5]

There are many portraits of people with Scottish surnames in the files of the Notman Studio, and many of them were undoubtedly not as successful as Mr McGibbon. We are left with intriguing questions about the individuals who are seen posed for their portraits, such as John Ritchie, photographed in 1886. In one hand Mr Ritchie holds a typically Scottish type of headgear, a balmoral. Is this a photograph of yet another prosperous member of Montreal's Scottish community, or is this man an example of an average Montreal Scot?

Two main questions drove the initial research for this study. The first concerned the origins of the Scottish immigrant population in Montreal. Where did they come from in Scotland? Since much of the historiography of emigration from Scotland focuses on Scottish Highlanders, it was decided to dedicate some time to discovering whether or not a significant population of Highlanders existed in Montreal during the nineteenth century. Published sources, the 1861 census of Montreal, and inscriptions in the Mount Royal Cemetery provided some preliminary answers.[6]

The second question involved the social composition of the Scottish community in Montreal. What did the average Scottish Montrealer do for a living? The 1861 census records provided some information about Scottish-born Montrealers, and a brief look at church registers at five-year intervals between 1835 and 1865 afforded a glimpse of the composition of Montreal's Scottish community over time. This study focuses on the period 1835–65, since these three decades represent a time of great development and change in Montreal and of growth and transition for the institutions of the Scottish community. It was in this era that many of Montreal's most renowned nineteenth-century Scottish immigrants arrived, obtained economic power and influence, and began to extend it from within this city.

The first survey for this study was based on a list of immigrants who lived in Montreal during the period. Their identities and place of origin were collected primarily from biographical information available in the Reverend Robert Campbell's *History of the Scotch Presbyterian Church, St Gabriel Street, Montreal.*[7] Of the 113 Scottish immigrants to Montreal who were examined, only 12 percent

Alex McGibbon, Grocer, in Shop Dress, Montreal, QC,
1866, William Notman. Courtesy of the Notman
Photographic Archives, McCord Museum of Canadian
History (I-22189.I)

John Ritchie, Montreal, QC, 1886, Wm Notman and
Son. Courtesy of the Notman Photographic Archives,
McCord Museum of Canadian History (II-81547.1)

were from the Scottish Highlands and Islands (table 15.1). Most were from the Lowlands, with a significant number coming from the cities of Glasgow and Edinburgh. Others came from the vicinity of Aberdeen and the northeastern coast. Because the survey relied on Campbell's book, it is likely to be weighted towards the more prominent members of the community, since Campbell has written mostly about those who held prominent positions in the church.

The 1861 census, which also reveals something about the origins of Scottish-born Montrealers, appears to draw from a wider range of the community. Although most of the Scottish-born simply listed Scotland as their place of birth, of the 1,386 records examined there were 115 separate instances in which a Scottish town or district was named. These records came from most of the wards in the City of Montreal and from people from various walks of life.[8] In this survey, a minority of the immigrants (only 14 percent) were originally from the Scottish Highlands or East Highlands. In 1861, it seems, the majority of Scottish-born Montrealers came from the urban centres of Glasgow or Edinburgh.

A final survey used the inscriptions on the monuments at Montreal's Mount Royal Cemetery. A total of 260 monuments were examined, with death dates ranging from the 1850s to the early twentieth century. An effort was made to obtain records from different areas of the cemetery. It appears from this preliminary survey that Scottish-born Montrealers were particularly proud of their origins.[9] The results of this search were quite similar to the results of the

TABLE 15.1
ORIGINS OF THE SCOTTISH IMMIGRANT POPULATION
IN MONTREAL (percentages)

Source	Aberdeen	East Highlands	Highlands	Edinburgh	Glasgow	Lowlands
Campbell and Rattray	4	5	12	12	19	48
Census of Montreal, 1861	8	3	11	23	31	24
Mount Royal Cemetery	4	5	12	12	29	38

other two surveys, with the majority of the inscriptions mentioning Glasgow and Edinburgh. However, it must be noted that the results are more than likely balanced in favour of those who were able to afford lasting granite monuments with fairly lengthy inscriptions.

All three surveys seems to indicate, then, that during much of the nineteenth century Scottish immigrants to Montreal were more often than not of urban or lowland origins.

Turning now to the second question, what was the social composition of the Scottish community in Montreal? Much has been written on the subject of the prominent Scots, but next to nothing has been written about the average Scottish immigrant who lived in Montreal during the first part of the nineteenth century.

This study of census records uses the occupational classification system devised by Michael B. Katz, who did a detailed study of census and financial records of people living in Hamilton, Ontario, from 1851 to 1861. Katz's book, *The People of Hamilton, Canada West: Family and Class in a Mid-Nineteenth-Century City*, examines the economic and social changes within Hamilton's ethnic groups over the decade. Katz measures, among other things, the economic and occupational mobility of various ethnic groups between 1851 and 1861. He discovers that a low percentage of Scottish Presbyterians remained poor over the decade and that a comparatively large percentage of Scottish Presbyterians became "well-to-do" during the same time period.[10] Presumably, the Scottish Presbyterians were also an economically mobile ethnic group in Montreal. There are numerous individual success stories of Scots immigrants to support the suggestion.

In 600 of the 673 records of male, Scottish-born Montrealers aged eighteen and over collected from the 1861 census, their occupations were classifiable according to Katz's system.[11] Only 103 people (or 18 percent) were classified as type 1, the highest category. This category included merchants, doctors, and clergymen – in other words, the typical Montreal Scots of the history books. A much higher number of people (193, or 32 percent) were identified as type 2, a category that includes clerks, bookkeepers, and grocers. People categorized as type 3 formed the largest group, which, with 219 people (36 percent), was slightly larger than the previous category. Type 3 occupations include artisans and tradesmen such as bakers, blacksmiths, and tailors. The glimpse of the community afforded by the census records of 1861 demonstrates that rich, successful businessmen and merchants did not make up the majority of the Scottish-born community living in Montreal. The census also shows, however, that an equally small percentage of Scots were in the two lowest-ranked occupational categories. A mere 4 percent of the 600 Scots were labourers in the lowest grouping (type 5), while a slightly higher percentage (10 percent) were classified as type 4 (i.e., carters or gardeners).

The urban origins of Scottish-born immigrants and the lack of a large number of Scottish-born labourers may perhaps be related to the extraordinary economic success of the Scots in Montreal in this period. It seems that a great number of the Scots immigrant population who settled in Montreal had the knowledge, trades, and skills that would help them to be relatively successful in an urban environment.

The 600 census records also revealed where the Scots in various occupations lived in Montreal (table 15.2). All the total classifiable records obtained for each ward were examined, and the percentage of each type of occupation was calculated. As would perhaps have been expected by those who are familiar with nineteenth-century Montreal, the impoverished St Anne Ward contained no type 1 occupations, while well-to-do St Antoine held the highest percentage

TABLE 15.2
OCCUPATIONS OF SCOTTISH-BORN MONTREALERS,
BY WARD (percentages)

Type	Centre	East	St Anne	St Antoine	St James	St Lawrence	St Lewis	St Mary	West
1	29	3	0	36	17	14	15	7	15
2	45	13	8	35	27	39	46	20	54
3	23	22	72	25	36	39	34	58	31
4	3	52	4	4	15	6	4	5	0
5	0	10	16	0	5	2	1	10	0

Sources: Types derived from Michael B. Katz, *The People of Hamilton, Canada West.*
Note: percentages based on 600 total classifiable records in 1861 census. Type 1 includes merchants, doctors, and clergymen; Type 2 includes clerks, bookkeepers, and grocers; Type 3 is composed of artisans and tradesmen such as bakers, blacksmiths, and tailors; Type 4 includes carters or gardeners; Type 5 is composed mainly of labourers.

of those occupations. St Anne Ward also contained the highest percentages of type 3 and 5 occupations.[12] Oddly enough, the East Ward had by far the highest percentage of type 4 occupations. This result is explained by the fact that the military barracks were situated in the East Ward and thirty Scottish-born soldiers were recorded as living in the area.[13]

Although the 1861 census was an ideal vehicle for examining the occupations of Scottish-born Montrealers, it was the first one that could be used for this type of study. The structure of the 1842 census was not detailed enough in this regard, and most of the records for the City of Montreal in the 1851 census appear to have been lost. It was therefore decided to examine church records with the help of Katz's occupational classification system, in order to obtain a broader picture of the Scottish community in Montreal before 1861.[14]

The examination of the religious institutions of Montreal's Scottish community was limited to the Scottish Presbyterian churches in Montreal. It appears that from 1835 to 1865 the majority of Montrealers of Scottish birth or ancestry would have belonged to one of the Scottish Presbyterian churches in the city. Because only a small proportion of the Scottish immigrant population belonged to other denominations, their numbers would not have been enough to form predominantly Scottish churches. In the 1842 census of Montreal, for example, most of the households examined contained at least as many Church of Scotland members as there were natives of Scotland. There are only 59 records of Scottish-born Montrealers in the remaining records for the 1851 census. Of them, 31 were listed as Presbyterian; 11 other natives of Scotland were listed simply as Protestants, and 8 others were said to be Church of England. The remainder included 4 Roman Catholics, 2 Wesleyan Methodists, 2 Episcopalians, and 1 Congregationalist.

Of the 1,386 records collected from various areas of the city in the 1861 census, there were 990 Scottish-born Montrealers (or 71 percent) listed as belonging to a Scottish Presbyterian church. Church of England members numbered 102 (7 percent), Roman Catholics 61 (4 percent), and Congregationalists 58 (4 percent). The numbers are considerably smaller for other denominations. With regard to the 1871 census, a preliminary look at 203 records of Scottish-born Montrealers residing in St Anne Ward revealed 142 Presbyterians (67 percent), 24 Church of England members (12 percent), 22 Wesleyan Methodists (11 percent) and 9 Roman Catholics (4 percent). Only a few other religious groups were listed.

Because the majority of Montreal's Scottish-born were Presbyterian, one might assume that the Scottish Presbyterian churches would have formed the nucleus and focal point of a united Scottish community. In fact, the situation was quite different. Montreal's Scottish Presbyterian churches, ministers, and congregations rarely agreed with each other over religious matters, and sometimes disagreed over temporal matters. One church in particular, the Saint Gabriel Street Church, was frequently troubled by internal strife. Religious conflict was responsible for many divisions within Montreal's Scottish community over the years. The history of the Scottish Presbyterian churches in Montreal shows ample evidence of bitter disputes within congregations. Divisions tended to occur over the choice of ministers, and the common pattern in Montreal seemed to be that those who preferred a more evangelical minister seceded from the main body of the congregation.[15]

The St Gabriel Street Church was attended by the elite of Montreal and until 1844 was arguably the most prestigious Presbyterian church in the city. The registers, however, reflect the use of the church by a broad spectrum of the population. For 1835, for example, not only merchants and gentlemen but also farmers, carpenters, cabinetmakers, blacksmiths, and shoemakers, as well as some labourers, are represented in the records (table 15.3). Comparatively few domestics and servants are listed, however. This pattern is consistent with the records of the other Scottish Presbyterian churches for this year and for subsequent five-year intervals until the survey ended in 1865. There were 1,267 records collected from Montreal's Scottish Presbyterian churches (at five-year intervals from 1835 to 1865) in which the occupation of the person was given and the person resided in Montreal.[16] Only thirteen domestics, one farm servant, and one groom were listed. Since an occupation was not generally attributed to women in the church records, the numbers of domestics and servants are undoubtedly slightly greater than the church records indicate.

The 1861 census records also show very clearly that at that time very few Scottish immigrants were ready to become servants or domestics in Montreal. Relatively few women born in Scotland were listed as servants or domestics, especially when contrasted with the great number of Irish-born Roman Catholic female servants and domestics seen working in the residences of wealthy Scottish immigrants. Of the 545 females aged eighteen and over, only 55 were listed as servants. Seven others were listed as domestics. Only 4 male servants were listed, and a mere 4 gardeners, 3 grooms, and 1 butler.

A history of the Saint Andrew's Society of Montreal written by Hugh Allan records an attempt made early in 1836 to establish a register office for Scottish immigrants looking for employment as servants. It was reported at the quarterly meeting in May that the idea had not been a success: "The applications for servants had been exceedingly numerous, amounting to above five hundred, but only two servants had applied for places, and it appeared on enquiry that very few Scotch persons would become servants, and the limited number who did, had no difficulty in obtaining places."[17]

TABLE 15.3
OCCUPATIONS OF MALES IN THE ST GABRIEL STREET
CHURCH RECORDS, 1835

Type 1	Type 2	Type 3	Type 4	Type 5
Forwarder, 1	Farmer, 10	Blacksmith, 4	Boatman, 1	Labourer, 13
Gentleman, 7	Founder, 1	Butcher, 1	Carter, 1	
Merchant, 7	Grocer, 1	Cabinetmaker, 4	Gardener, 2	
Surgeon, 1	Tavern Keeper, 2	Carpenter, 9	Quarrier, 1	
		Chandler, 2		
		Cooper, 2		
		Engineer, 2		
		Engraver, 1		
		Joiner, 2		
		Shoemaker, 7		
		Tailor, 2		
Total, 16 or 17%	Total, 14 or 15%	Total, 44 or 48%	Total, 5 or 6%	14%

Sources: As in table 15.2, the occupational categories were developed by Michael B. Katz in *The People of Hamilton, Canada West*. This table gives further examples of the types of occupations that Katz placed in each category.
Note: This table shows the type of information available in church records for the study of the Scottish Presbyterian community in Montreal. Ninety-two church records were gathered from a total of 235 records in which the people were not known to be from outside Montreal. Not all church records gave information on the person's occupation. The records were also edited to remove double and triple listings of one individual in the same year.

In "Varieties of Scottish Emigration," Eric Richards provides a possible explanation for the apparent reluctance of Scottish emigrants to become servants. He suggests that by this period, Scottish emigration had become more a "migration of rising expectations" and less an exodus fuelled by desperation.[18] This may well explain why the glimpse of the composition of the Scottish community in Montreal afforded by Presbyterian Church registers, as well as the 1861 census, shows a relative absence of servants and domestics from 1835 through to 1865.

Over the thirty-year period, some Montreal churches seem to show a predominance of one of Katz's occupational types, and in one instance at least, one type of occupation. In 1835, for example, the Secession Church, which appears to have been the smallest congregation of Montreal's four Scottish Presbyterian churches, had a relatively high percentage of carpenters or joiners in the register.[19] Seven carpenters and one joiner are listed, combining to form 23 percent of the occupations in that year. There are only a few representatives of the upper classes (a merchant, a lawyer and a surgeon), and there are no labourers. The names in the Secession Church records are almost entirely those of tradesmen.

In his *History of the Scottish People, 1560–1830*, T.C. Smout explains that in Scotland, the Secession Churches "drew their main support from lower down the social scale than the ministers of the establishment."[20] Certainly this trend appears to be reflected in Montreal's Secession Church (later known as the Erskine Church), as the records reveal a similar profile, with a high percentage of type 3 occupations at each five-year interval up to and including 1845 (table 15.4).

A comparison of the occupational profiles of Montreal's four Presbyterian churches in 1835 is revealing of the Scottish community as a whole, as well as of the characteristics of the individual churches (table 15.5). St Gabriel Street, St Andrew's and St Paul's, all affiliated with the Established Church of Scotland, have a similarly high percentage of type 1 occupations, while the Secession Church shows an extremely high percentage of type 3 occupations. The percentages for types 4 and 5 appear to be comparatively low in all four churches. This data is derived from a preliminary study of the baptisms, marriages, and deaths in a given year. Ideally, the records for two or

TABLE 15.4
OCCUPATIONS AT MONTREAL'S SECESSION CHURCH,
1835–65 (percentages)

Type	1835	1840	1845	1850	1855	1860	1865
1	9	10	2	8	23	8	18
2	23	15	19	57	27	40	34
3	68	55	65	33	38	46	38
4	0	15	2	2	7	3	5
5	0	5	12	0	5	3	5

Note: Types derived from Michael B. Katz, *The People of Hamilton, Canada West.* See table 15.3 for occupations representative of each type.

TABLE 15.5
OCCUPATIONAL PROFILES OF MONTREAL'S
PRESBYTERIAN CHURCHES, 1835 (percentages)

Type	St Gabriel	St Andrew's	St Paul's	Secession
1	17	15	18	9
2	15	33	37	23
3	48	46	23	68
4	6	6	8	0
5	14	0	14	0

Note: Types derived from Michael B. Katz, *The People of Hamilton, Canada West.* See table 15.3 for occupations representative of each type.

more consecutive years would be combined in order to even out any potential imbalances. It was decided, nevertheless, to speculate on the small glimpse of the community that was afforded by these church records.

Another comparison of the occupational profiles of Montreal's Presbyterian churches was made for the year 1845. At that time, Montreal's four Scottish Presbyterian churches had been joined by a fifth, called the Free Church or the Côté Street Church.[21] The St Gabriel Street Church had also become a Free Church at that time.[22] When the 1845 church records are examined using Katz's occupational classification system, the two Free Church congregations appear to have had a similar social composition. Fifty-seven percent of the classifiable church records revealed type 3 occupations (tradesmen, such as carpenters or blacksmiths) in both the St Gabriel Street and Côté Street Free Churches. St Andrew's and St Paul's Church records each show far fewer tradesmen, with 21 percent and 22 percent, respectively, classified as type 3. St Andrew's and St Paul's also have higher percentages of type 1 and type 2 occupations than do the two Free Churches. The 1845 church records do suggest that the Free Church tended to attract more people of lower occupational rank or status than the Church of Scotland. The occupational profiles of the two Free Church congregations do appear more like that of the Secession Church, which also had a high percentage of tradesmen in 1845 (65 percent).

Reverend Campbell notes that St Gabriel lost old members of the congregation to St Andrew's Church, which became "what St Gabriel Street Church had unquestionably been before, the Scotch church of Montreal, by way of eminence."[23] A look at the church records does confirm that St Andrew's did seem to benefit from the disruption. The records for St Andrew's for 1845 show a large peak in numbers, while the records for St Gabriel Street show a dramatic drop. After 1845, the St Andrew's registers maintain, on average, a larger number of records of baptism, marriage, and death per year than any other Scottish Presbyterian church in Montreal, until 1864.

The late 1850s and early 1860s seem to have been a time of renewed growth within the churches of Montreal's Scottish Presbyterian community if the increase in the total number of churches is considered an indication of the growth of the congregations. Industrialization of the city meant that the population was increasing in new areas of the town. Two new churches were founded to serve Montreal's growing working-class districts of Point Saint Charles and the Saint Joseph suburbs. It may be reasonable to assume that these new churches would have served a large Irish-born population of workers on the Lachine Canal in this period, given the low percentage of Scottish-born labourers and residents of the St Anne Ward in the 1861 census.

The period from 1835 to 1865 was characterized by an increase in population and the development of industry and commerce in the City of Montreal. The growth of Montreal's Scottish community, as reflected in the establishment of Presbyterian churches, does not seem to have occurred at an even pace. In the early 1830s the number of Scottish Presbyterian churches in Montreal had doubled, presumably because of a substantial increase in the population. Then, the Scottish Presbyterian community appears to have slowed its development through the 1840s and early 1850s. One new Free Church congregation was formed in Montreal in 1844. In the late 1850s, another period of growth seems evident, mainly in the new working-class communities in the industrializing areas near the Lachine Canal, where the two new churches were founded, at first as mission stations.

It is important to mention that information gleaned from church records shows a slightly different picture of the population than do the census records in which the Scottish-born were selected. The majority of the Scottish-born in the census were Presbyterian, but Presbyterians in the church records certainly include not only Scottish-born individuals but also Canadians of Scottish and Irish descent and others such as Irish-born Montrealers. It should also be noted that the growth and change in the Scottish community, as seen in the founding of new churches, could also have been influenced by additions to the population of people who were not Scottish-born Presbyterians.

Even a brief examination of church records and the 1861 census such as was afforded by this study demonstrates that the Scottish community was much more complex than is generally acknowledged in the available literature. It was composed of people from various occupations and social levels. Over the thirty-year period chosen for this study, the occupational profile of each church, as seen through the church registers, shows many variations. The growth in the number of Presbyterian churches appears to have coincided with the growth of the Scottish community and is likely to have been at least partly due to the arrival of Scottish immigrants to the city. The church records certainly demonstrate that Montreal's Presbyterian churches were composed of people from different occupational and social strata. Census records indicate that in 1861 many of Montreal's Scots lived in the St Antoine district, while St Anne Ward was practically empty of Scottish-born residents. The census and church records both show clearly that the Scots in Montreal were not all rich merchants and businessmen, contrary to the conclusion that might easily be drawn from so many sources. Relatively few members of the Scottish community were able to build a commercial empire and maintain a huge house in the Square Mile. The average Scottish immigrant in Montreal was much more likely to be a clerk than a merchant, or a carpenter than a manufacturer. There were, however, relatively few Scottish-born servants, labourers, and workers at the lower end of the social scale.

Census records and other sources also suggest that immigrant Scots in Montreal tended to be of urban and Lowland origins. Comparatively few Highlanders seem to have settled in the city. It is not yet possible to quantify the success of Scottish immigrants in Montreal. Further studies similar to Katz's study of Hamilton would be useful in this regard. It is certain, however, that many Scottish immigrants were highly successful in their new home.

NOTES

1 Pierre Berton, *The National Dream: The Great Railway, 1871–1881* (Toronto: McClelland and Stewart 1970), 319.
2 Mrs R.W.S. MacKay, *MacKay's Montreal Directory* (Montreal: Owler & Stevenson 1861), 227.
3 Lynda Price's *Introduction to the Social History of the Scots in Quebec, 1780–1840* is the only modern published work to include a brief examination of Montreal's Scottish community. It is also one of the few sources of information on urban Scottish communities in Canada. Unfortunately, her

compilation is quite limited on the subject of the Scots in Montreal. The book makes it clear that there were decided class divisions within the Scottish community, but major errors in the footnotes and appendices make the text difficult to follow.

4 The McCord Museum website (www.mccord-museum.qc.ca) provides access to over 45,500 images from the Museum's Notman Photographic Archives.

5 E. Brian Titley, "Alexander McGibbon," in *The Dictionary of Canadian Biography*, vol. 13, 1901–1910, Ramsay Cook, general ed. (Toronto: University of Toronto Press 1994), 638.

6 Mount Royal Cememtery, founded in 1852, was Montreal's major Protestant cemetery.

7 A few more names were collected from W.J. Rattray's *The Scot in British North America*.

8 A complete survey of the records for the City of Montreal in the 1861 census was next to impossible because of time constraints; however, a fairly large representative sample was deemed necessary for this preliminary survey (in this case, one-third of the 3,235 Scots listed in the census). In choosing records of Scottish-born residents of Montreal, an attempt was made to survey each district in Montreal, in order to obtain records of Scots of varying socioeconomic levels, beginning at the first record for the area and ending when it was felt that enough Scottish-born residents had been collected. Some large districts or wards, such as St Anne Ward, surprisingly, did not yield very many Scots at all. In this case the entire ward was surveyed, yielding fifty-two usable records (males aged eighteen and over with an occupation listed). In other cases, such as Centre, East, and West Wards, the districts themselves were very small, remaining from the time Montreal was a walled city, and were easily searched in their entirety. Other wards, such as St Antoine and St Lawrence, were very large, and contained many Scots. In these cases, the search was abandoned after over 300 records were obtained in each, as it was felt that there was a fair sampling made of the different streets in the area, from the east to the west end of the ward. In St Antoine, the records may be biased towards the more average resident, as the records surveyed tended to be further south than the mountainside homes of the more privileged Square Mile residents. In other large wards, less densely populated with Scots, at least 100 records were collected from each (St James and St Mary).

9 More often than not, it seemed, if a town or district of birth was named, it was the monument of a Scot.

10 Michael B. Katz, *The People of Hamilton, Canada West: Family and Class in a Mid-Nineteenth-Century City* (Cambridge, MA: Harvard University Press 1975), 165.

11 Occupations that could not be classified included those not listed under Katz's system (e.g., storeman), as well as those Katz felt were unclassifiable, such as servants' and women's occupations.

12 A preliminary survey of some 200 records was undertaken for St Anne Ward for 1871 for purposes of comparison in this paper. There was still a high percentage of persons with type 3 occupations, but a lower percentage with type

5. There seems to have been a considerable increase in the number of Scots living in this area by 1871, however, since 200 records were collected quickly and without any difficulty. In contrast, only 123 records were collected from the entire St Anne Ward in 1861.

13 Some of the soldiers were recorded as living in the Montreal Barracks, others in the Quebec Gate Barracks, and others on St Helen's Island.

14 Any doubles of the same person found in a given year (such as when the father's name and occupation appears with the birth and burial of same child) were eliminated, so as to try to keep the records from becoming wrongly weighted.

15 For more information on the history of the St Gabriel Street Church and the congregations formed from it, see Reverend Robert Campbell's *History of the Scotch Presbyterian Church, Saint Gabriel Street, Montreal.*

16 Or more precisely, the person was presumed to have lived in Montreal when no other town or city of residence was listed.

17 Hugh Allan, *St Andrew's Society of Montreal* (Montreal: St Andrew's Society 1844; reprint 1856), 13.

18 Eric Richards, "Varieties of Scottish Emigration," 478.

19 The register contains only forty-one records (twenty-six baptisms, six burials, and nine marriages).

20 T.C. Smout, *A History of the Scottish People, 1560–1830,* 221.

21 For a discussion of the Free Church in Canada, see Richard William Vaudry, *The Free Church in Victorian Canada, 1844–1861.*

22 Reverend Robert Campbell, in his *History of the Scotch Presbyterian Church*, details the events of 1843–44 and their impact on the St Gabriel Street Church.

23 Campbell, *A History of the Scotch Presbyterian Church*, 509.

Acknowledgments

This book sprang from a colloquium held in May 2002 at the Mc-Cord Museum of Canadian History in Montreal. The event, entitled Character and Circumstance: The Scots in Montreal and Canada, would not have been possible without the support of the Social Sciences and Humanities Research Council of Canada and Le Ministère des Relations internationales du Québec, as well as the efforts of our co-organizers, Victoria Dickenson, Executive Director of the McCord Museum, Suzanne Morton of McGill University, and Claude Morin of the Université de Montréal. We would like to thank all the conference participants for their learned papers and lively debates and discussions, all which fed into this volume directly or indirectly. We are grateful to Dr Dickenson for committing the McCord to this book project during the colloquium and to the Canadian Museum of Civilization for its cooperation and support. Moira McCaffrey, Director of Exhibitions and Research at the McCord, kept the project alive for three years, and Melanie Martens brought her dedication, tact, and editorial talents to the preparation of the manuscript. We appreciate the willingness of McGill-Queen's University Press, particularly Phil Cercone, to undertake this publication, and we thank the staff of the press and two anonymous referees for their advice and help. Any flaws that remain are the responsibility of the contributors and the editors.

We are of course most grateful to our contributors, without whom the book would not exist. They demonstrated patience and precision at every stage throughout the long evolution of the manuscript. To them we say a heartfelt *móran taing dhuibh*.

Contributors

EDWARD J. (TED) COWAN, Professor of Scottish History,
University of Glasgow

J.M. BUMSTED, Fellow of St John's College and Professor of History,
University of Manitoba

GEORGE R. DALGLEISH, Curator of Scottish Decorative Arts,
National Museums of Scotland

MARJORY HARPER, Reader in History, University of Aberdeen

H.P. KLEPAK, Professor of History and Warfare Studies, Royal
Military College of Canada

GILLIAN I. LEITCH, doctoral candidate, History, Université
de Montréal

RODERICK MacLEOD, Faculty Lecturer and Director of the Quebec Protestant Education Research Project, Department of History, McGill University

DOUGLAS McCALLA, Canada Research Chair in Rural History, University of Guelph

HEATHER McNABB, Cataloguer and Technician, McCord Museum of Canadian History

IRENA MURRAY, Director and Sir Banister Fletcher Librarian, British Architectural Library, Royal Institute of British Architects

JANET MURRAY, researcher and author, Halifax

JOCK MURRAY, (MD), Professor Emeritus, Humanities and Medicine, Dalhousie University

CATH OBERHOLTZER, Conjunct Professor, Department of Anthropology, Trent University

PETER E. RIDER, Atlantic Provinces Historian and Curator, Canadian Museum of Civilization

EILEEN STACK, Communications Officer, McCord Museum of Canadian History

RENÉ VILLENEUVE, Associate Curator of Early Canadian Art, National Gallery of Canada

SUZANNE ZELLER, Associate Professor of History, Wilfrid Laurier University

Index

Italicized locators denote illustrations and tables. Locators that contain *n* denote endnotes. Place names with no country specified are in Canada.

Abbott, Maude, 188, 190
Aberdeen, Scotland, 24–6, 27, 33, 244, 249. *See also* University of Aberdeen
Aberfeldy, Scotland, 18n13
Aboriginal peoples. *See* Native peoples
Aboyne, Scotland, 26
Acheson, T.W., 77, 82, 83, 85, 95n20
advertising, 12, 26–7, 28, 157, 163n27
agriculture. *See* farmers, land

Aitken, Max, xviii, 82
Alexander, William, 4–5, 14
Allan, Hugh Jr, *158*, 160
Allan, Hugh Sr, 77, 160, 212, 215, 216, 218–19
Allan Line, 134
Almon, William, 197
American and British Associations for the Advancement of Science, 177
American Civil War, 46–8
American War of Independence, 44, 45, 125
Anatomy Act, 197, 199n21
Anchor Line, 32
Anglicans: education, 228, 230, 232, 233, 240n1; in Montreal, 142–3, 233
anthropology. *See* ethnography

apprentices: medical, 186, 188, 190–1, 193; of merchants, 76, 78, 85
Arbroath, Scotland, 125, 137
Archibald, John Smith, 209n1
architects, 154, 201–2, 209n1, 236
architecture: Quebec, 201–3, 206–9; Scottish style, 34, 36
Arctic, 6, 7, 14–15
Argenteuil, 228
Argyll and Sutherland Highlanders of Canada, 50
Armour, James S.S., 148n11
Armour, Robert Jr, 173–4
Armour, Robert Sr, 173
Arnoldi, Peter, 141
assisted passage, 29
associations, 174, 176, 177, 202, 212–15. *See also* cultural associations, emigration societies, historical societies, medical associations, "national" societies, sports clubs
Assynt, Scotland, 35
Astor, John Jacob, 63–4, 67
Atlantic Canada 56, 196–7
Atlantic crossing, 23–4, 26, 29, 31–2.
Ayrshire, Scotland, 192

The Backwoodsman, 8
Baconian tradition of science, 171, 172, 178
bagpipes, 6, 8, 32, 50, 55, 56
ballads. *See* songs
Ballantyne, Robert Michael, 65–7, 72, 73
Balmoral, Scotland, 109, 149
Bank of Montreal, 77, 82, 92
banking: bank shares, 89; bankers, 82; clerks, 91, 92; incorporation, 90; networks, 78, 80, 85; in Scotland, 78, 80; Scottish prominence, 48, 242; Scottish tone of in Canada, 91–2.
Barnston, George, 175, 176
Barnston, James, 175–6
Barra, Scotland, 29–30

Barry, James Miranda Stuart, 189, 199n12
beadwork, 100, 102–4, 106, 110–16, 121n41
Beattie, Judith Hudson, 118n11
Beauport, 189
Beaver Club, 70–2, 71
Belfast, 23, 25
Bell, Andrew, 175
Bell, Robert, 175, 178
Bennett, Margaret, 24
Bethune, Angus, 6
Bethune, John, 233, 234, 240
Bigsby, Jeremiah, 174
Black, Edward, 231, 233, 240
Black Watch: regiment, 41, 45, 47, 48, 54, 59n28; of Scotland, 50; sett, 162n14
Blackwood's Edinburgh Magazine, 3, 8, 10, 16n2
Bland, John, 209n1
Bogle Corbet, 8, 11
Bon Accord, 24–6, 34
Bo'ness, Scotland, 129, 131
Bonnie Lassies, 157
booking agents, 33
Botanical Society of Montreal, 176
botany: medical, 186; study of 5, 7, 17n18, 172, 175–6
Bovey, Captain, 51
Brantford, 80–2
Britannia pottery, 130, 132
British Army, 41, 45, 48–9, 50
British Columbia: exploration and fur trade, 5–7, 15, 17n12, 18n13, 61, 63–5; railways, 79; writers, 16
British Empire: and Canadians xviii; female emigrants civilizing, 32; geological discourse, 172; God's intentions for, 175; mercantilist policies, 78; military, 41, 44–7; nineteenth century, 46, 49; Scottish participation, in xviii, 11, 78. *See also* Crown, loyalty to; identity, British
Brockville, 31
brooches, 122–9, 145, 146, 154

Brown, George, 84
Brown, John James, 154
Brown, Robert, 15
Brown, William, 32, 35
Bryce, George, 67–8, 74n1
Buchanan, Alexander, 29
Buchanan Harris & Cos, 87–8
Buchanan, Isaac, 84, 88
Buchanan, Peter, 87–8, 93
Burley, David, 83
Burnham, Dorothy, 112
Burns Clubs, 36
Burns, Robert, 10, 16, 216
Burnside University, 192
Bury, 24
business: apprentices, 76, 78, 85; as-
  sets linked to place, 87–8, 90, 93;
  connections in Britain, 84–5,
  87–8, 90, 91–3; defined, 83–4;
  failures, 86, 88–9, 93; hierarchies,
  80, 83, 93; as male domain, 84;
  percentage of Scots in the business
  world, 80–2, 92, 95n20; prominence of Scots, 23, 48, 76–7,
  80–2, 89, 92, 242; Scottish tone of
  Canadian business, 91–2. See also
  corporations, credit, economic development, fur trade, merchants,
  succession
Bytown, 84

Caldwell, William, 191, 192
Caledonian Society, 154, 243
Calgary Highlanders, 52
Cameron Highlanders of Ottawa,
  52
Campbell, James Dykes, 132
Campbell, Marjorie Wilkins, 69–71,
  73
Campbell, Robert, 244, 247
Campbell, Wilfred, 188, 190
Canada Company, 8, 12
Canada Land Company, 24, 174
Canada West, 8. See also Ontario,
  Upper Canada
Canadian Armed Forces, 40, 50,
  52–7

Canadian Expeditionary Force,
  50–2
Canadian Institute, 175
Canadian Medical Association,
  197–8
Canadian Museum of Civilization,
  111, 112, 113, 114, 138, 140
Canadian National Railway, 27
Canadian Pacific Railway, 77, 79
Canadian Scottish (regiment), 54
Canadian Sports (pottery), 130, 131
"Canadianized Scotchmen," 11
canals, 10, 77, 175
Canloan program, 53
cap badges, 151, 153, 154, 158
Cape Breton: churches, 35; emigra-
  tion to 29, 35, 57n4, 119n21;
  militia; 49; Scottish identity in, 23;
  Scottish military in, 41; taken by
  Britain, 57n4; tourism, 36
Cape Breton Highlanders, 49
Caribbean region, 6, 80, 87–8, 94
Catholic Church, 143–5, 146, 178
Catholic communities, 35, 227,
  232–3, 236, 237, 250
Cattermole, William, 8–9
censuses, 82, 243–4, 247–50, 252,
  258n8
characterization of Scots, 12, 31, 34,
  64–5, 69–72, 77, 86, 91, 161n6
charity, 36, 109, 218–21, 230. See
  also the poor
chartered companies, 90–1
Chartist ideals, 16
Chesapeake, 78, 80, 94
chiefs, 44, 47, 64–5
children: building wealth for, 88, 90;
  clothing, 107, 108, 111, 123–4,
  150, 156, 157–9; of fur traders, 7,
  100, 110; protective symbols for,
  105, 123–4; rooting sojourners in
  Canada, 88. See also Home Children
Chisholme, David, 173–4
Christ Church (Montreal), 142–3
Christianity, 168, 175, 178, 239. See
  also religion

churches: assisting immigrants, 26; as clan and landmark, 229; ecclesiastical silver, 142–5; funding, 35; records, 249–51; Saint Andrew's Society march, 216, 217; Scottish identity, 34–6. *See also* religion
Church of Scotland, 13, 250, 254
clans, tartans, 157, 161nn8, 11, 162n23, 163n27. *See also* families
class: in Canada, 24, 33; and churches, 252–4, 257; commerce and professions, 83–4; education, 238–9; fur trade, 64–5, 68, 80; in Montreal, 47, 252–4, 257n3. *See also* chiefs
clergymen: as historians, 67, 244; migration, 27, 35, 86; as scientists, 175; as teachers, 36, 171, 230–1, 233. *See also* churches, missions, religion
clerks: bank, 91, 92; canals, 10; fur trade, 62, 64, 65, 66; merchants', 76, 78, 85, 93
clothing: children's, 107, *108*, 111, 123–4, 150, *156*, 157–9; men's, 107, *108*, 150, 152, 159, 162n14; Native peoples', 100, 102, 104, 106–10, 112–14, *115*, 119n25, *128*, 129; used, 109; women's, 107, *108*, 123–4, 154–5, 157, 162n21. *See also* fancy dress, fashion; Highland costume, military uniforms, tartan
Clouston, Edward, 82
Clouston, James, 111
coal, 171, 174, 177
coats of arms. *See* heraldry
Cochran, Robert, 130, 134
Cold War, 53–4
collectors, 100, 102, 110–12, 117n6, 203
commerce. *See* business
community building, 90
Confederation: and education, 236–7; era as high point of Scottish influence, 15–16; politicians, 77
Conservatives, 222–3

contractors, 84, 236
Cooper, J.I., 222
corporations, 90–1
covenant chain, 124
Cowan, Edward, 83
cradleboards. *See* tikanagans
crafts. *See* embroidery; Native peoples, crafts; silversmithing
Cranbrook Institute of Science, 105, *107*
credit, 78, 85, 88, 89–90, 91
Cree. *See* James Bay Cree
crown as decorative motif, 124, *126*, *127*
Crown, loyalty to, 45, 58n9, 211–12, 215, 217–18
Cruikshank, Robert, 125, 135n8, 138–42
cultural associations: demonstrating Scottish identity, 34, 36, 150, 213; Highland societies, 150, 161n8; literature and history, 67, 173; maintaining links with Scotland, 38n22, 213. *See also* Saint Andrew's Society
curling, 213

Dalhousie, Earl of, 173, 191, 196
Dalhousie University, 196–7, 199nn20, 22
dance, 56, 154, 221, 226n35
Dawson, George Mercer, 178
Dawson, John William, 168–73, 176–8, 234, 240
debt, 87–8, 90
decorative motifs: Christian, 146; English, 138, 141–2, 145, 146; Masonic, 146; Native, 100–9, 113, 119n21, 146; Scottish, 105, 123–4, 126–7, 138, 139, 146
defence, 47
Delftfield Pottery, 129
design, 201. *See also* architecture, decorative motifs, *particular design styles*
DeWolf, James, 197
Dickson, Thomas, 9
Dickson, William, 9

Dinwiddie, Robert, 129
diversity of "Scots," 72–3
doctors: administrators, 188, 190; artists and writers, 190; early doctors in Canada, 187–90; explorers, 5; fur trade, 100, 114; military, 187–90, 192; naturalists 7, 18n13, 175; politicians, 196; ships' surgeons, 188, 189, 193; social prominence, 188, 190, 198; teachers, 191–3, 197. *See also* education, medical; hospitals; medicine
Dougall, John, 232, 235, 240
Douglas, David, 5–7, 18n14
Douglas fir, 5, 18n13
Douglas, James, 6, 189
drinking, 8, 70, 72, 221, 226n37, 232
Drummond, Thomas, 7
Drummond, W.H., 190
Dumfries, Scotland, 7
Dumfries Township, 9
Dundee, Scotland, 209n2
Dunlop, William "Tiger," 3, 8, 11, 12, 174
Duperron-Bâby, Jacques, 138, 140, 147n5
Durham Report, 232

East, Ben, 105, *107*
Eastern Townships (Quebec): education, 228, 240n1; Gaelic language and culture, 23, 24, 35; immigrants to, 35, 36, 226n33; land companies, 24; Scottish identity in, 23, 34, 35
Eastmain, 114, 118n11
economic development, 78, 90–1
Edinburgh School of Applied Art, 203
Edinburgh, Scotland: emigrants from, 9, 65, 247, 249; fashions, 157; luckenbooths, 123; medicine, 184–7, 191, 197; museums, 117n6; silversmiths, 124. *See also* *Blackwood's Edinburgh Magazine,* University of Edinburgh
Education Act, 232, 234, 237

education, medical, 183–7, 190, 190–3, *194–5*. *See also* apprentices, medical
education, postsecondary 5, 56, 171, 178, 184–6. *See also* education, medical; *particular institutions*
education, public: charity, 230; funding, 228, 230–2, 235, 237; for girls, 238; high school, 233–4, 238; prominence of Scots, 242; public lectures, 172, 230; and religion, 232, 236, 239; Scottish approach, 168, 179, 228, 230–2, 234, 237, 239. *See also* school boards
Elgin, Lord, 223, 226n40
Elmslie, George, 25–6
Elora, 8
embroidery: Cree, 99–102, 110–11, 114–15, 121n40; emulating tartan, 150, 152; Scottish, 119n21, 159; types, 162n17
emigrant guides, 8–10, 12–14, 31, 32
emigrant regiments, 45
emigration. *See* migration
emigration agents, 11, 26, 29, 31. *See also* booking agents
emigration societies, 27, 32–3
engineers, 83, 172, 175
entrepôt trade, 78, 85, 90
entrepreneurship: defined, 83; heading one's own business, 87, 93; James Bay Cree, 109–12; Scots' image as enterprising, 12, 77, 86, 91, 92, 147; turning exile to, 36–7
Essex and Kent Scottish, 52
Esson, Henry, 230–2, 240
Established Church of Scotland, 253
ethnicity: ethnic histories, 68; ethnic identity, 82–3, 229; paternal versus maternal, 95n24; structuring community and networks, 93; treatment of by historians, 68–9, 72, 73. *See also* censuses; fur trade, Scottish presence; identity, Scottish

ethnography, 14, 102, 106, 117n6
evolutionary science, 178
exhibitions, 112, 150, 162n21, 202
exiles, 34, 36–7. *See also* migration,
　unwilling

Fairie, John, 152
families: encouragement and assis-
　tance to emigrate, 24, 26, 85–6,
　93; hierarchy of kinships, 93;
　maintaining links with Scotland,
　38n22; mercantile and banking,
　80, 84, 85–8, 91, 94; military
　service, 44; primogeniture, 87;
　rooting sojourners in Canada, 88,
　93. *See also* children, marriage,
　succession, tartan
fancy dress, 154–5, 157
Fargues, Thomas, 190
farmers, 23–7, 28, 29–32, 86. *See
　also* land
fashion: Highland themes, 108–9,
　120n28, 150, 152, 155–9; maga-
　zines, 110, 121n40; producing,
　111–12
Fenians, 46–7, 48
Fergus, 8, 25, 34
Fergusson, Adam, 8, 24–5
Ferrie, Adam, 86
Ferrier, James, 222, 233–4, 236, 240
feudal culture, 65, 67–8. *See also*
　chiefs
5th Regiment the Royal Highlanders
　of Canada (Black Watch), 50
5th Royal Battalion. *See* Royal Light
　Infantry
finance. *See* banking, credit
Findlay, Robert, 202, 209n1
Finlay, Jacques Rafael, 6
1st and 2nd Battalions, the Black
　Watch (Royal Highland Regiment)
　of Canada, 54, 56
1st and 2nd Canadian Highland
　Battalions, 54
First Nations. *See* Native peoples
Fleming, James, 132
Fleming, Sandford, 15, 175

Flett, Mrs, 110
floral designs, 102–4, 106, *113*, 114
Forfarshire, Scotland, 7, 125, 137
Fort Garry, 66
Fort George, 5–6
Fort Langley, 6
Fort Resolution, 7
Fort Walla Walla, 6
Fort William, 64–5, 68
42nd Foot. *See* Black Watch
48th Highlanders of Canada, 49, 54
forwarders, 84
Fraser, J.B., 197
Fraser, John Arthur, 158
Fraser, Simon, 6
Fraser Highlanders, 41, 44, 45,
　58n7, 69, *151*
Fraser River, 6
Fredericton, 36
Free Church of Scotland, 35, 253–4,
　255
free trade, 90
French Canadians: architecture,
　206–9; as clients of Scottish busi-
　nesses, 138, 140–2, 146; educa-
　tion, 193, 196, 229, 231; in the
　fur trade, 6, 62, 63, 65, 69, 138;
　loss of *seigneuries*, 44; politics, 70,
　212, 214; in Scottish cultural ac-
　tivities, 56
friends encouraging and assisting
　migration, 24–6
frugality, 86, 91
fur trade, 60–74; children of traders,
　7, 100, 110; clubs, 70–2, 71; con-
　flict portrayed as and Cree culture,
　99–100, 107–11; demobilized sol-
　diers in, 69; doctors, 100, 114;
　English versus Canadian, 62–3,
　72, 73; ethnic mix, 6, 95n24, 110;
　families, 85–6, 138; historiogra-
　phy, 61–73; leaders, 77, 85–6; nat-
　uralists, 175; raw materials for
　study of, 61, 63–5, 68, 110–11,
　114; Scottish presence, 60–2,
　65–70, 72–3, 77, 242; and tartan,
　107–8; trade goods, 106–10, 123,

124–6, 128–9; writings on, 60–4, 65–70. *See also* Hudson's Bay Company, North West Company
Fusiliers Mont-Royal, 48

Gaelic language, 12–13, 23, 26, 29, 34–5
Galbraith, J.S., 68
Galloway, Scotland, 6, 10
Galt, 9
Galt, Alexander Tilloch, 77, 82
Galt, John, 3, 8, 9–10, 11, 12
garrisons, 44, 48–9, 188
Gatineau Valley, 12
geological surveys, 168, 171, 176–7, 178
geology, 168–77
geometric designs, 105, *106*, 119n21
Georgian design, 138, *139*, 141, 146
Gilkison, William, 8
Gladman family, 110, 112, 114, 120n37, 121n49
Glasgow: bankers, 80; emigrants from, 12, 23–4, 88, 247, 249; emigration agents, 26; medicine, 184, 185; merchants, 76, 78, 80, 87–8, 90, 129–30; planters from, 6; potteries, 129–30, 132; shipping lines, 134; silversmiths, 124. *See also* University of Glasgow
Glenbow Museum, 118n11
Glengarry County, 6, 12, 23, 35, 52, 58n9
Glengarry, Scotland, 58n9
Goderich, 8
Gordon, John, 29–30
Gordon, Robert (of Kenmure), 4–5, 14
government: and immigration, 23–4, 26–7, 28, 29. Scots in, 6, 242, 244. *See also* politics, prime ministers
Gow, Ian, 203, 210n10
Graham, Andrew, 14
Grant, Albert, 114

Grant, Cuthbert, 6
Grant, Dorothy, 114
Grant, George, 15
Grant, Josephine, 114
Grant Collection, *103*, 105, *113*, 114
Greenock, Scotland, 129
Greenshields, John, 221
Guelph, 8, 9. *See also* University of Guelph

Halifax, 80, *81*, 197. *See also* Dalhousie University
Halifax, Earl of, 57n4
Hall, Archibald, 192
Hamilton, 50, 83, 86, 95n16
Hamilton, Robert, 88
hardiness, xvii, 41, 44, 64, 161n6
Hargrave, Letitia, 120n37
Harris, Robert W., 87–8
heart brooches, 123–9, 146
heart design, 105–7, *113*, 122–9, *139*, *145*, 146
Hebrides: Hebrideans, 72–3; Hudson's Bay Company staff, 74n1; immigrants from, 23, 24, 29; nostalgia about, 3; shipwrecks, 31–2
Hector, 31, 32, 36
heirs. *See* succession
heraldry, 123, 142, 147n10, 216
Herman, Arthur, 167, 168, 177–8
hierarchies, 80, 83, 85–6, 93. *See also* class
High School of Montreal, 233–4, 238
Highland Clearances, 24, 28–9, 45, 58n9
Highland costume: compared to Native dress, 41; establishment of, 150, 161n9; as fancy dress, 154–5, 157; as fashion, 107–9, 149–60; feminized, 155, 157, 162n21; fur trade, 6; influence on Native dress, 107–9, 120n28; military, 41–3, 48–53, *151*, 152; popularity, 120n28, 149–50; proscription, 120n28, 161nn8, 9; ritual role,

150; Saint Andrew's Society, 216; Scottish identity, *153*, 157, 160, 244

Highland culture: architecture, 36; dance, 56, 154; equated to Scottish culture, 160, 161n12; feudal culture in the fur trade, 65, 67–8; games, 36; popularity, 108, 109, 120n28, 149–50, 161n12; speeches, toasts and sayings, 72, 218, 221; writings about, 150. *See also* Highland costume

Highland identity. *See* identity, Scottish

Highland Lassie, *155*, 157

Highland Light Infantry of Canada, 52

Highland regiments: Canadian, 45, 48, 49–50, 52–5, 59n26; influence on Highland costume, 150, 151, 152; prestige of, 49, 50, 52, 53, 151; reserve, 55; Scottish, 41–4, 53, 57n2, 57; setts, 162n14. *See also particular regiments*

Highland societies, 150, 161n8

Highlands: distinctiveness of Highlanders, 72–3; immigrants from 23, 244, 247, 249. *See also* military service, 44, 58n5; *particular place names*

historical societies, 67, 173

Hogg, James, 3–4, 10

Holiwell, Charles A., 133

Holmes, Andrew Fernando, 191, 193

Home Children, 31, 32

Hôpital général de Québec, 145, 188, *206–8*

Hopkins, Edward Martin, 118n17

hospitals 193, 197, 202. *See also particular hospitals*

Howison, John, 11

Hudson's Bay Company: business structure, 90–1; clerks, 65, 80, 110; compared with the North West Company, 62; employees' places of origin, 6, 62, 65, 68, 74n1, 85–6; family networks,

85–6; hierarchy, 80, 85–6; influence on Cree culture, 99–100, 107–11; Montreal District, 118n17; sales shop, 110, 111; trade goods, 129; traders and factors, 5, 7, 80, 114. *See also* fur trade, marriage, to Native women

humanism, 203

Huron Tract, 24, 174

Hurvey, Mrs, 121n40

identity, British, 211–12, 215, 217–18, 223, 224

identity, Canadian: literary, 10, 11, 16; Scottish elements, xvii, xix, 56, 160

identity, ethnic, 61, 82–3, 229

identity, religious, 34, 35, 229

identity, Scottish: in advertising, 157, 163n27; aid for immigrants, 219; as Canadian identity, xviii, xix, 56, 160; complexity of, 72–3, 82–3; demonstration of, 34–5, 46, 72, *153*, *158*, 160; elements adopted by non-Scots, 56, 57, 159, 167; Highland culture as, 160, 161n12; ignored in manuscript accounts, 61; lost, 33–5, 38n22; politics, 223; pride in, 247; reinvented, xix–xx, 10, 36–7, 55, 65, 68, 83, 150, 160; religion as element of, 34–6; retained, xx, 33–6, 38n22, 247; societies, 211, 214–15, 222; vis-à-vis British culture, xvii, 178. *See also* churches, Gaelic language, Highland costume

Idiens, Dale, 102

immigration. *See* migration

immigration agents. *See* emigration agents

industrial elite, 77, 82, 86, 92, 94n9, 95n20

industry: as aspect of Christianity, 168; industrialization of Canada, 174, 175, 255; industrialization of craft, 140, 146; industrialization of Scotland, 78, 90, 129, 132,

171, 179; investment in, 91
International Boundary Commission, 174
Inverness, Scotland, 26, 124, 202
investments, 89, 91. *See also* banking
Irving, Washington, 63–5, 68
Isle of Lewis, Scotland. *See* Lewis, Scotland

J. & M.P. Bell, 130
Jacobites, 44, 45
James Bay Cree, 99–121; artifacts in museums, 100–6, 109, 111–15, 117n6, 120n35; arts and crafts, 99–102, 104–7, 110–16; cottage industries, 109–12, 116; decorative motifs, 100–9, *113*, 119n21; marriage to fur traders, 100, 110, 114, 120n37; visual symbolism, 108–9
Jarvie, Agnes, 88
jewellery. *See* brooches, cap badges
John Bland Canadian Architecture Collection, 201, *206–8*, 209nn1, 7
John Marshall & Co, 130, *131*
Joseph, Abraham, family, *155*, 157, 159
journals, 17n11, 18n14, 65, 173, 192, 203

Karras, Alan, 85, 87, 93, 94
Katz, Michael B., 83, 248
Killarney, 34
kilts: Canadian frontier, 6; children's, *156*, 157, *158*; as fashion, 150, 157, 159; feminized, 155, 157; military, 42–3, *51*, 52–3
Kincardineshire, Scotland, 33
Kingston, 172
kinship. *See* families
Kirkcaldy, Scotland, 129
Knowles, Elspet, 33
Korean War, 53, 55

Lake Megantic, 35
Lake Superior Scottish Regiment, 53
Lanark and Renfrew Scottish, 52

land, 23–7, 44, 86–90, 93
land companies, 24, 174
Landemann, George, 70, 72
landscape, 4–5, 14–15, 32, 41
Langdon, John E., 135n10
language. *See* French Canadians; Gaelic language; linguistics; Native peoples, languages; Scots language
Laurentians, 228, 229
Laval University, 178, 193, 196, 197
Lawrie Todd, 9, 11
Lawson, George, 176
lawyers, 83
lectures, 26, 27, 172, 230
Lefroy, John, 100, 102, 112
Lewis, Scotland, 24, 35, 36
linguistics, 14
Lingwick, 24
literacy, 168, 228
Literary and Historical Society of Quebec, 173
Liverpool, 78
Lizars, Daniel, 9–10
Loch Broom, Scotland, 31, 35
Loedel, Henry, 191
Logan, William Edmond, 168–72, 176–8
Logie, William, 192
London: commerce, 78, 87, 90, 91; exhibitions, 112, 150, 162n21; gold- and silversmiths, 125, 137, 142; Highland societies, 161n8; Hudson's Bay House, 111; medicine, 190; Royal School of Mines, 178; Scots born in, 82
Lorne Scots, 52
Louisbourg, 41
Lovat, Lord, 69
Lower Canada, 229–30, 231. *See also* Quebec
Lowlands: distinctiveness of Lowlanders, 72–3; emigrants from, 23–4, 27–8, 62, 160, 244, 247, 249; farmers, 24; Masonic lodges, 5. *See also particular place names*
Loyalists. *See* United Empire Loyalists

loyalty, 64. *See also* Crown, loyalty to
luckenbooth brooches, 122–9, 146
Lyell, Charles, 171–2, 177

Mabane, Adam, 188
MacCallum, Duncan, 197–8
McCord Museum of Canadian History: about, 161n2; clothing, 150, 152, *154*, *159*, 163n27; fur trade, *71*, *106*, 114–16, *126*, *131*; Native culture, *106*, 114–15, *116*, *126*; pottery, *131*, *133*, *134*. *See also* Notman Photographic Archives
McCulloch, Thomas, 171
Macdonald, Archibald, 6
Macdonald, Finnan, 6–7
Macdonald, John A., 77
Macdonald Stewart, 157, 163n27, 173
Macdonald, William C., 173, 179
MacDonell, Alexander, 62
Macdonell, Bishop, 3
Macdonnell family, 58n9
MacDougall, George, 6
McDougall, John, 86
MacDougall, Robert, 11–14, 15
McDowell, Duncan, 91
McGibbon, Alexander, 243–4, 245
McGill College: founding, 233–4; graduates, 192, 198; patrons, 173; preparatory school for, 238; prestige, 233; principals, 168, 233–4; sciences, 172–3, 175, 178–9. *See also* McGill Medical School, McGill School of Architecture, McGill University
McGill, James, 9, *71*, 77
McGill Medical School, 190–3, *194–5*, 230
McGill, Peter, 89, 215, 222
McGill, Robert, 235, 240
McGill School of Architecture, 201, 202, 206, 209n1
McGill University, 201, 202, 203, 206. *See also* McGill College. McGill Medical School, McGill School of Architecture

McGillivray, Duncan, 5
McGillivray, Simon, 6
McGillivray, William, 6, 77, 85
McInnes, Donald, 86
McIntyre, Duncan, *153*, 154–5, 160
MacKay, Donald, 92, 93
McKay, Donald, 119n27
Mackay, Jean Baptistes Desportes, 6
McKay, Thomas, 84
Mackenzie, Alexander (fur trader, explorer): exploration, 5–6; as fur-trade leader, 70, 77–8; on Native peoples, 14; origins of, 62, 85; writings, 61
MacKenzie, Alexander (historian), 29, 36
Mackenzie, Alexander (prime minister), 56, 84
Mackenzie, Donald, 5, 7
Mackenzie, Norman, 35
Mackenzie, Roderick, 61, 63, 73
Mackenzie sett, *151*, *152*, 162n14
McKenzie, Tait, 190
Mackenzie, William, 82
Mackenzie, William Lyon, 84
McLachlan, Alexander, 16
MacLennan, Hugh, 70
MacLennan, William, 154
MacLeod, Donald, 29
Macleod, John, 5, 6
Macleod, Murdo, 33–4
Macleod, Norman, 6
McLeod, Norman, 35
MacLoughlin, John, 5, 6, 18n15
Macmillan, David S., 94
MacMillan, James, 6
MacPhail, Andrew, 36
McPhail, Andrew, 190
MacTaggart, John, 10–11, 12
McTavish, Emily, 118n11
McTavish Frobisher & Co, 126
McTavish, George Simpson, 118n11
MacTavish, John, 7
MacTavish, Simon, 6
McTavish, Simon, 77, 85
MacVicar, Donald Harvey, 236, 240
McVicar, Robert, 7
magazines, 8

Malcolme, David, 13
Malloch Collection, 105, *106*, 114–15, *116*
Malloch, William Bell, 114
Manchester University Museum, 119n23, 120n35
Manitoba, 50, 66, 67
manufacturing. *See* industrial elite, industry
maps, 175, 177
Maritimes. *See* Atlantic Canada
marriage: age at time of, 88, 95n24; to Native women, 15, 66, 88, 95n24, 100, 110, 114, 120n37; postponed, 88; presents, 123, 134; rooting sojourners in Canada, 88, 93; in Scotland as goal of sojourners, 88; of Scots to non-Scots (other than Native), 88, 95n24; wives' roles in business, 84
Marsden, William, 197
Masonic lodges, 5, 17n10, 146
masons, 84
Masson, L.R., 61, 67
medical associations, 184–7, 197–8
medicine: Edinburgh model, 186–8, 191, 193, 196, 198; as male domain, 189; Scotland as leader in, 183, 190, 198. *See also* doctors; education, medical
Melville Church, 35
Menzies, Archibald, 18n13
merchants: in Canada, 80–2, 89–90; clerks, 76, 78, 85, 93; in Scotland, 76, 80, 87–8, 93
Metropolitan Museum of Art, 140
migration: advertising, 12, 26–7, 28; age and family status, 85, 86, 91; assisted, 23–4, 26, 29; Canada as destination for Scots, 12–13, 22–3; chain migration, 24; families, 86; financial situation, 12, 26, 29, 36, 218, 226n33; heirlooms, 122–3; image and reality, 31–3; leaders, 23, 32; motivations for, 4, 23, 27–9, 33, 85–6, 252; on-migration, 34, 35, 90, 125, 192, 218; place of origin in Scotland, 244,

247, 249; quantity over the years, 27, 45, 49, 57, 90, 125; temporary, 85, 87, 88; unwilling, 23–4, 27–31, 34, 45; by way of England, 125; writings about, 8, 11, 16. *See also* apprentices, clerks, emigrant guides, emigration agents, emigration societies, *particular place names*
military culture, 40–57
military service: barracks, 249, 259n13; Canadians in Scotland, 53; medical staff, 187–90, 192; officers trained in science, 173; popularity of, 44, 58n5. *See also* soldiers, demobilized
military uniforms, 46, 48. *See also* Highland costume
militia, 45, 47–50, 52–5, 57, 59n28
mining, 12, 91, 171, 174, 177
missions: Scottish influence on Cree material culture, 99, 107, 109, 120n30; urban, 255
Mitchell, Elaine, 73
moccasins, 100, 104, 110–11, 114–15, 121n43
Montgomery's (Montgomerie's) Highlanders, 41, 45, 58n7
Montreal: architecture, 201–2; banking, 77, 82, 92; barracks, 249, 259n13; cemeteries 244, 247, 258n6; censuses, 243–4, 247–50, 258n8, 252; churches, 229, 238, 247, 250–7; class, 47, 252–4, 257n3; commerce (post–fur trade), 77, 81, 84, 86, 92; cultural life, 173; elite, 80, 89, 92, 138–42, 157, 168, 214, 242–3, 251; families, 86; growth, 90, 242, 244, 255; hospitals, 191–3; mayors, 152, 222; medicine, 190–6; militia, 47–9, 51, 54, 152; "national" societies, 211–14, 216, 217, 223; North West Company, 61, 67, 70, 124; opportunities for immigrants, xviii–xix, 13, 26; pottery trade, 132; power centre of Canada, xix, xxiii, 92, 242–3; property owners,

237; publishers, 12, 130, 173; receiving homes for female immigrants, 33; schools, 171, 229–39; science, 168, 174, 177, 178–9. *See also* McGill College; Scots' influence, 10–11, 80, 92; silversmiths, 124–6, 137; wards, 249–51, 258n8. *See also* McGill College, particular churches, Square Mile, Saint Andrew's Society (Montreal)

Montreal Gazette, 173

Montreal General Hospital, 191, 192, 193

Montreal Herald, 12, 173

Montreal Light Infantry, 46

Montreal Medical Institution, 193

Montreal Museum of Fine Art, 144

monuments, 9, 25, 203

Moodie, Susanna, 8, 11

Moose Factory: Cree material culture, 99, 102, 104–5, 109–11, 114, 118n11; people from, 82, 114

Morrin, Joseph, 196

Mount Royal Cemetery, 244, 247, 249, 258n6

Muirkirk, Scotland, 12

multiculturalism, 73, 75n35

Murray, Alexander, 175

Murray, James, 44

museums. *See particular museums*

music. *See* bagpipes, dance, songs

Napoleonic Wars, 28–9

nation building, 77

National Arts Survey of Scotland, 203–6

National Gallery of Canada, 138–41, 143, 145–6

National Museum of the American Indian, 114

National Museums of Scotland, 101, 106, 127

"national" societies, 211–14, 216, 217, 223

Native peoples: clothing, 100, 102, 104, 107–9, 112–13, 119n25; commonalities with Scots, 13–15, 41, 108–9; crafts, 99–121; and the fur trade, 62, 68, 102, 109–12; jewellery, 124–6, 128–9; languages, 13, 62; place names, 13; spiritual beliefs, 109; study of, 5, 14, 62, 102. *See also* decorative motifs; James Bay Cree; marriage, to Native women

NATO, 53, 54, 55

natural history, 5, 171, 174, 175. *See also* botany

Natural History Society of Montreal, 174

naturalists, 5, 7, 14, 17n13

neoclassical design, 138, 141–2, 145, 146

networks: academic, 209n2; church, 229; commercial, 76–7, 85–7, 91, 93, 222; community, 93; credit, 78, 80; medical, 197–8; scientific, 173–6; social, 167, 173–6, 214, 220–2. *See also* families

New Brunswick, 32, 33, 35, 36, 82, 83

New France, xviii, 41, 44, 57n4, 61. *See also* French Canadians

New Glasgow, 228, 229

Newfoundland, 45, 58n7, 59n26, 176

newspapers: links to Scotland, 38n22; promotion of Canada in Scotland, 23, 24, 27; publishers, 12, 84, 173, 232; Saint Andrew's Society reports, 214–15, 216, 220, 223. *See also particular newspapers*

Niven, Frederick, 16

Nobbs, Percy Erskine, 201, 202, 209n1

noble savage, 161n6

Noctes Ambrosianae, 3–4, 17n3

Noctes Ambrosianae Canadiensis, 8

North Nova Scotia Highlanders, 54

North West Company: base in Montreal, 61; compared with the Hudson's Bay Company, 62; family networks, 85; partners, 62, 64–5, 67–8, 71, 74n1, 85; writings about, 61–5, 67–70

northern Canada, 64, 117n6, 175,

176. *See also* Arctic, fur trade
Northwest, 5–7, 61–2, 65–6, 176
Northwest Passage, 7
Norway House, 7
Nor'Westers and Loyalist Museum,
    103, 105, 112
nostalgia about Scotland, 3, 10, 16,
    70, 125. *See also* identity, Scottish
Notman Photographic Archives:
    about, 161n2, 243, 244; images,
    42, 51, 79, 151, 153, 155, 156,
    158, 169, 170, 194–5, 221, 245–6
Notman, William, 84, 86. *See also*
    Notman Photographic Archives
Nova Scotia: Department of Educa-
    tion, 172; eminent people from,
    168; immigrants to, 31, 34, 45;
    militia, 49, 54, 58n7; tourism,
    36–7. *See also* Cape Breton
novelists, 8, 11, 16, 66

occupations, 243, 248, 251, 252–7,
    258n11. *See also particular occu-
    pations*
Ogilvie, Alexander Walker, 157,
    162n24
Ogilvie, Mrs Alexander Walker,
    154, 157
Ogilvie Flour Mills, 162n24
Ontario, 52, 53, 80, 81. *See also*
    Canada West, James Bay Cree,
    Upper Canada
Orkney, Scotland: distinctiveness of
    Orkneymen, 72; explorers from,
    7; Hudson's Bay Company staff,
    63, 65–6, 68, 74n1, 80
orphans. *See* Home Children
Orwell, 23, 36
Ottawa. *See* Bytown
Ottawa Valley, 23–4, 52, 228

Parker, Daniel MacNeil, 198
partnerships, 78, 80, 87, 89, 93.
    See also North West Company
passage. *See* assisted passage;
    Atlantic crossing
Peel, Dufferin, and Halton Regi-
    ment, 52
Perth, 49, 175

Perth Regiment, 49
Perthshire, Scotland, 8, 193
Peterson, William, 202, 209n2
photographs: dressing up for, 153,
    154, 156, 158; as ethnographic
    sources, 107–8, 112, 114, 118n8,
    119n25, 152–8; photographers,
    84, 107, 133; transferred to pot-
    tery, 133–4
physicians. *See* doctors
Pictou, 31–2, 34–7, 49, 171–2, 197
Pictou Highlanders, 49
Pitt Rivers Museum, 100, 118n17,
    119n23
place, assets linked to, 87–8, 90, 93
place names, 4–5, 13, 34
plaids, 119n26, 120n28, 150, 153,
    158, 163n27
poetry, 7, 10, 12, 16
polar explorers. *See* Arctic
politics: Scots in, xix, 8, 56, 77;
    Saint Andrew's Society, 211–12,
    215–18, 222–3
poor, the, 29–30, 36, 186–7, 218,
    226n33. *See also* charity, upward
    mobility
population, percentage of Scottish
    origin, xvii, 48, 242, 243
Portneuf, 130, 131
potato famines, 29
pottery, 129–34
Presbyterians: churches, 147n11,
    229, 250–7; clergymen, 67, 196;
    communities, 35, 250
prime ministers, 56, 77, 229
Prince Edward Island: Catholic com-
    munities, 35; immigrants to, 27,
    33, 45; militia, 58n7; Selkirk set-
    tlement, 23–4, 25, 27, 35–6; twen-
    tieth-century immigration, 27
Princess Louise's Regiment, 50
Pritchard, James, 80
professional standards, 184, 197,
    201
protective symbols, 105, 108–9,
    123–4
Protestantism, 178, 228, 229,
    233–4, 239. *See also particular
    denominations*

public health, 186, 187
public image of Scots, 31, 34, 77.
  See also characterization of Scots

Quarrier's Orphan Homes of Scotland, 31
Quebec: architects, 201–2; churches,
  35, 229–30; disbanded soldiers,
  44–5; education, 227–30, 232,
  239; Gaelic language, 35; James
  Bay, 99, *108*, 114; merchants, 80,
  81, 132; militia, 49–50; pottery,
  130, 132; settlement schemes, 45;
  souvenirs, 132–4. *See also* Eastern
  Townships, *particular towns and
  cities*
Quebec City: fashion, 157; immigrants disembarking at, 26,
  29–30; medicine, 188, 189, 193,
  196; receiving homes for female
  immigrants, 33; scenes of on pottery, 132–4. *See also* Hôpital
  général de Québec
Quebec Medical Society, 197
Quebec Times, 29–30
Queen Victoria, 108, 109, 149–50,
  157
Queen's Own Cameron Highlanders
  of Canada, 50
Queen's University, 172, 176, 196

Rae Collection, *101*
Rae, John, 7, 14–15, 100, 102, 104,
  105, 110, 112
rags-to-riches. *See* upward mobility
railways, 26, 27, 77, 79, 90, 91
Rebellions of 1837, 46, 222–3, 232
Reciprocity Treaty (1854), 46
Red Hackle, 48
Red River settlement, 7, 65
Redpath family, 89, 173
Redpath Library, 201
religion: civic, 236–7; denomination
  of military groups, 41; and educa-
  tion, 232, 236, 239; and language,
  35; and medical schools, 187; and
  modernity, 168, 178, 239; of
  Montreal's business elite, 92; Na-
  tive beliefs, 109; religious identity,
  34, 35, 229. *See also* Christianity,
  particular denominations
remittances to Scotland, 16, 24, 26
Renton, Jane. *See* Vincent, Jane
  Renton
reserve soldiers, 54–5
Rhind, James, 202, 209n1
Rhynes, Robert, 27
Rich, E.E., 68–9
Richardson, James, 175
Richardson, John, 7, 14–15
Rideau Canal, 10, 175
Rideau Valley, 12, 23–4
Ritchie, John, 244, 246
Robert Cochran & Co, 130, 134
Robertson, Colin, 68
Robertson, William, 191, 192, 193
Roman Catholic. *See* Catholic
  Church, Catholic communities
Romanticism, 161n6
Ross, Alexander, 79
Ross, Bernard Rogan, 111
Ross, James Clark, 6
Ross, John, 6, 32
Roy, Thomas, 175
Royal Architectural Institute of
  Canada, 203
Royal Canadian Air Force, 55
Royal Canadian Navy, 55–6
Royal Canadian Regiment, 56
Royal Colleges of Physicians and
  Surgeons of Scotland, 184–7
Royal Commission on the Ancient
  and Historic Monuments of Scot-
  land, 203, *204–5*
Royal Grammar Schools, 230–1,
  233, 234
Royal Highland Emigrant Regiment,
  45, 58n7
Royal Highland Regiment of Cana-
  da (Black Watch), 47, 58n7
Royal Infirmary (Edinburgh), 185,
  188, 191
Royal Institution for the Advance-
  ment of Learning, 228–9, 230,
  233, 238, 240n1
Royal Light Infantry, 47, 48, 49,
  58n15
Royal Military College of Canada, 56

Royal Museum of Scotland, 171
Royal Newfoundland Regiment, 59n26
Royal Ontario Museum, 100, 112
Royal Scots, 41, 42–3
Royal Scots of Canada, 48, 50
Royal Scottish Museum, 202
Royal Society, 17n10
Royal Victoria Hospital, 202
Royals. *See* Royal Light Infantry
Rum, Scotland, 29
Rupert's House, *108*, 118n11
Rupert's Land, 68, 74n1. *See also* Hudson's Bay Company
Rutherford, Ernest, 179

Saint-Ours family, 138
Saint Andrew's Day, 214–15, 216, 224, 225n14
Saint Andrew's Society: British loyalty, 211–12, 215, 217, 224; networks and socialization, 214, 220–2; politics, 211–12, 215–18, 222–3; prestige and power, 217, 220, 222; Scottish identity, 36, 215–18; symbols and rituals, 216–18, 219, 220–1, 224, 226n37; welcome to immigrants, 32, 252; women, 216, 218, 220, 221, 226n35
Saint Andrew's Society (Fredericton), 36
Saint Andrew's Society (Montreal): charity, 36, 218–21, 226n33, 252; history of, 212, 214–15, 222, 252; newspaper coverage, 214–15, 216, 220, 223; officers of, 154, 157, 215, 222, 243
Saint Andrew's Society (Saint John), 32
St Andrews University, 184, 185
St Ann's, 35
St Gabriel Street Presbyterian Church, 26, 148n11, 230–1, 244, 251, 253–4, 256
Saint John, 33, 80–3
St John River, 32
school boards, 227, 234–9
schools: charity, 230; demonstrating

Scottish identity, 34, 36; emigration promotion in, 27; learning materials, 172. *See also* education
science: Baconian, 171, 172, 178; democratization of, 5; evolution, 178; exploration of Canada, 5, 175; and industrialization, 174, 175, 179; journals, 17n11; military officers trained in science, 173; practical, 171, 172; scientific societies, 67; Scotland as leader in, 5, 17n10, 168, 183, 190, 198, 230; social-scientific networks, 173–6; Victorian, 171, 175. *See also* botany, geology, natural history
Scotch Colony, 32, 35, 36
"Scotch Yankey," 11
Scotland: economic development, 78, 80, 129, 132, 171, 179; places of origin of emigrants, 72–3, 244, 247, 249. *See also* identity, Scottish; *particular place names*
Scotland-Canada symbiosis, 4, 10, 44
Scots in the North American West, 1790–1917, 73
Scots language, 10, 19n33
The Scotsman in Canada, 68, 188
Scott, James, 12
Scott, Walter 6, 9–10, 19n31, 213
Scottish Enlightenment, 5, 14, 17n7, 167, 168, 169, 171
Scottish identity. *See* identity, Scottish
Scottish regiments, 41, 44
Scoular, John, 5
Seaforth Highlanders of Canada, 50, 54
Secession Church, 252–4, 256
second-generation (and later) Scottish Canadians: in commerce, 77, 81, 82, 94n9; in science, 171, 175–8; Scottish ethnic identity, 83
seigneuries, 44, 89
Selkirk, fifth Earl of: settlement schemes, 12, 23, 24; writings about, 67, 69; writings by, 62–3, 73
servants, 31, 32, 33, 251, 252
Service, Robert, 16

settlement schemes, 4, 23, 32, 44–5, 57n4, 62
setts, 152, 162nn14, 23
Seven Years' War, 41, 44, 125
77th Foot. *See* Montgomery's (Montgomerie's) Highlanders
78th Foot. *See* Fraser Highlanders
shepherd's check, 119n26, 119n27
Shetland, 72, 74n1
ships: disasters, 31–2; immigrant, 31; reconstructed for tourism, 36; Royal Canadian Navy, 56; shipping lines, 32, 134; ships' surgeons, 188, 189, 193; timber, 26, 31–2
shopkeepers, 83, 126
silver objects. *See* silversmithing
silversmithing: domestic articles, 138–42, *208*; ecclesiastical works, 142–5; fur trade, 124–9, 145; innovative, 138, 140, 143, 145, 146; jewellery, 122–9; pierced work, *126–7*, *138*, *139*, 142–3, 145–6; in Scotland, 124
Simpson, Aemilius, 6
Simpson, George, 6, 77, 85–6, 102, 109–10, 118n17
Sinclair, John, 8
Skakel, Alexander, 171, 174, 230, 233, 234, 240
skating, 154, 157
Skye, Scotland, 23, 33
Slave Lake, 7
Smith, Donald, 68, 77, 78, 79, 86, 91
Smith, Donald (Lord Strathcona): collection of Cree artifacts, *104*, 118n15
Society for the Promotion of Public Education, 231–2
sojourners, 85, 87, 87–90, 93. *See also* apprentices; clerks
soldiers, demobilized, 6, 44–5, 58n4, 69, 86. *See also* veterans
songs, 3, 9, 68, 70, 221
South Uist, Scotland, 29–30
souvenirs, 112, 114–16, 121n43, 125, 132–4
spirituality. *See* religion
sports, 34, 130, 154, 157, 213

sports clubs, 34, 213
Square Mile, 92, 234, 238, 258n8
Starnes, Henry, 152
Stephen, George, 77, 78
Stephenson, John, 191, 193
Stirling, Earl of. *See* Alexander, William
stone masons, 84
Stonehaven, Scotland, 33
store system, 129, 135n14
Stormont, Dundas and Glengarry Highlanders, 52
Strachan, John, 3
Strathcona, Lord. *See* Smith, Donald
Strickland, Samuel, 8
Stuart, Charles, 114, 118n15
Stuart, John, 6
succession, 87, 88, 89
sugar trade, 6
surveyors, 112
Sweeney, Robert, 89
Szasz, Ferenc, 73

tartan: Cree motifs similar to, 109; for educational institutions, 56; fabric types, 119n26, 119n27, 150, *154*, 161n11, 162n21; family and clan connections, 157, 161nn8, 11; as fashion, 108–9; 120n28, 150, 152, 155, 159; military, 46, 55, 56; Native people wearing, 107–9, 119nn24, 25; origin of the word, 161n11; research into clan-specific tartans, 161n9; as trim, 46, 107. *See also* Highland costume, setts
"tartanization," 36, 150, 152
Taylor, Andrew Thomas, 201, 209n1
Taylor, Lou, 162
Taylor, Nancy, 121n43
teachers, 86, 187, 191–3, 202
Temiskaming, 114, 118n16
temperance, 232
Terrebonne, 228
theatrical garb, 155, 157
thistle: cap badges, 154; embroidery, 119n21, *159*; James Bay Cree, 100–4, 114, 117n7; Saint Andrew's Society, 118n17, 216–17, 219

Thomas, Francis T., 132
Thompson, David, 6
Thompson, James, 26
Thompson, Judy, 111–12
Thompson, Scott, 119n25
Three Years in Canada: An Account of the Actual State of the Country in 1826-7-8, 10
thrift, 64
tikanagans, 105, 106, 107, 115, 116
timber ships, 26
tobacco, 78, 129, 157, 163n27, 173
Tolmie, William Fraser, 7
Toronto: growth, 90; medicine, 196; militia, 49, 52; pottery trade, 132; receiving homes for female immigrants, 33; science, 175; servants in, 33. *See also* University of Toronto
Toronto Scottish, 52
tourism, 36–7. *See also* souvenirs
trade goods, 106–10, 123, 124–6, 128–9
traders, 6, 78, 84–5, 87–8, 90. *See also* business, entrepôt trade, fur trade
Traill, Catherine, 8
transfer-printed pottery, 132–4
transportation. *See* Atlantic crossing, canals, railways, ships, travel
Traquair, Ramsay: McGill School of Architecture, 201, 202, 206; publications, 209n6; on silver-smithing, 125, *208*; works by, 203, *204–5*, 206, 209n5
travel, for migrants within Canada, 29–30, 218–20
travel writing, 8–10, 14, 18, 61
Tulchinsky, Gerald, 86
Tupper, Charles, 196, 197–8, 199n21
Twenty Years in Canada West, 8

Union of 1707, 78
United Empire Loyalists, 58n8, 69, 70, *81, 82*, 190
United States: Canada between Britain and, 176–7; on-migration
from, 85, 86, 189, 240n1; on-migration to, 34, 192. *See also* American Civil War, American War of Independence, War of 1812
Université de Montréal, 196
University College Dundee, 209n2
University of Aberdeen, 171, 184, 192
University of Edinburgh: ethnography, 102, 117n6; fine art, 209n2; graduates, 86, 168, 173–5, 188–9, 192–3, 196, 197; medicine, 184, 185–7, 188, 189; prestige of, 86, 187, 198; science, 168, 171, 175, 178–9; technology, 172
University of Glasgow: engineering, 172; graduates, 7, 9, 171, 174, 197; medicine, 184; memorial to James McGill, 9; science, 179
University of Guelph, 9
University of Manitoba, 67
University of Toronto, 172
Upper Canada: commerce, 84; medicine, 196; population born in Scotland, 95n16; settlement, 8, 10, 24–6, 29, 30, 45, 58n9, 218. *See also particular towns and cities*
upward mobility: in commerce, 77, 85–6; of immigrants to Montreal, 13, 248–9, 257; labourers becoming farmers, 26; of Scottish Presbyterians, 248; through family networks, 85–6, 93; through industry and frugality, 86
urbanization, 90

Valentine, Hugh Allan Inglis, 209n1
Vallée, Louis Prudent, 133
Vancouver, 50
Vancouver Island, 6, 15
Varennes, 143, 145
Vaudreuil, 143
veterans, 44–5, 54, 58nn4, 7, 69
Victoria, Queen. *See* Queen Victoria
Victoria General Hospital (Halifax), 197
Villeneuve, René, 135n8

Vincent, Harriet, 114
Vincent, Jane Renton, 110, 114,
   120n37, 121n40
Voltigeurs de Québec, 49–50

Wallace, William Stewart, 69
War of 1812, 44, 46, 173
Waterloo Regiment, 52
Waterston, Elizabeth, 16
Watkins, Edwin A., 109
wealth, 88–91. *See also* investments,
   upward mobility
weather, 13, 64
weavers, 23–4, 27–8
weddings. *See* marriage
West Coast. *See* British Columbia
Western Canada: Highland settlements on the prairies, 23, 34, 35;
   history of Scots in, 6–7, 68, 73;
   militia, 52. *See also* Northwest,
   particular provinces
Westmount, 202
whisky. *See* drinking
wholesalers, 84–5

Wien, Tom, 80
William Bennett & Co., 130
Williamstown, 112
wills, 88
Wilson, Andrew, 12
Wilson, Daniel, 172
Wilson, George, 117n6
Wilson, James, 175
Wilson, John, 3–4
Winnipeg, 50
winter, 13, 64, 130
women: clothing, 107–8, 123–4,
   154–5, 157, 162n21; cottage industries, 110–14; education, 189,
   238; female emigration societies,
   32–3; magazines for, 110; in medicine, 189; occupations, 84,
   110–14, 189, 251, 252, 258n11;
   in Saint Andrew's Society, 216,
   218, 220, 221, 226n35. *See also*
   marriage
World War I, 50–2
World War II, 52–3